My Road To Berlin

M R T B
$4.50

The Autobiography of

AS TOLD TO LEO LANIA

In this unusual autobiography, Willy Brandt, the world-famous mayor of Berlin, tells the exciting and dramatic story of his life. MY ROAD TO BERLIN is, as Brandt himself puts it, "two stories, my own and that of Berlin, since the two cannot be separated from each other."

Born in extremely poor circumstances, fatherless and poverty-stricken in the town of Lubeck, Brandt fled from Germany just after Hitler came to power. He sought refuge in Norway, where he soon made his mark in the Labor party. When the Nazis took over and occupied Norway, Brandt was imprisoned as a Norwegian soldier. After the war—by then he was a Norwegian officer—he was offered the post of Norwegian ambassador to Paris. Instead of accepting the appointment, Brandt gave up his Norwegian citizenship, his rank, and career to return to bombed-out Berlin "in order to help build democracy in my native land." Rising in the ranks of the Social Democratic party, Brandt became in a few years the mayor of Berlin and a recognized political leader of Germany.

3 1148 00026 8102

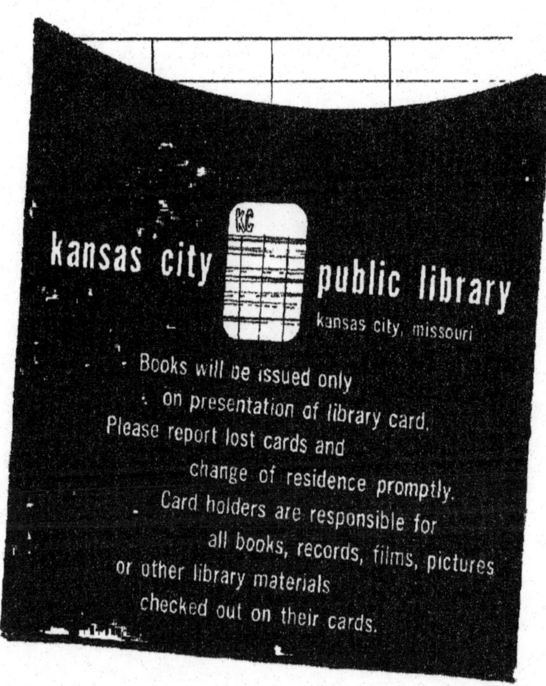
kansas city public library
kansas city, missouri
Books will be issued only
on presentation of library card.
Please report lost cards and
change of residence promptly.
Card holders are responsible for
all books, records, films, pictures
or other library materials
checked out on their cards.

MY ROAD TO BERLIN

DOUBLEDAY & COMPANY, INC.
GARDEN CITY, NEW YORK
1960

My Road to Berlin

WILLY BRANDT, Mayor of Berlin

as told to Leo Lania

Library of Congress Catalog Card Number 60–10666

Printed in the United States of America
First Edition

Design: N. Sylvester

Contents

List of Illustrations

Following page 144

MY ROAD TO BERLIN

CHAPTER ONE

A Berliner in New York

1

A hard, cold rain swept angrily around the street corners; it whipped the walls of the buildings which, smooth and unassailable like the ramparts of a huge fortress, mocked its fury; it stung the faces of the people like a thousand needles. They pressed themselves against the walls, seeking protection under umbrellas and marquees. It was a poor protection; against this kind of rain, there was no defense, but the people did not budge. Four and five rows deep, they stood along the edge of the sidewalks on both sides of the street—men and women, young and old, workers, office girls, executives. They yelled, clapped, many waved with small flags: thick red horizontal stripes and a broad white stripe in the middle showing a bear standing on its hind legs—the coat of arms of the city of Berlin

Most of the windows of the thirty- and forty-story buildings were open; up there heads and faces formed bright spots in the gray curtain of rain. The rain turned to snow. It fell from all the windows—a colored snow, like confetti: it was snowing paper. Presently the narrow gorge of Lower Broadway was covered with a thick layer of paper scraps.

It was noon, February 10, 1959. Slowly I drove along Broadway toward City Hall I stood in the open car, but I felt no cold, I hardly noticed the rain. Forms and figures mixed and dissolved, my eyes focused on some patches of color: the flags on the street poles and lampposts—the red-white-blue of the star-spangled banner, the black-red-gold of the German Federal Republic, the red-white of the city of Berlin. The applause of the crowd was like the surf of the ocean. Some shouts rose above the noise. "Hi, Willy!" "Good luck, Willy!"

In front of Trinity Church my eyes fell upon an elderly man. Bareheaded, without a topcoat, he stood on one of the steps; judging from the expensive cut of his suit, he might have been a banker or broker. Now he raised his umbrella, and, waving it, he shouted in a thin voice: "Hurrah for West Berlin!" Those around him joined in—a group of laborers in their overalls, dripping wet; some Negroes, construction workers, tin hats on their heads, their faces like polished ebony, their voices deep and resonant: "Hurrah for West Berlin!"

No, I felt neither cold nor rain. I felt quite warm, sheltered, as if I were not driving through the strange streets of New York but through my own Berlin.

Once more I glanced at the man on the steps of Trinity Church. He did not look at all "American", from his looks and attire one might have taken him for a European, perhaps an emigrant—he might also have been Jewish How many among these men and women, the employees and the workers, had come to America but a few years ago, victims of the Hitler madness, Jews and Christians alike? For thousands of them, Germany had once been their home—later it became their hell. Now Broadway was their special domain.

I understood: this ticker-tape parade with which New York usually greets only heads of state was actually not meant for me, the governing mayor of Berlin; it was, rather, an impulsive demonstration by which the mayor and the people of this unique city, that has more Germans than Frankfort or Stuttgart, more Italians than Florence, more Jews than Israel, wanted to show their sympathy with the men and women of Berlin—with the Berlin which although conquered by the brown dictatorship had never been converted to the new creed, had to pay the heaviest penalty for the crimes of the Nazis, and which now, still bleeding from many wounds, was holding the front of freedom and human dignity against the red dictatorship. And who could better appreciate the gravity and significance of this struggle than those who had been its victims? Because they had not forgotten the past, could never forget it—these New Yorkers and my Berliners had the same claim on the future.

This was my third visit to America.

In 1954—as a member of Parliament—I had been here for the first time, to see the greatness and the huge possibilities of this continent, to study this country and its institutions; I had been a guest who could hardly digest the outpouring of American hospitality. In the beginning of 1958 I had come again, then as the elected representative of Berlin, the purpose of my visit was to confer with the responsible leaders in Washington, to give lectures in New York and Boston, to accept an honorary degree in Philadelphia, but above all, to express my thanks for all that the United States had done for my city.

This time I had a special mission. And it was still more difficult for me to maintain myself in the whirlwind of exciting impressions and fascinating experiences. Every hour was filled to the brim with discussions, conferences, and press interviews—from the moment of my arrival at International

Airport, Idlewild, through the few days in Washington, until the hour of this parade in New York. For this time I was the bearer of a special message, forced by circumstances to represent the cause of Berlin and freedom on the Washington scene—on the stage that dominates the world.

I had accepted this role not lightheartedly. Berlin lies a hundred and ten miles behind the Soviet front, whereas a distance of three thousand miles separates this front from Washington and New York. Could I reasonably expect Americans to have the same intense feeling about the fate, the worries and difficulties, the hopes and desires of Berlin?

And might not the past, those unholy thirteen years of the "thousand-year Reich," prove an unconquerable wall of mistrust? In the postwar era America had consistently shown its intention not to make free Germany atone for the crimes of the Nazis. The American people has made sacrifices to enable the Federal Republic to rise from the ashes—and not only sacrifices of goods and money. During the Russian blockade American and British fathers and sons risked their lives to save Berlin from starvation and total ruin.

Yet, all through these years, only a relatively small part of the American people had been directly affected by the events in Berlin; this time it was different. The Berlin crisis could easily involve the whole United States. Was it not naive to believe that the American people as a whole would be prepared to defend Berlin, even if this defense implied the risk "to die for Berlin"?

How long ago was it that millions of Frenchmen refused "to die for Danzig," that the League of Nations left Ethiopia at the mercy of Mussolini and did not dare oppose the Japanese war lords in China, that the premiers of France and England were hailed as apostles of peace when they returned from Munich in 1938? And even recently, the people in the Soviet Zone of Germany and in Hungary had the same experience: no nation wants to die for another—not for anti-Fascists or for anti-Communists, not for Hungary, not for the Poles or the Jews. Why should America be an exception in the case of Berlin?

Certainly, I was quite convinced that there was no need for a war to hold Berlin. The men in the Kremlin were no less interested in avoiding a war than the West; both knew that victory would have to be paid for by suicide, and at the end "the survivors would envy the fate of the dead." The real danger was that the Soviets might think they could by a mere *threat* of war bring the crisis to a head and force the West to withdraw from Berlin The more ruthlessly the Communists showed their determination to reach their goals, even at the cost of war, the more firmly the democratic nations tried to preserve the peace at any cost. What did the freedom of two and a quarter million of West Berliners count against the mutilation and the atomic death of several dozen million Americans? Would the latter understand that Berlin was not just another town in faraway Germany, but an advanced bridgehead of the free nations? That they had to be prepared to stand up for the freedom of Berlin, if they did not want to die for New York or Chicago?

To bring home this realization to the Americans—and to the other democracies—seemed the more difficult as the Communists defended their demands with arguments which impressed the uninformed as logical and reasonable. Was the "German Democratic Republic" not a reality? When the citizens of the Federal Republic traveled to Berlin, when the Berliners traveled to western Germany, their documents were controlled at the border by officials of the Soviet Zone Why should the Americans, or the British, or the French, refuse to accept the same procedure? Was it worth bringing on a conflict because of such "formalities"? Russia was willing to grant West Berlin the status of a "free city." Did it really matter whether 11,000 or 3000 Allied soldiers were stationed in Berlin? All that the Soviet government wanted was the removal of a dangerous source of conflict! Berlin was the cause of one of the severest crises of the postwar period. Berlin endangered the peace of the world; therefore the status of Berlin had to be changed. Wasn't that plain common sense?

The Communist argument was as logical as that of the boy who murdered his parents and then pleaded extenuating circumstances on the ground that he was an orphan. Berlin had not brought on the crisis, but the Soviets had manufactured it in order to use it as a pretext for their political offensive. They felt—not without cause—the existence of a free Berlin within the Communist orbit was an embarrassing disturbance. Too great was the contrast between the work of reconstruction, the rhythm, the pulsating economic and intellectual life in West Berlin, and the gray desolation between the ruins of the East sector. The number of men and women fleeing daily to the West—more than two millions within ten years—spoke a clearer language than all Communist statistics about the accomplishments in the Soviet paradise. Deprived of the right to vote, the people of the East Zone voted with their feet. This election, too, had to be abolished. But above all, the Russians intended to demonstrate by the anticipated withdrawal of the Western powers from Berlin that the borders of the Soviet empire were now "definitely" at the Elbe and Werra rivers.

When I took the plane to America I did not fancy that I could give special information to the President, Secretary of State Dulles, or his officials in the State Department, which they did not already possess. They all were too well acquainted with the Communist phraseology, they could easily distinguish between falsehood and truth. They all knew what was at stake in Berlin. What, then, could I hope to accomplish with my trip, with the dozens of conferences, discussions, and speeches?

"Propaganda for Berlin?" As far as the determination of the Berliners was concerned, to make all, even the most painful sacrifices for the defense of their rights—and of justice—that was not necessary for me to stress. The courageous conduct of the Berliners during the blockade was not forgotten, and only a few months ago—in December of 1958—the citizens of my city had decisively defeated the Communist foreign legion in a secret ballot.

I was the mayor of Berlin, not the Foreign Minister of the Federal Republic. I had neither the authority nor the right to speak on behalf of Bonn and to make—or even discuss—agreements, which fell under the competence of the Federal government.

What I really hoped to accomplish on my trip—which took me from America to Asia and which was followed by visits to London, Paris, and other European capitals—was to make it as clear as possible to the peoples of the free nations that Berlin would not surrender even in the—quite unthinkable—case that the West would forsake us. The democracies might expect that in the face of the daily growing danger the people of Berlin would make their fight dependent on certain American guarantees. I wanted to dispel such a misunderstanding. Berlin did not ask any reward for its unflinching attitude. The people of West Berlin know what the United States with their British and French allies have meant, and still mean, to them. We owe it to the Western democracies that Berlin can live in freedom, that it can live at all. From this fact Berlin derives no rights, but rather an obligation. To make clear to the Americans that they could always rely on the Berliners, that was one of my tasks.

I was also the bearer of a second message. Berlin was not only determined to defend its right to live, but it was also not at all panic-stricken, or desperate. To state this fact seemed to me especially important in view of the alarming reports in the world press. In the postwar years the Berliners had proved their tenacity, their will to work, their energy and determination, and for it they had earned approval and admiration. They also had steady nerves. The people at the Berlin front awaited the coming events with greater composure than many millions in the Western hinterland.

However, the Berliners were no gamblers; they fear and detest war. Who was in a better position to know what war meant than the men and women of battered and scorched Berlin! Yet, who was also in a better position to know what the loss of freedom meant!

And finally: just before the Soviet Premier had started his campaign for the end of the Four Power agreements on Berlin, the world press had published reports about a rebirth of Nazism and anti-Semitism in Germany. The foreign observers were wrong to believe that the sympathizers and fellow travelers of the man from Braunau could again play an important role in Germany, or even regain influence. On the other hand, it would be wrong and childish to deny that there are still Nazis left in Germany—and not only in Germany.

The distrust abroad was rather understandable if one thought of the shortcomings of some German courts, for example, or some German schools, or if one realized how a considerable part of the German nation lived quite indolently from day to day—between yesterday and tomorrow, without yesterday and tomorrow. Small wonder, that in the midst of the crisis questions were raised abroad, anxious, sometimes bitter and unfair questions. They had to be answered.

This was, in my opinion, the only honest answer: certain manifestations of the Nazi spirit cannot be denied, and as isolated as they may be, their danger must not be underestimated. It is bad enough that here and there the swastika has appeared again, that synagogues have been desecrated, that Jewish co-citizens have been molested, that vicious pamphlets have turned up. That must not be minimized; that, we in Berlin do not want to minimize. All of us have every reason to be ashamed. But how could one reasonably expect that a madness, to which admittedly half or more of the German people had succumbed for over ten years, would disappear within a short time without leaving a trace? It is true that many among our people banned from their memory what should have been kept alive. I personally have never believed in the therapeutic effect of "letting grass grow over the past." But in all modesty I want to point out that the world political crisis, the tensions of the Cold War have not been the best possible climate for eradicating the heritage that was handed to us in 1945. The yardstick for the strength or weakness of the German democracy and the reliability of the new Germany was not the number of Nazi provocations, but the determination of the politically responsible forces to expose such cases fearlessly and to prosecute and punish the incorrigibles. In this respect the parties of the Federal Republic, the authorities of the Bundesländer, and the press had to be commended There was not a single important newspaper in western Germany which did not immediately seize upon any case of anti-Semitism and which did not attack any sign of neo-Nazism with all force. That was *one* guarantee that the new Germany was worthy of the trust of the democratic world.

The *second* guarantee was—Berlin. Through bitter experience it has learned the lesson that any new totalitarian threat must be met at once with unwavering determination. In order to understand, however, what this city means for the future of a new Germany—and of a free Europe—it is necessary to see Berlin not only as an outpost in the Cold War, not only as a bulwark *against* the further advance of communism, but also to appreciate the role which Berlin is called upon to play in the struggle *for* democracy. To evaluate this role correctly Berlin should not merely be regarded in its relation to our immediate present and its problems, but in the perspective of the last forty years.

What are forty years in the life of a city, of a nation? Well, these years count double or threefold, as one must admit. And they hold the key to an understanding of the present, they answer the question about the future—Berlin's, as well as Germany's.

Hardly any other capital has been so often misunderstood as Berlin. Even the Germans themselves have always had a complex and antagonistic attitude toward this city. Paris is France, the Englishman sees in London the symbol of the national character—Berlin, so we have been told over and over again, "is not Germany." In that respect Berlin shares the fate of New York, which is supposed to be "not America," not typical of the way of life and the aspirations of the overwhelming majority of the people, contrary to the national character, hostile to it.

When the King of Prussia was proclaimed the Emperor of Germany, Berlin was made the capital of the Reich. Thus the city became by necessity the symbol of the Wilhelminian era: aggressive, dynamic, ruthless in the pursuit of its own interests, cold, efficient but without imagination, always pushing forward but in reality without a goal; faithful to its duties but obdurate; authoritarian, militaristic. Prussia and her *Junkers* had imposed their hard will upon the peace-loving, easygoing, and life-enjoying German states in the south and the west of the Reich. Up north, in the "sandbox of Brandenburg," life offered the people very little. It was therefore logical that they became enthusiastic about death. Berlin was the Sparta—Munich the Athens of the new empire.

Berlin was seen in this light not only by foreigners—Munich, Frankfort, Dresden looked upon that city with irony and often with scorn. It had surpassed them in influence and power, a typical parvenue. "Berlin is accused always of becoming something and never being something," a German historian once declared.

It is not easy to establish when and how a myth was born. Many circumstances and factors contribute to its growth: hurt sentimentalities, the feelings—real or imagined—of endured injustice, concrete events and intangible moods, falsehood and truth. Yet, one thing is sure: myths have a longer life and are more powerful than reality.

The myth of Berlin as a stronghold of Wilhelminian militarism could not even be shaken by the fact that it was the home of prominent liberal intellectuals and the center of the rising labor movement, less Byzantine and more republican than most of the other cities in Germany.

The Berliners had more than once revolted against the autocratic rule of the mighty. Yet, when people spoke of 1848, they first thought of Frankfort and Vienna, whereas at the mention of Berlin they remembered instinctively the picture of the imperial family—Wilhelm II and his five sons, each in the uniform of another branch of the armed services, marching in step down Unter den Linden in 1914, at the beginning of World War I.

Four years later Berlin was "the stronghold of the Spartacists," although Hamburg or Leipzig could easily contend with Berlin for this title. The mutiny of the sailors in Kiel, the proclamation of a Soviet Republic in Munich, the bloody riots in Hamburg, in the Ruhr Valley, and in the industrial districts of Central Germany were regarded as passing events in a time of general confusion—the Communist excesses in Berlin were taken as a conclusive proof of the rootlessness of its population.

The insubordination of the workers was said to correspond to the lewdness of the upper middle class. "Berlin, the city of sin"—this catchword united the upright citizens of the provinces in their abhorrence of this "sink of corruption" and in their determination to share in the vices which Friedrichstrasse und Kurfürstendamm had to offer. The *Reeperbahn* in Hamburg offered entertainment of a much more disreputable kind. Every big city is a natural hotbed of prostitution, sexual aberrations, and criminality; Berlin was no exception. But since the poisonous elements of the big city could also be found in Berlin, the whole city was said to be a regular morass.

The myth of the sinful, rootless, corrupt, anti-national Berlin was an effective weapon in the hand of Goebbels. Hitler and his accomplices knew very well why they had no love for Berlin. They demanded blind faith—the Berliner is by nature "bright" and always a skeptic; they wanted to keep the people in a perpetual state of delirium—the Berliner is sober; they served pathos—the Berliner scoffs at bombast, he simply refuses to take braggarts and boasters seriously. Therefore, he has been accused of cynicism. But are not most cynics thwarted idealists? At any rate, the Berliner doesn't like to make a show of his feelings; he rather hides them behind a biting wit. It is a caustic wit which, like a corrosive acid, reduces false gold to talmi.

It is dangerous to generalize and to assign uniform characteristics to a whole nation, or even a city. Rightly it has often been pointed out that most Berliners were not born here; they came from Breslau, Pomerania, or Vienna, not to speak of a French element, the descendants of the Huguenots who found asylum here after their expulsion from France. This does not alter the fact, however, that Berlin's specific way of life has molded its inhabitants in quite a particular manner and formed their character. Climate and traditions had much to do with it, and also the struggle for existence which was harder here than in most other cities—but also more rewarding.

How great Berlin's creative energies are, the world realized most clearly in the twenties.

Eight years passed between the end of the great economic crisis that robbed the mass of the German people of their material possessions, and the brown barbarism that robbed them of their souls: after war, revolution, and inflation eight short years of relative peace and limited security. The respite was sufficient to make Berlin the intellectual and artistic metropolis of Europe, more openminded than Paris, more cosmopolitan than London.

For eight years Berlin was leading in modern music, architecture, in drama and films. Here everyone who had something to say or to show could be sure of finding support and an interested audience. No doubt, there were swindlers and mountebanks who took advantage of Berlin's passion for everything modern. Every new approach or trend was hailed as important, just because it was new. Much of what was written, published, and produced was immature, and remained an experiment. But even those experiments stimulated artists, dramatists, producers, architects in the whole world; Erwin Piscator's productions, Ernst Toller's and Bert Brecht's plays, the atonal music of Schönberg, and the modern architecture which Gropius promoted, the paintings of the expressionist and abstract school—for all these artists Berlin was an important laboratory. The influence of that period is still felt today.

Berlin's great and positive accomplishments are, of course, no excuse for the errors, offenses, and crimes of the following years. It is true, the majority of Berlin's population resisted the lures and threats of the brown seducers longer than other towns; the convinced Nazis were—even in the years of Hitler's great successes—a minority among the Berliners. But there were plenty of fellow travelers and cowards—as everywhere in Germany. Heroes and martyrs were scarce—in Berlin just as elsewhere.

The thesis of the collective guilt of the German people is not only unfair but also wrong—though it is understandable why the victims and witnesses of Hitler's maniacal tyranny cried for revenge, and demanded atonement without making a distinction between Germans and Nazis.

The German people have the right to reject the thesis of their collective guilt, but they cannot escape the collective responsibility for the great catastrophe. The majority of the Germans took no part in the crimes of the Nazis; much too late did they realize the truth. However, a whole generation has to bear the responsibility for the acquiescence in the rise to power of a band of criminals.

This responsibility the Berliners share with the rest of the Germans.

Collective responsibility implies that the citizen must feel accountable for the national affairs and the actions—or omissions—of his political representatives, of the authorities and the government. In good times, when full employment, prosperity, and rapidly increasing comfort turn your thoughts exclusively toward the acquisition of a refrigerator, a television set, a motorcycle, or a car—treasures we hardly expected ever to possess and which are now suddenly within our grasp—there is little interest left for the welfare of others. Everyone regards himself as the architect of his own good fortune, you take every success as the well-deserved reward for your own ability and toil; proudly, even haughtily, you look down on those who live in less favorable circumstances. After all, it is their fault, you have no time for them and don't want to have your pleasures spoiled by their complaints. No, there is no time to look back, nor to ask questions; no time for self-criticism.

The symphony of the "Wirtschaftswunder" sounds much louder than the voices of the warners—they are only discordant notes in the general rhythm. One praises "rugged individualism," and means egoism. Collective responsibility? "Collective" has something to do with communism—better keep away from all politics. One wants to be responsible only for the dazzling accomplishments of the present, not for the sinister events of the recent past. Those years should be forgotten, anyhow.

Such an attitude is human. One finds it in Berlin as well as in the west of Germany. But there is an essential difference. In Berlin the past is a living present. Here it cannot be forgotten.

In the west the division of Germany is a deplorable fact which one has to accept, no matter how sad that may be. In Berlin the division is felt as an insufferable pain; it cannot be dulled by neon lights, skyscrapers, and the fancy goods in the shop windows. The border cuts through every second family.

This doesn't mean that the Berliners are bent on revenge and indulge in a cheap nationalism. For the men at the front war is not an exciting adventure, no "bath of iron." An American saying is that there are no atheists in fox holes. Be that as it may, the men in the fox holes have, no doubt, a better instinct for the real values in life. To them democracy is not a vague formula but something real, all the more precious because they have gained it only by hard, practical experience.

How Berlin acts in good and bad days, in boom and recession is of particular importance to the whole of Germany—and not only to Germany. The capital of a united Germany—and this Berlin will and must be someday again—can exert a guiding influence on all democratic forces in Europe.

Every day Berlin tries anew to show itself worthy of this task, conscious of its close relationship with the people on both sides of the Iron Curtain: with the countrymen in the free Federal Republic and with the captive Germans in the East Zone, and last but not least, with the democratic nations whose friendship and support Berlin can only expect if its people prove by their deeds that they have learned from the mistakes and errors of the past.

There is no better way of proving it than by accepting a collective responsibility for the defense of freedom and justice—the freedom and the rights of the individual.

The Berlin of 1945 was a terrible example of the price a nation has to pay if it shirks this responsibility.

The Berlin of 1960, on the other hand, is an example of the strength and the spiritual power people can acquire, provided they find the way to self-criticism and truth. It is only due to that inner strength that they have been able to perform those feats of endurance and reconstruction that have astonished the world and even themselves.

2

I do not know how many of the New Yorkers who greeted me so enthusiastically understood the example and the lesson of Berlin fully and clearly. Nevertheless, I would like to believe they all felt that what united them with Berlin was more than expediency.

New Yorkers seemed to me very much like Berliners. They have the same instinctive aversion for bombast and pomp; they have natural wit, a refreshing irreverence which is never a sign of envy or enmity, but the natural way to make one feel a friend among friends: "Good boy, Willy!" "Good luck, Willy!" "*Mach's gut,* Willy!" Berliners and New Yorkers speak the same language.

I am not a Berliner. I was born in Lübeck, I spent many

years in foreign countries, a critical period of my life in Norway and Sweden. It was only after the end of the war that I became a Berliner. But since my early youth I have been devoted to what Berlin stands for today. And it was not accidental that I returned to Berlin in 1946. The decision to link my fate with the fate of Berlin was as well considered as it was inevitable.

Norway, where I had fled in 1933, meant more to me than an asylum. It was my second home. In 1940, Hitler robbed me of my home the second time. I worked for a free Norway and a democratic Germany. When I made up my mind to devote all my energies to the reconstruction of Germany, I did not choose Germany in preference to Norway—I chose a future upon whose realization the fate of all of us depends —not only Germany's or Norway's.

How I reached that decision and why I became a Berliner, is the story of my life. Or rather, two stories: mine and Berlin's. They cannot be separated from each other.

1

CHAPTER TWO

A Boy Called Herbert Frahm

1

Of the boy Herbert Ernst Karl Frahm I have only a vague recollection. I know that he was born in Lübeck just before Christmas 1913, on December 18. The mother was very young, a salesgirl in a co-operative store. He never knew his father, not even who his father was. And he did not want to know. He carried the name of the mother; the father was never mentioned at home.

Home was a modest worker's flat, one room and a kitchen, but to him it was not a home. Since the mother could take care of him only after working hours, he was, during the first years of his life, left all day long in charge of a woman who lived not far from where the mother was employed. He was often alone, left to himself for many hours. He had practically no playmates.

When Herbert was four or five years old the war entered his life for the first time. The war appeared in the shape of a man in a muddy soldier's coat. The man smelled of sweat, wet leather, powder and oil. The odor fascinated Herbert, as did the rough cloth of the heavy coat, the leather belt, the long bayonet. He climbed quickly on the lap of the man whom he called "Papa." He let himself be kissed, the bristly beard tickled him. He liked the soldier from the very beginning. From then on the three lived together and the little apartment became a home.

But not for long. "Papa," who was the widowed grandfather, remarried. Herbert went to live with him and his wife, whom he called aunt. He didn't like her too much.

To Grandfather, on the other hand, he became very much attached. This was a simple honest man and an excellent storyteller. He could answer all questions and answered them gladly. Mother visited them once or twice a week. She tried to spoil the boy within the limits of her modest means.

Grandfather had grown up in the country, as a laborer on one of the big estates of a famous count in Mecklenburg. Grandfather's father had still been treated like a bondsman and had been whipped more than once. Corporal punishment was given even for a slight offense. Grandfather, however, revolted against the landlord's rule.

Until then it was the custom that just before an election to the Parliament the landlords had brandy distributed among the laborers. On election day the men had to come to the house of the overseer. There in the living room a big soup tureen stood in the middle of a table. The men passed in front of the overseer, who sat behind the table and took down their names. They had to put their ballots into the tureen, one on top of the other. Thus, the landlord could easily ascertain later how each laborer had voted.

When Grandfather approached the table he overturned, as if by accident, the tureen, the ballots scattered, the overseer fumed and cursed, but there was nothing he could do: he could not find out which ballot belonged to which worker.

Grandfather had outwitted him, for he was a follower of August Bebel, the leader of the Socialists, one of the first party members in the village.

Later Grandfather moved into town and became a worker in a factory. After the war he found employment in the Lubeck Draeger-Works. He was a truck driver.

A few years later Herbert had probably the strongest experience of his childhood.

The workers in Lübeck went on strike. The strike led to a general lockout. Those were bad days.

Herbert was eight or nine years old, old enough to understand the difference between rich and poor. He knew that he belonged to the poor, that there was much that was beyond his reach. But real misery he had not yet known. Now suddenly hunger was standing in the kitchen, like an evil landlord.

"Are you hungry, my boy?"

Herbert had stopped in front of a bakery and was staring longingly at the bread and the rolls. Never before had they seemed so crisp. The smell from the shop made him slightly dizzy. In confusion he turned around.

The boy immediately recognized the gentleman who had spoken to him. He was the "Herr Attorney General," one of the directors of the Draeger-Works.

Herbert swallowed with difficulty. Then he nodded.

Whereupon the director took him by the hand, led him into the store, bought two loaves of bread, and gave them to him. "Here you are, my boy," he said.

Herbert turned on his heels and ran as fast as he could. He was afraid the gentleman might change his mind and take the bread away from him.

He arrived at home out of breath. And breathlessly he told his grandfather of the unexpected luck.

Grandfather became very serious. "Take the bread back!" he said. "At once."

Herbert did not understand. "Back . . . ? The Herr Attorney General gave them to me."

"Gave them . . . ! A striker accepts no gifts from his employer. We will not let ourselves be bribed by our enemy. We are no beggars, to whom one throws some alms. We ask for our right, not for gifts. Take back the bread, immediately."

Never before had Herbert seen his grandfather so hard and so angry. Great was his confusion, yet still greater his shame. Should he not have known? He had listened carefully to the discussions at home between Grandfather and his relatives and fellow workers. Now, of course, he could do nothing but carry out the order. In fact, it was more than an ordinary order; it was rather a mission which Grandfather entrusted to him. He felt like a soldier who was sent with a message into the camp of the enemy.

Proudly he marched back to the bakery, haughtily he put the bread on the counter. "Here—we don't want it!" he shouted. The triumph he felt made him forget even the hunger. This childhood experience strengthened the bond between Herbert and his grandfather.

Herbert was a good student, the best in his class. He learned easily, he was an avid reader. But he liked even more to listen to Grandfather's tales about the war and about the future when there would be no wars, about the misery in the country and how the Social Democrats would end all misery forever.

Like his schoolmates, Herbert found his heroes in the world of the fairy tales and legends. Unlike most of his friends, he had, however, heroes of his own: August Bebel and Ferdinand Lassalle, the leaders of the new Social Democratic party.

To Grandfather socialism was more than a political program; it was rather a kind of religion. It would make all men brothers, eliminate all injustice from the world, even the money would disappear. Herbert never tired of listening to these prophecies, and his heart beat faster when Grandfather started to sing the revolutionary songs of the workers, the "Marseillaise," the "March of the Socialists."

Those were hectic years. It was said the Social Democrats were in power—but did they really have power? Their leader, Fritz Ebert, was President of the Republic—but mostly the will of the other parties prevailed. Grandfather and his friends always spoke about the danger that the clock of history might soon be turned back. This fear they never lost.

In 1920 the Kapp Putsch, a reactionary coup of the military in Berlin, was crushed by a general strike of the workers.

In 1921 the Communists staged a coup. It too was unsuccessful.

In 1922, after the assassination of Walter Rathenau, the Foreign Minister of the Republic, the pent-up wrath of the workers exploded in huge demonstrations.

At one of these occasions the workers of Lübeck disarmed and interned the police and formed a militia. Grandfather was on duty in one of the police stations as a clerk behind the desk, a red badge around his arm. Herbert was permitted to take Grandfather his lunch.

He found Grandfather and his comrades in great excitement. A republican guard had caught a man who had answered the call of nature at a street corner. The man was a worker! How could he behave so lowly! At once the punishment was meted out—a sound thrashing on his behind. That would teach him to remember proletarian dignity and republican discipline.

In 1923 the inflation reached its climax. The ten-year-old boy did not understand its causes. This strange word "inflation" that everyone used—the way the words "war" and "revolution" were still used—acquired a concrete meaning when you had to buy your provisions immediately after you got your pay check, since the next day the money had lost its value. When the new mark was introduced the pupils were asked to collect all the old paper money and to bring it to school. Big laundry baskets full of bank notes were brought. For each ten billion marks the collector got a candy stick. It cost a pfennig in the new money.

When he was thirteen Herbert, in recognition of his good marks, was admitted to a *Realschule* (high school). He was granted a scholarship. The following year he entered the Johanneum, a senior high school of great reputation.

At that time his mother married. Her husband was a tall, sturdy, warmhearted bricklayer who hailed from Mecklenburg and was a Social Democrat like the grandfather. Herbert called him uncle.

It was in those days that Herbert heard for the first time the name of a man who was allegedly his father. The name sounded Swedish or Danish or Norwegian. The boy was not interested. Or was he?

I don't know. I remember no more than the few episodes just described. An opague veil hangs over those years, gray as the fog over the port of Lübeck. Figures and faces are like shadows—they rise to the surface and disappear again, like flotsam on the waves of the northern sea.

It is hard for me to believe that the boy Herbert Frahm was—I, myself.

2

The four years which I spent at the Johanneum were an important period in my life, not so much for the very good education I received, but because I entered for the first time a world which, though not hostile, was strange to me. There were few boys from the working class.

There were also few teachers who were sympathetic to the young Republic.

I was more interested in the youth movement than in school. During the previous years I had belonged successively to the children's group of the Workers Sport Association, to the Social Democratic *Kinderfreunde* (children's friends), to the Workers Mandolin Club. Later I joined a group of the "Falcons," a kind of boy scouts. As a leader of that group I entered the Socialist Workers Youth. That was in 1929.

During the first years at the Johanneum I was among the best students. Later on I began to neglect my studies; I played truant.

Still, it would be unfair not to pay tribute to some teachers to whom I owe much. Outstanding among them was Professor Eilhard Erich Pauls, my teacher in German and history.

He was a Frisian, and the free spirit of the peasants and fishermen of his native land was reflected in his teaching method and in his relationship with us students. With his pince-nez and his bushy mustache he looked like the typical German professor, but he was not at all typical of the average teacher, who, conscious of his intellectual superiority and of his social standing, scorned the common people and mourned for the "good old days" of the Kaiser. He gave no lectures in the usual sense, he never addressed us ex cathedra, but used to walk up and down the classroom, turning each lecture into an informal discussion, always stimulating, always provoking contradiction and debates. Although he himself was a conservative, he gave me a chance to win the highest mark at the final examination in history by allowing me to write a paper on August Bebel.

German and history were my favorite subjects. I did not share the enthusiasm of some of my schoolmates for poetry. I was not carried away by the rhythm and the melody of the poems which we had to learn by heart. I was interested in novels which "had something to say," in biographies, and first of all in reports on social conditions which gave you a better insight into political problems. Andersen Nexo, the Danish novelist, Erich Maria Remarque, Thomas Mann were my favorite authors.

I decided to become a journalist. Already, at fourteen, I had written little pieces for the local Social Democratic paper, the *Volksboten* (the *People's Messenger*). I won a prize, a copy of Fenimore Cooper's *Leatherstocking Tales.* Encouraged by this success, I tried my hand at short features and little essays.

Little as I was paid for my literary efforts, this was my first self-earned money. Eagerly I began to chase after incidents and events which I could turn into a story. I lacked professional knowledge, not zeal.

Once I came across two men fishing in the River Trave. Here I saw an opportunity to show the social significance of a seemingly innocent hobby. My pride about this accomplishment in the field of "social realism" was rudely jolted when the Workers Fishermen Association sent a protest to the newspaper against the "nonsense" I had written and accused me of "reporting something I knew nothing about." From then on I thought it more advisable to stick to political matters.

Politics was my favorite dish. Even in school I grasped at every opportunity to start a political discussion. Professor Kramer, our teacher in English and French, had sympathy with the rebellious spirit of the one Socialist in class and did not object too strenuously. (Years later, heartbroken and in despair about Hitler's triumph, he committed suicide.)

Once Kramer told us of a mass meeting of the unemployed which he had attended. The men had "cried for bread," he said ironically, but actually "what they wanted was the sausage for that bread." Whereupon I replied: "And why not?

Why should the unemployed be satisfied with a piece of dry bread?"

This remark—and many others of a still more inflammatory nature—prompted Professor Kramer to send for my mother. "Keep your son away from politics," he advised her. "The boy is gifted—what a pity, politics will ruin him."

At our final examination we had the right to choose between three themes. One was taken from history, one dealt with Goethe, the third was based on the statement of a student who was going in for his high school diploma. "When we look back on our years at school we must say they gave us nothing for our future life."

Only two students chose that theme. One, because it offered him a chance to win the sympathy of the Board of Examiners by refuting this heretical thesis. The other one was I. I tried to prove the student was not so wrong. Nevertheless, they let me pass. After all, I had been an outstanding student for many years, I had been given a scholarship, it would have put the school in a bad light if I failed.

In large measure my troubles at school were the result of my acquaintance with a man not connected with the school. His activity and example had a strong impact on my thinking and my work—and not only in those years. He exercised a lasting influence on my whole life.

Professor Pauls put me on the road to journalism. Dr. Julius Leber made me a militant democrat and a liberal socialist.

3

I joined the Socialist Youth by necessity, as it were. Mother, her husband, and Grandfather were all active members of the Social Democratic party and of the trade unions. I was born into socialism, so to speak. But that doesn't mean I was spared troubles and errors trying to find my own place in the socialist organization.

The youth movement attracted me primarily on account of its romanticism: it meant hiking and camping, close comradeship, life in tents, songs at the open campfire. I was a good swimmer but did not go in for athletic records. Once I entered a 5000-meter race and won—for I was the only contestant.

I loved nature. We went on long hikes, visited the North Sea and the Baltic. We spent a summer on an island near Andernach on the Rhine, where the "Falcons" had a camp. What a romantic landscape! I fell in love with the charming hills, with the old castles and ruins, with the mystic legends attached to them.

We did a lot of reading and sat up long into the night, discussing the meaning of life and solving the riddle of the universe. Still more important was the practical democracy we learned from our living together. We had to face tasks which we could master only through our co-operative effort. We began to understand the importance of organization and of voluntary discipline. We realized how many—seemingly unimportant—details had to be considered in order to make people of different background and opposite temperaments work together in the interest of a common cause And we learned to help ourselves. In our youth movement we had to rely on our own ability and means; we did not expect to be helped or supported by the state.

The youth movement was a good training. I showed a certain gift for organization, I was a good speaker, and already at sixteen I was given a responsible position. Temporarily I was president of the organization in my district.

In 1930 I was admitted to the Social Democratic party as a regular member. I was not yet seventeen, and to become a member one had to be at least eighteen years old. An exception was made in the case of the "contributing editor" of the *Volksboten.* Julius Leber was my sponsor.

Julius Leber was editor in chief of the *Volksboten*, the uncontested leader of the Lubeck Social Democrats and deputy to the Reichstag.

He hailed from Alsace, and he looked like a Latin, with his sharply cut features, a high forehead, burning eyes, the strong jaw and a soft sensual mouth. When he stood on the platform his rhetoric and his expressive gestures made one think of a Roman tribune.

He was born in a little village in Upper Alsace and grew up in very modest, not to say proletarian circumstances. After finishing the village school he was admitted to the high school; the parson had intervened on behalf of the unusually bright boy. Soon he gave up his studies, since he had to go to work. Again someone who recognized his abilities came to his rescue: Leber was granted a scholarship at the *Oberrealschule* (senior high school) in Freiburg. He earned his living by giving lessons to fellow students and contributing articles to different papers. In the same manner he worked his way through the universities of Strasbourg and Freiburg, fighting a never ending battle against hunger and want.

In 1914 he volunteered for the Army. At the front he was commissioned a lieutenant and was decorated several times for bravery. As an officer of the newly created German Army he took an active part in the suppression of the Kapp Putsch. Presently he resigned his commission and acquired a doctor's degree in political science.

He was thirty when he came to Lübeck and found a job on the editorial staff of the *Volksboten*. Soon he was recognized as the most outstanding personality in the labor movement of northern Germany.

Leber was an "intellectual," yet the little people, the workers, regarded him as one of their own. He expressed what they had at heart, he had an unerring instinct for their aspirations and hopes. He had their confidence, for they felt rightly:

here was a man who knew what he wanted and wanted it passionately. Here was a man who never compromised, not a fanatic, but a real fighter.

The front experience had formed him. He was convinced that "personality, strong will, and strong hearts had a heavier weight than the dead apparatus of a political party." This point of view brought him in conflict with the bureaucrats of his party. He reproached the leaders with stifling the creative energies of the youth; he called them "captives of outdated formulas and slogans."

With equal determination he fought against the radicals who in pursuing their socialist goals declared democracy "old hat," not worth defending. As internationalists they equated love of one's country with shallow nationalism Leber criticized the weaknesses of the Weimar Republic but vigorously upheld the thesis that "socialism without democracy was inconceivable "

"One has tried," so he said in one of his articles, "to prove that there is a conflict between authority and order on the one side, and freedom and justice on the other. We, however, will never forget that freedom and justice, authority and order are dependent on each other; they complement each other The fullest freedom under a system of anarchy where the state has no authority to intervene practically means slavery for the weak and poor—turning justice into highest injustice "

As an Alsatian he was much concerned about the relationship between Germans and Frenchmen—"the people on the right and the left side of the Rhine who mix like the vine from both banks."

Since he asserted that a sovereign state could not remain defenseless and that therefore the German Republic should be permitted an army, he was denounced as a "Rightist."

The Left accused him of betraying the principles of the

class struggle. He wanted the Social Democratic party to be "a home for the youth of the middle class who in the war had lost its way and was searching for a new fatherland." Not only the Left scoffed at this strange socialist who was traveling his own special road to socialism.

We members of the Socialist Youth were, naturally, "Leftists." But that did not affect my personal relationship with Leber. I had grown up without a father; there was an emptiness in my life—Leber filled it.

I had many friends but not one who was really close to me. This was probably my fault; I felt it difficult to confide in other people. From my early years I had maintained this reserve. Accustomed to live within myself, I found it not easy to share my sentiments and inner thoughts with others.

Leber was to me more than a teacher or older friend. I would have never admitted that I lacked self-confidence, but secretly I had my doubts. Leber dispelled them by giving me recognition and encouragements. His occasional praise meant all the more to me because he also never hesitated to criticize my youthful impetuosity. He did it with a slight amiable irony. He treated me as his equal. He took me seriously.

The year 1930 brought decisive changes. The Social Democrats left the Federal government; in the last few years they had lost much of their influence, which was anyhow always weaker than their opponents asserted.

There were also other changes, one could see them in the faces of the people. Even the well-known scene of the streets of Lübeck underwent a change. Most of our older and more experienced party members did not realize what was going on. We, the young ones, saw more clearly. We met the Hitler youth in our meetings and in private sessions, we clashed with them, we fought them with words and fists.

These incidents were not to be taken seriously, we were

told. The Nazis were a small sect and in Lübeck certainly not a danger To some extent that was true.

In September the Nazis entered the Reichstag, a hundred and seven men strong; they had become the second strongest party

In the previous elections the Nazis had won not more than twelve seats—now 6 4 million people voted for them. Their unexpected victory deepened the disappointment about the failure of the parties of the Left. In the ranks of the Socialist Youth more and more voices were raised against the leadership of our party. It was accused of a large measure of responsibility for this disaster. The accusations became more and more violent, the criticism against the policy of retreat and compromise more and more bitter:

Republic? "It favors its sworn enemies and persecutes its followers." Social reforms? "Sedatives to paralyze the activity and energy of the masses." The Social Democratic deputies had voted for the construction of an armored cruiser, "but the enemy was in our midst." Democracy? "An empty word." The number of unemployed rose from month to month, millions of them were completely hopeless. They asked for work, and the government put them off with subsidies which were "too little to live on and too much to die on."

The crisis demanded revolutionary measures, but the Social Democratic leaders, in our opinion, offered nothing but resolutions. "No wonder the Communists took advantage of that situation. Maybe they were not wrong after all: under a proletarian dictatorship the workers could at least hope to secure their existence and to render harmless the enemies of the people."

Lubeck had one of the strongest Social Democratic organizations in all Germany, and it remained a bulwark of the progressive forces. But even here one could see now an ever growing number of citizens, of young people, of unemployed with the swastika in their lapel. Slogans which up to then had only adorned the recesses of public lavatories now openly appeared on the walls of many buildings, on huge banners: "Germany arise! Death to the Jews!" The SA, or storm troopers, the armed bands of the Nazi party, made their contribution to the "rejuvenation" of Germany by beating up and killing their opponents. Many a street became a battlefield.

One evening in an outskirt of the city there was a scuffle between an SA troop and some of our comrades. Some of our friends were wounded, a Nazi was killed. A trial ensued, and I was one of the defendants. In this case I had not been even near the fight. I was acquitted "for want of proof." My good Professor Kramer found it, nevertheless, a disgrace that a student of the Johanneum had to appear in court under the accusation of manslaughter.

In spite of the growing power of the Nazis, Leber rejected any alliance with the Communists. He fought with equal vigor both the hammer and sickle and the swastika. In the case of everyone else such a "rightist" attitude would have met with scorn on our part. In the case of Leber we made an exception. We could not help admiring his strong personality. Nobody could suspect him of being inclined to compromise. Even his most bitter enemies had to respect his personal courage.

Only much later did I realize that the "Rightists" of the type of Leber and the youthful and impatient "Leftists" in the German Social Democratic party were much closer to each other than we assumed in those days, when we were separated by walls of ideologies and dogmas.

There was, however, one point on which we could never agree—Leber's attitude toward the military. We had grown up in the anti-militaristic tradition of the German labor movement, we had been taught to distrust the "reigning class," whereas Leber knew that in order to gain power the Social

Democrats had to either win the sympathy and allegiance of the Army or remain without influence.

As passionately as Leber stuck to his principles, he always defended our right to express our own opinions freely and openly. Fairness was one of his main characteristics.

One day a party magazine published an article by a prominent Socialist leader Disgusted with the nefarious tactics of the Communists, the man, a deputy of the Reichstag, compared the famous Karl Liebknecht with Adolf Hitler and declared that they were not different from each other. I was enraged; Communist or no Communist, Liebknecht in World War I had fought most heroically for peace, he had been an idealist, a humanitarian, he had been murdered in the most brutal manner. Immediately I wrote a letter to the editor, in which I heaped scorn on that deputy's head. My letter appeared in the next issue of the magazine.

The following day I was called into the office of the party secretary. He told me my letter was inexcusable, I had committed a breach of party discipline, and Leber wanted to have a serious word with me.

When we entered Leber's office the secretary at once launched his attack against me. Leber let him speak. He nodded a few times, never looked in my direction. At last he asked the secretary to leave the room. Now we two were alone. For a moment he remained silent I squared my shoulders, I was not going to give in. Even Leber would not succeed in making me recant my accusations.

At last he said softly: "You know how to write. But why don't you let your articles lie on your desk for at least one night before you send them off to press? The next morning, looking at your manuscript, you yourself will probably find that some rewrite might be in order. As a result your articles will improve, don't you think?"

Leber spoke without irony. I had been prepared to meet

an accusation, instead I received friendly advice. I left the room much less sure of myself than I had been when I entered.

Not all our discussions ended as peacefully. The radicalization of the Left, furthered by the provocations of the Nazis and by the growing economic crisis, widened the gap between the Youth and the party leadership. In the fall of 1931 the break became inevitable.

4

In the summer a friend and I took a trip to Scandinavia, to Norway. It was my first independent journey to a foreign country. True, I had been to Denmark in 1927, but at that time my trip had been sponsored by a welfare organization and I had been under the care of a family in Vejle. Now I could decide for myself where I wanted to go and what I wanted to see.

We went to Copenhagen, and from there we took a freighter to Bergen. I was enthusiastic about the beauty of Norway, the fjords, the glaciers. Here nature was really wild, we could hike for hours without finding a trace of modern civilization. The mountains of Germany with their thickly populated valleys and their fertile pastures seemed tame in comparison.

The Norwegian people made even a stronger impression on me. The simple farmer had natural dignity, was conscious of his worth and quite well educated. What surprised us young Germans most was to see how even the poorest farmer and worker regarded himself an equal to any other citizen

In later years, during my long stay in Norway and Sweden, I studied the history of these people, I learned to understand their social and economic institutions, the background and moving forces of their political lives. My first visit was too short and I was too young to gain more than a superficial view of the country and its inhabitants. It was enough to show me the principal differences between the political and social conditions in Germany and Norway.

The people with whom I discussed politics—and most of them understood either German or English—seldom used the word "democracy"; they used the word "*Folkestyre*" instead. That means "government of the people." Democracy in the modern sense, based on the sovereignty of the people and expressed in free elections, is in Norway not much older than in other Western European nations *Folkestyre* in the sense of the active participation of the individual in the administration and control of public affairs is deeply rooted in the conscience of the Nordic peoples. In contrast to most of Europe, the Scandinavian peasants never lost their freedom. There, feudalism never existed. Probably my strongest experience on that trip was the realization of the complete lack of pride of class and rank, which in the Weimar Republic was hardly less dominant than under the Kaiser, in spite of the revolution and the influence of the Democrats and Socialists.

I thought it natural that every Social Democrat regarded himself not only as a political opponent, but also as a personal enemy of the Conservative. I will never forget a talk I had with a Danish Social Democrat who had just returned from Germany. In Berlin he had visited the Reichstag. He was very pessimistic about the future of German democracy. The reason he gave for his skepticism surprised me very much.

In the restaurant of the Reichstag, so he explained, he had seen small signs on the different tables: "For members of the Center party only," "For members of the German Nationalist party only," etc. He said: "In a country where the deputies cannot eat their lunch together, it must be very hard to establish democracy."

For my Danish friend this was indeed an astonishing custom. In Copenhagen the deputies wandered from the *Folketing* (Parliament) to the so-called *Snapseting*, a dining room where they sometimes talked politics but most often left politics alone and talked about their garden and their children, or simply enjoyed a few drinks together. The Norwegian deputies were teetotalers; in the Parliament, however, the institution of separate party benches was unknown. All the deputies from the same district sat together.

I was, of course, a republican. I was convinced that progress, democracy, and social justice could only prevail under a republican system of government. The Scandinavian democracies, on the other hand, had no quarrel with the monarchy. Norwegian friends told me the following anecdote:

After the first great victory of labor in the elections of 1927 the King thought it logical to offer the government to that now strongest party. Some of his conservative counselors objected and pointed out that there were many Communists in the Labor party Whereupon King Haakon dryly replied: "Gentlemen, I am also the King of the Communists."

5

In the fall of 1931, Nazis and German Nationalists, storm troopers and *Stahlhelm* (steel helmet), a reactionary veterans' organization, united. The followers of Hitler hoped to overthrow the hated Social Democratic government of Prussia. But in spite of their alliance with the Conservatives and though supported by the Communists, their referendum, aimed at the dissolution of the Prussian Diet, failed. Now the most reactionary circles, the rich landowners and industrialists, financiers and officers, Schacht, the Minister of Finance, and General Seeckt, the head of the German Army, thought the moment opportune for "direct action." The answer of the Social Democrats to that threat was the formation of the "*Eiserne* front" (iron front), a concentration of different workers' sports organizations and of the *Reichsbanner*, a democratic veterans' association.

At the very same time the left-wing, Social Democrats, broke with the party; disciplinarian measures of the leadership provoked the split. A few deputies, a number of active party locals, and, last but not least, a great part of the Socialist Youth formed a new Socialist Workers party. From the practical point of view the new organization was destined to remain without influence. At that time we did not realize it. We wanted to believe in a new beginning, in the possibility of preventing a catastrophe at the last minute.

In Lübeck only a small number of older Social Democrats but many young comrades joined the new party. Leber tried to prevent me from following them. Was I completely mad, he asked. This time he lost his superior calm, which until then he had always shown in our personal discussions. The new party was an association of cripples, he asserted. They wanted to be revolutionary? They were impotents who, conscious of their physical and intellectual incapacities, escaped into radicalism. "In spite of your youth you can appreciate a good book, a good drink, the favors of a beautiful girl. You are quite normal, you don't belong to that band of sectarians."

I thought Leber unjust and protested more violently than I had ever dared before. We separated in bitterness.

I left the Social Democratic party. The direct consequences were hard on me. I suffered from my break with Leber. I could also no longer work on the *Volksboten*. The income from my other journalistic endeavors was minimal.

This was not the only material disadvantage of my joining the new party. I had planned to go to University, Leber had offered to help finance my studies. That was now out of question.

I could not complain about a lack of work. The new party made me, in spite of my youth, a political instructor. As organizer and speaker I was on the go day and night. But all my work was honorary. How should I earn my living?

I took a job with a firm of ship brokers in Lubeck. There I came in close contact with people who later proved useful to me: sailors, fishermen, longshoremen. I made good friends with the Scandinavian "clients." Between my political activity in the evening and my work for the firm during the day, I found no time for meditation and self-pity That was good. My life was hard, but I felt strong enough to master it.

*

CHAPTER THREE

Flight to Freedom

1

On July 20, 1932, the democratic forces once more had the opportunity to stop the bold advance of the Nazis in an open battle. It was probably their last chance. It was not taken

In the elections for the Prussian Diet, in April of that year, the government of Otto Braun remained in the minority. There was no majority for a government of the Right either. The anti-republican parties held 193 seats, 163 of which had been captured by Hitler. The parties of the so-called Weimar coalition—Democrats, the Catholic Center, and Social Democrats—elected 163 representatives. The Communists, fifty-seven men strong, were the tongue of the balance. Thereupon, in July, Herr von Papen, the Chancellor of the Reich, by means of emergency decrees and proclaiming martial law, dismissed the Prussian government. This was the open violation of the Constitution.

In the evening of that day I addressed a public meeting

called by the socialist workers in Lübeck. We—and not only we—expected the Social Democratic party to mobilize the masses for the defense of their last stronghold, to form a union with all parties and groups opposed to a Hitler regime, and to offer resistance to von Papen's *coup d'état*. Severing, the Prussian Minister of Interior, could still count on the police, at that time the only reliable republican force in Germany. The *Reichsbanner* and the other units of the "*Eiserne* front" were ready for action. A bold initiative of an active republican leadership would have probably rallied even the Communist workers to their side. Berlin was still a stronghold of democratic socialism, the power of the trade unions still unbroken.

Prussia seethed with indignation. On July 20, von Papen had treated the duly elected ministers as if they were hired hands on one of the estates of his fellow *Junkers*. He had threatened to throw them out of their offices if they did not leave peacefully. Many Prussian towns were eager to take up his challenge. Ernst Reuter, for instance, the noted mayor of Magdeburg, whose sober judgment and self-possession was generally recognized, wanted to give his police the order to march on Berlin.

Severing declined his offer. The Executive Committee of the Social Democratic party, on the one hand, called on its followers "to prepare themselves for a decisive fight," and on the other hand warned them "to beware of rash actions." Against von Papen's violation of the Constitution an appeal would be made to the Supreme Court.

It is doubtful whether the democratic forces could have remained victorious in an open battle against von Papen. Hitler and his storm troopers would have come immediately to his support. They would have had the German Army at their side, which in numbers and arms was by far superior to the Prussian police. The storm troopers and the reactionary *Stahl-*

helm were much better armed than the "*Eiserne* front." A general strike seemed hopeless to the Social Democratic leaders. The unemployed cannot strike, and there were nearly five million of them. In utter despair many had deserted to Hitler, who promised them everything: bread, work, jobs—even uniforms.

Today, however, it should be evident that the active resistance which the republican leaders regarded as "senseless" would definitely have made sense. Even though the fight might have cost many lives, it would at least have proven to the world that a great part of the German people believed in democracy, it would have united the republican forces and banished the general feeling of defeatism and hopelessness which—later on, even more than at that moment—demoralized the democratic Left and facilitated the stabilization of Hitler's dictatorship.

To be defeated in a battle, heroically fought against tremendous odds, is tragic; to surrender without a fight makes the tragedy a farce. It robs the victim of his last, most precious possession: his self-respect.

On that twentieth of July the backbone of the opposition against Hitler was broken.

As yet the republicans were not fully aware of the magnitude of the catastrophe. The violence of the Nazis, intoxicated with their triumph, provoked active resistance—in spite of the appeals of the leaders for discipline and reserve. Force was met with force in every public meeting, in the streets of every town; even in the Reichstag the deputies of the Left and Right fought each other with fists and inkwells.

And then we of the Socialist Workers party saw that in those decisive hours we in Lübeck could count on Leber as on no one else. Wherever there was a stiff fight, he was always on the spot.

We arranged a mass meeting at which Julius Leber proclaimed the order of the hour:

"We are in the midst of a counterrevolution. But we declare: our movement is stronger. History is on the side of freedom, and freedom will be with you as long as you fight for it.

"Today quite a few may ask, what the future will bring.

"I tell you: the final decision rests with you It is up to you to decide whether to call off the fight or to go on fighting. I say: we shall fight to the end.

"Victory or no victory, if one fights for liberty one doesn't ask what tomorrow will bring."

Suddenly everyone was on his feet. Men and women, their clenched fists raised, shouted themselves hoarse. My heart stopped, and then began to beat madly. I felt it in my throat. I wanted to jump on the platform, to squeeze Leber's hand. I had found him again. I had never lost him.

At this moment the Nazi SA stormed into the hall. They attacked with cudgels and life preservers, hitting men and women indiscriminately. But it was Leber whom they wanted. Suddenly he stood alone and unprotected on the platform. Presently he grabbed a chair, smashed it to pieces, and, using one of its legs as a weapon, he fought himself free.

There were many such bloody clashes in the following weeks. It almost looked as if these demonstrations of republican energy and determination made a strong impression on the minds of the wavering and undecided.

In the November elections the Nazis lost two million votes. In Magdeburg, Ernst Reuter sounded the call to action:

"Forward to the attack! Attack in all streets, in the factories, in every meeting—wherever we republicans have an opportunity to speak to the seduced and misled people!

"Attack against the demagogues and adventurers who are leading the nationalistic movement! Down with the government of Herr von Papen and his aristocratic clique who think they can rule and reign over us."

In the beginning of December, Herr von Papen resigned. The reality of the economic crisis was a fence which the gentleman rider could not take.

General von Schleicher became Chancellor. He intimated that he wanted to co-operate with the trade unions, he promised jobs for the workers and a liberal agrarian program for the distressed farmers.

At the same time a crisis developed in Hitler's party. The SA insisted the Fuhrer should carry through the promised revolution and seize by force the supreme power; one wing of the party, headed by Gregor Strasser, the influential Chief of Organization, afraid to be overrun by the wild adventurers, sought contacts with the Conservatives, who for their part had also become afraid of the mob. They stopped their subsidies, the Nazi party got into financial troubles, it could no longer meet its obligations. Hitler himself seemed undecided.

Was this the turning point?

Then the East Prussian *Junkers*, violently opposed to von Schleicher's agrarian program, helped Hitler out of his mess. They persuaded the old President von Hindenburg to drop Schleicher and to put Hitler in his place. These gentlemen, who always had a very high opinion of their political acumen, were sure they could keep "this vagabond house painter" firmly under control. To many high officers he was nothing but "a Bohemian corporal" who would quickly learn to obey orders. The masters of the heavy industry and high finance did not doubt for a single moment that they had the "Braunauer" in their pocket. They helped him out of his mess so that he could get rid of the trade unions and do away with the "lousy Republic." As soon as he had done the dirty job, they would give him the sack—they thought.

So came the thirtieth of January.

We young and radical Socialists, though we had quite a few wrong notions of our own, at least did not share the illusions of those reactionary politicians who had entered Hitler's cabinet, nor of their backers and employers. But we, too, strongly believed the Hitler regime would only last a short time. The Nazis would prove incapable of fulfilling their promises; that must be their undoing. The nation "of the best-trained and best-organized workers" could never be enslaved. Germany was not Italy.

The first of February, two days after Hitler had been appointed Chancellor, Julius Leber was arrested

On his way home from a session with some friends he was held up by a band of storm troopers The comrades of the *Reichsbanner* who accompanied him as his bodyguard offered fierce resistance. Leber was severely injured; with a cut nasal bone, he was carried off. One of the assailants was killed in this fight. Although he and his friends had acted in self-defense and in spite of his immunity as a member of the Reichstag, Leber was imprisoned.

The workers of Lübeck were highly incensed. In every factory they met and demanded the proclamation of a general strike in order to enforce Leber's release.

I was a member of a delegation that was to present those demands to the chairman of the local branch of the Free Trade Unions. When we put our resolution on his table he refused even to read it and asked us to take it back at once. Did we not know that according to the last decrees strikes were strictly forbidden, against the law?

In the next two weeks I hardly went to bed. The fire of resistance had to be kindled. I thought—and I was right in this assumption—that there must be many more workers in other towns and cities who felt as we did. A one-hour protest strike for Leber's release was carried out in impressive discipline.

Then, on the nineteenth of February, Lübeck saw one of the most powerful demonstrations in the history of the city. Fifteen thousand people gathered on the Burgfeld. The threats of the new rulers could not frighten them, the icy cold did not scare them away.

At the intervention of his wife, Leber was allowed bail and released from prison hospital for a few days. He was allowed to attend the meeting under the condition that he would not make a speech.

When he appeared on the platform with a bandaged head, unbroken, unbent, he shouted only a single word: "Freedom!"

The people took this shout for more than a demand—it was a vow. No, the fight had not ended—now it began.

This was not the last of our illusions. Actually, this was the last free demonstration in Lübeck. It was also the last time I saw Leber.

2

Nine days later, the twenty-eighth of February, was the day of the Reichstag fire. But in spite of swindle and terror, the elections of March 5 did not give Hitler the majority he had hoped for.

On the following Sunday a national convention of our party was to be held in Dresden. The Social Democratic party was already "illegal." To escape the police I had to conceal my identity. My not very ingeniously chosen disguise consisted of a colored student's cap. I traveled under my party name of Willy Brandt.

In Berlin I had to change trains. It was my first visit to this city. With mixed feelings I wandered through its streets.

Like many of us who lived in the provinces I felt rather antagonistic toward Berlin. We were full of admiration for its astonishing vitality; at the same time we distrusted the German capital, even while we Socialists knew of the proud tradition of Berlin's labor movement. In Berlin there was always "something going on." During the last years we had followed with great interest what Berlin had to offer—culturally, politically, historically.

On the other hand, we could not help feeling superior to the people of Berlin. Its much heralded tempo—was it not in fact a senseless haste? I shared the widespread prejudices against the Berliners, against their alleged megalomania, their coldness which excluded any real human relationship. I would always prefer my Lübeck. The older I got, the more I learned to value and love its beauty. There we had tradition. At every step the churches, the old Gothic houses with their high gables, the proud mansions recalled to one's mind a great historic past—the power of the Hanse. Lübeck had style, Berlin . . . ?

The first impression seemed to confirm my doubts. Barbarically adorned with swastika flags, the Friedrichstrasse looked as vulgar as a carnival, the Kurfürstendamm as ostentatious as the made-up mistress of a war profiteer. Uniforms were everywhere. Marching storm-trooper columns, their yelling, the shattering noise of their motorcycles filled the streets. The whole city seemed to be an army camp.

The cafés of the intellectuals, a landmark of the western district of Berlin, were half empty. Most of the regular customers, noted artists and writers, were absent Those who sat here spoke only in a whisper, suspicious looks followed me. Suspicion and fear were like a poisonous fog—it depressed me, it compressed my chest, I felt that I was suffocating.

I went to the Wedding, the district where the workers lived. What a contrast! Ugly and bare they were, those endless streets with the large tenement houses and the sunless back yards. But on that day they looked as if they were illuminated by an inner light. No flags, no banners relieved the general grayness—it was as if the houses wanted to show that they were not ashamed of their poverty; their nakedness had the dignity of a great sorrow.

My feeling of impotent rage at the triumph of the Nazis gave way to a feeling of close affinity with the common people of Berlin. The careworn women, the worn-out workers walked with their heads down. A strange silence filled the streets—heavy and sad. This mute protest touched me deeply. Only here and now did I fully realize the extent of the catastrophe—much clearer than I had in Lübeck.

The conference for which we met in a little restaurant in a suburb of Dresden was nothing but a series of fatal news items. Some friends were missing, they were in prison or in protective custody. We heard of tortures, of murder. A few of our comrades had been shot—"trying to escape." We had always told each other we had to expect the worst, but actually we never wanted to believe that this "worst" could ever happen. Well, it was even worse.

Incredulously and with mounting exasperation we listened to the first reports about the persecution of the Jews. The humiliations and beatings were nothing in comparison with the horrors of the following years, but already appalling in their malice and senseless brutality. Active opponents of Hitler fell as victims of their resistance like soldiers on the battlefield. But here were human beings, the majority of whom had not even taken part in the political struggle, and they were now persecuted and tortured only because they were born as Jews.

Until then I had very little contact with Jews. In Lübeck there were few of them. At the Johanneum I had only one or two Jewish schoolmates; on Saturday they used to be absent from school, we others never teased them on account of it. In the socialist movement we identified anti-Semitism

—the socialism of the idiot, as Bebel called it—with the detested Nazism. It would have never occurred to us to make a distinction between the few Jewish comrades and those of another faith. After all, what distinguished them from us was nothing but their religion, and they were as little "religious" as the rest of us. Race? A Hitler swindle which nobody would fall for—we thought. There had never been a "Jewish problem" in Lubeck. Now, however, Dr. Fritz Solmitz, the political editor of the *Volksboten* and Leber's assistant, was driven in a mock parade through the streets, an obscene sign around his neck, before they deported him and drove him to death. And we could not help him.

When I just said I was not religious, I meant that organized religion did not appeal to me, I kept aloof from public worship. In my early school days I regularly attended the divine services for children—to the regret of my grandfather, who subscribed to the militant anti-clericalism of the founders of the Social Democratic party. In high school I began to take a great interest in the history of religion and thought of myself as a freethinker. However, those of my friends who took a certain pride in confessing their atheism were rather repugnant to me. As a boy I never stayed awake brooding upon the question whether God existed or not; there is no mystic strain in me. But I knew that there will always be behind all questions still a last one that cannot be answered. The ethos of Christianity appealed to me. A true Socialist was, in my opinion, not a worse but a better Christian. His practical work in the interest of tolerance, justice, and the love for one's fellow men must be more pleasing to God than lip service and solemn ceremonies.

Owing to this point of view, my friends and I regarded the persecution of the Jews not only as reprehensible and detestable but also as anti-Christian.

On the way to our meetings, which took place in different

saloons or private apartments, we felt like soldiers on a dangerous patrol. Our Germany, our home, had become enemy territory. Whom could we still trust?

A group of former Communists, expelled from their party on account of their "right deviations," had joined our Socialist Workers party. Some of them—Jacob Walcher and August Enderle, former steelworkers, and the writer Paul Froehlich—became my friends. They were old hands at "illegality", war and revolution had taught them the art of conspiracy, whereas we others had no notion what underground activity entailed. We had much to learn from them in this respect.

It was decided that while the secret executive committee of our group was to remain in Berlin, some bases should be established abroad; from there we hoped to inform world public opinion about the true situation in Germany, to smuggle anti-Nazi pamphlets into the Third Reich, to gain support—spiritual and material aid—for the victims of the terror. Oslo was to be one of these bases, for we felt very close to the Norwegian Socialist party; they subscribed to the same program and followed our political line.

Paul Froehlich was appointed head of the Oslo office, and I was charged with the task of organizing his secret trip from Lübeck to Norway.

But in spite of careful preparations we failed in this enterprise. We had planned to transport Froehlich in a fishing boat from the isle of Fehmarn, in Holstein, to Denmark. At the last moment he was arrested on the island. His disguise as a fisherman was not convincing.

Thereupon our Central Committee decided that I was to be in charge of the Oslo office, particularly since I could no longer stay in Lübeck, anyhow. I had been warned of my imminent arrest and had to expect the worst. It was impossible for me to hide in another German town, for I had no profession which could cover my political activity; and how could I earn my livelihood?

As much as I was tempted by the great adventure, it was not easy for me to say good-by to Lubeck. There was a girl with whom I was very much in love. Gertrud was much more optimistic than I was. She was sure she would join me in Oslo not later than two months hence Gertrud's understanding and courage eased the pain of my parting from my native town and from my friends.

First I went to nearby Travemuende, where a hiding place had been arranged in a fisherman's house. Even here my escape was nearly brought to naught.

I was careless enough to accompany the fisherman to a bar for a glass of beer. There I ran into a former comrade who had deserted to the new masters and who obviously knew at once what my intentions were. To turn around and to run away was out of question. I behaved as if I had not the slightest cause for fear, greeted the boy very warmly, kept him company for a few minutes. Those were long and anxious minutes.

When I left, I didn't know: would he follow me, call the police, betray me?

At midnight I breathed more freely when the fisherman took me to his boat. It was a small cutter, equipped with motor and sails. I found a hiding place behind boxes and cordage. The customs inspector did not find me.

At early dawn we set sail—direction Roedbyhavn, a little town on the Danish island, Lolland.

It was the worst journey of my life. The weather was awful, the seasickness was sheer torture.

When we landed I could hardly stand on my feet. A few cups of strong coffee, to which my friend had added a large dose of brandy, brought me back to life.

Thus I landed in the free world with a brief case and one hundred marks.

The same day I took the train to Copenhagen. I reported to the Danish Youth Federation and was directed to the author Oscar Hansen, an editor on the party organ in whose apartment I was very cordially received. A few days later I continued my journey by boat to Oslo.

Even in Copenhagen I realized how difficult it was to give foreigners a clear picture of the events in Germany. My Danish friends intimated they thought the stories about the cruelties in Germany very much exaggerated. The Germans were a cultured people, were they not? Wasn't the judgment of the refugees "too subjective," even warped? It must be. Were we not too pessimistic when we declared that Hitler would plunge the world into war?

On the other hand, much of what I told the friends abroad was, no doubt, in many respects inadequate. My theory about Hitler's rise to power was rather schematic: He was "a lackey of high finance," National Socialism "a rebellion of the lower middle class"—a simple but much too primitive explanation. Our criticism of the labor movement was hard and often a little self-complacent I lacked the right perspective. To be sure, I was not yet twenty years old.

3

As soon as I arrived in Oslo I paid a call on Finn Moe. He was the foreign editor of the *Arbeiterbladet,* the organ of the Norwegian Labor party, an experienced politician, human and eager to help a comrade in need. After the war he became Norway's representative in the United Nations and chairman of the Foreign Affairs Committee of the Storting.

Thanks to his intervention I was granted a small monthly allowance. It came out of a special fund which the Norwegian trade unions had established for the purpose of aiding needy comrades in their own country. Since I volunteered for some clerical work in the secretariat, I got the double rate—thirty kronen a week and an additional allowance for my rent. My life was very modest, but I found it not at all harsh or depressive.

Within a few months I was able to forego any further financial aid. I had taken up my journalistic career, my articles, distributed to a few dozen papers, and the features I wrote for the trade-union magazines provided an income large enough to make my material existence secure.

Very soon I decided that I didn't want to be a refugee.

I was chairman of the Refugee Federation. Much as I was concerned with the sorrows and troubles of my companions in misfortune, I realized the necessity of taking roots again, I did not want to be an outsider. My youth had something to do with this decision. I refused to live in a spiritual and political isolation.

Oslo was not a large and not a typical refugee center. Yet, here, too, in the course of a few years a peculiar "refugee atmosphere" developed The emigrants were like people who had missed the train and passed the time of waiting with memories of the past and with dreams of the future. Thus they lost their interest in the present, in what happened outside their narrow circle. Dependent entirely on each other, they became excitable and bitter. There were daily quarrels which depressed me because of their senselessness. Long sessions had to be held to discuss complaints and protests, matters of utter futility.

Just prior to the outbreak of the war, for instance, I had to settle a dispute between two groups of Austrian refugees. On further consideration I found out that the whole dispute stemmed from the world-shaking problem as to whether or not one group had received a few shirts less than the other from the allocation of some gifts which a charitable organization had provided.

The debates about the guilt of the German Left did not make much more sense. Mostly they were held in a vacuum, and were dominated by personal prejudices and the urge—humanly understandable but utterly useless—to justify one's own position. I shared the view of Ernst Reuter, who in his Turkish exile where he lived as a government official and university professor once stated:

"In Prague"—where the Central Committee of the Social Democratic party-in-exile had established itself—"they are writing a lot of articles, trying to prove conclusively that we have nothing to learn from the events of the recent past. But after a lost political battle nobody must think we can begin again where we have left off."

A topic that was passionately discussed at every meeting of the left-wing Socialists was the NAP, the Norwegian Labor party. Thanks to a program of practical measures against the economic crisis, the party had won the elections, and according to an agreement with the Farmers party it took over the government in the beginning of 1933. Was that permissible? Was it not against the Socialist principles? I shall never forget the warning of a comrade who, by quoting a lot of dogmas and Marxian theorems, proved to me that I would "never reach the summit because I was carrying in my knapsack the heavy burden of the NAP."

I tried earnestly to keep in close touch with Germany; at the same time I deemed it equally important to take roots in the political life of Norway as quickly as possible. In my case it meant active collaboration with the Labor party, primarily with its Youth Federation. That was impossible without a sound knowledge of the Norwegian language. I could already read it. A few weeks later I could speak it well enough to make myself understood. And a few months after my arrival

I made my first public speech in Norwegian. Soon I mastered it as if it were my mother language.

The Socialist Youth was nothing less than sectarian In contrast to Germany, it was a mass movement. The young people met at social gatherings, they did not let politics interfere with their enjoyment of light entertainment—music and dance. The youngsters had a sound knowledge of Scandinavian and world literature, they were much interested in the intellectual trends of Western Europe and America As an "expert on foreign affairs" I was more and more in demand. Whatever my audience learned from my lectures, I learned at least as much from their questions and the discussions.

My work with the Norwegian Youth Federation belongs to the happiest chapters of my life. There I made friends with men and women who later were to assume a high responsibility for the affairs of their country: Rakel Seweriin, who became a deputy and Minister for Social Affairs; Nils Langhelle, in later years Minister for Defense and President of the Parliament; Halvard Lange, the present Foreign Minister, well known and much liked far beyond the confines of his country.

My collaboration with the Norwegian Youth movement was, I must admit, not without frictions. I committed a grave mistake. Without a clear understanding of the local political situation I joined an opposition group. Its criticism of the official party policy was not without validity; in fact, the leading members of the group later on gained high and influential positions in government and public life. For the time being, however, my association with these men brought me into a temporary conflict with the leaders of the Labor party with Martin Tranmael, the dynamic force behind Norway's labor movement—today its "grand old man", Oscar Torp, then the Chairman of the party; the present Prime Minister, Einar Gerhardsen.

The Norwegian Labor party belonged then to the radical left wing of the international Socialist movement. But called upon to master the practical problems of the administration of its country, it had to liberate itself from dogmas and theories which could no longer be applied to the swiftly changing world situation. In those years I could not quite grasp the deeper causes and the historic meaning of this evolution.

My friend Jacob Walcher was mainly responsible for my joining the opposition group I just mentioned.

In the summer of 1933 he arrived in Oslo for a short visit. He was on his way from Prague to Paris, where he was to establish the Executive Committee of the Socialist Workers party. We discussed ways and means of how to strengthen the underground in Germany. Money was needed. Could we get it in Norway? From what sources? Walcher brought me in contact with a group of Norwegian intellectuals, *Mot Dag* (toward a new day), radical Socialists who had broken with Moscow and played an important role in Oslo's social and intellectual life.

My encounter with that circle and its leader, Erling Falk, was one of my most interesting experiences of that period.

Falk was a sort of high priest of intellectualism. His followers sat at his feet like the disciples of a religious order. Students, writers, scientists belonged to that group; they formed a truly socialist elite. For many years they had a strong influence on the political thinking of the rising academic generation.

I owe these men much: stimulating hours, literary discoveries, a broadening of my intellectual horizon. The group also published a workers' dictionary on which I collaborated. But after a relatively short period of time I left this circle because I could not stomach its intellectual arrogance.

In 1936, *Mot Dag* joined the Labor party—without Falk,

to be sure, who was not admitted and who because of his illness had lost the leadership of his group.

I saw Falk for the last time in 1940, shortly before his death in a Stockholm hospital. In the face of the imminent catastrophe—Hitler's war—he had made peace with his opponent Tranmael. With all due respect for his and his friends' efforts and accomplishments, I parted from them with the firm belief that in the world of today there is no place for ivory towers to which intellectuals can retire to lead a life of splendid isolation. On the other hand, my encounter with Falk and his friends strengthened my determination to improve my education. I recognized the need of acquiring a more solid knowledge for my political activity than the one you could gain from pamphlets and party leaflets.

In September 1934 I matriculated at the Oslo University. I passed an examination in philosophy and signed on for lectures in history. From a fugitive I had become an "academic citizen." My political work and the war prevented me from bringing my studies to an organic conclusion.

4

How could we help our friends in Germany? This question occupied us political refugees incessantly; it gave me many a sleepless night.

Up to a certain extent we could and did speak on behalf of our comrades who were condemned to silence. This was our simple obligation and a patriotic duty. No doubt we could have discharged it more effectively than we did.

We tried not to lose our personal and political contacts with our native country. We met as often as possible with our German comrades, exchanged ideas, comforted each other. Copenhagen was a good place for conferences with friends from Lübeck and other parts of northern Germany.

To reach our friends inside Hitler's Reich we wrote our

letters in invisible ink and secret code. We manufactured "illegal" newspapers and pamphlets and smuggled them across the border; unfortunately only a small number of our publications reached their destination, even though we employed all the well-tried devices: the suitcase with a false bottom, the "filled" binding of a book.

We used other tricks, too. Once one of our Norwegian friends, a reserve officer, made a trip to Germany. He put his uniform atop everything else in his suitcase, and in that uniform we had sewed in the secret material that he was supposed to deliver to our comrades. The trick paid off, for the customs official was so impressed with the uniform of a genuine officer, he didn't even dare touch it.

Perhaps I should state explicitly that all our work in my Oslo office was honorary. Our friends in Germany risked their lives; it was out of the question for us to accept payment for our activity.

Whatever money we collected—and it was not little—we sent to our Committee in Paris and it was used exclusively on behalf of the victims of Hitler's terror: to support the families of the prisoners, for their legal defense . . . sometimes just to cover the funeral expenses of the victims.

Once in a while we could do more—thanks to the help of our Norwegian friends.

I remember, for instance, a trial that was held at the end of 1934; the underground leaders of the Socialist Workers party—among them my friends Max Koehler and Stefan Szende—were the defendants. They had to expect heavy penalties, probably a death sentence.

We tried everything to save them. The Berlin authorities were deluged with protests. In Norway we mobilized a number of high judges and lawyers, among them the later mayor of Oslo, Brynjulf Bull, who signed a petition. It was read in the courtroom during the trial, and the German judges mistook it for an official intervention of the Norwegian lawyers' association. The Attorney General fumed, but it proved effective. Our friends were fortunate enough to find judges who were still not completely under the thumb of the Nazis, though they were certainly not in sympathy with the "Socialist traitors." The process ended with relatively light sentences. And thanks to the pressure of our campaign and the presence of observers from abroad, the defendants even had the chance to refute the minutes of the preliminary investigation and actually expose in the courtroom the marks of the beatings they had endured in the Gestapo headquarters.

That was in 1934. It was a gratifying but not a typical case. Soon the Gestapo strengthened its control over the police and the judicial authorities and made sure that such "blunders" never occurred again.

Another case in which we successfully intervened had to do with the noted pacifist Carl von Ossietzky. As the editor of the *Weltbuhne*, a widely read political and literary weekly, he had fought valiantly for years against the secret rearmament of Germany. Because of his disclosures he had been hated and persecuted by the reactionary and militaristic circles long before Hitler. Twice he had been put on trial and imprisoned. The Christmas amnesty of 1932 set him free.

Two months later he was arrested again, this time by the Nazis. He was one of the first among the "criminals" who, on the night of the Reichstag fire, were rounded up by the Gestapo.

He spent many years in different concentration camps. It was a miracle that he, a feeble and sick man, could survive those years at all. At last, in 1936, he was, by then suffering from an incurable disease, transferred to a Berlin hospital. For in the meantime the "case Ossietzky" had gained worldwide attention and for once Goebbels had to bow to public opinion in the Western democracies.

I don't think I can subscribe to every article Ossietzky wrote in the *Weltbühne* prior to 1933; yet I am proud that I was able to take an active part in the effort to obtain the Nobel Peace Prize for this victim of Hitler, this courageous anti-militarist, the "first gentleman of the German press."

The idea originated in 1934 among some of Ossietzky's friends in Strasbourg. They hoped that such an outstanding honor and the international publicity might lead to his release. I was asked to enlist the support of prominent personalities in Norway and Sweden. But it was too late to submit Ossietzky's name to the committee which had to choose the winner for that year.

The following year many more famous personalities came to our support. However, in 1935 no Peace Prize was given. In 1936 nearly one thousand people of international renown and fame nominated Ossietzky. In Switzerland, a hundred twenty-four parliamentarians supported his nomination. It was partially due to my hard work that sixty-nine members of the Norwegian Storting and fifty-nine deputies of the Swedish Riksdag signed a formal petition on his behalf. In close co-operation with Kurt Grossmann, the secretary of the "German League for Human Rights," and with the journalist Hilde Walter in Paris we succeeded in turning the "affair Ossietzky" into a world-wide movement.

Former Nobel Peace Prize winners like Jane Addams and Norman Angell, politicians, scientists, famous authors rallied to our side. Thomas Mann, Professor Albert Einstein, Hellmut von Gerlach spoke for "the other Germany"; from France came the voices of the novelist Romain Rolland and André Philip; England was represented by Clement Attlee, the authors Aldous Huxley, J. B. Priestley, H. G. Wells, Virginia Woolf, and the philosopher Bertrand Russell.

On November 23, 1936, came the long-awaited decision. The five-man committee gave Carl von Ossietzky the Nobel

Peace Prize for 1936. Among the five was Martin Tranmael; another was Christian Lange, the father of Halvard Lange, the future Foreign Minister. The chairman of the committee was the former Minister of Justice Frederik Stang, a highly respected Conservative.

Ossietzky was much too ill and too weak to accept the prize in person, even if the Nazi government had given him the permission for the trip abroad. He died in May 1938. At least we had the satisfaction of knowing that we had helped make his last two years a little easier for him. And we had also succeeded in inflicting a heavy moral defeat on Hitler. He was so furious about the great honor that was bestowed upon "the noted traitor Ossietzky" that he issued a special order: henceforth no German citizen would "ever" be permitted to accept a Nobel Prize.

When I was informed about the successful outcome of our campaign, in November 1936, I was no longer in Oslo. I heard about it in Berlin.

*

CHAPTER FOUR

With the Underground in Berlin

1

The knowledge of our impotency in the face of the ever growing power of Hitler's dictatorship was bitter agony. At first many of us had thought it improbable that the "thousand-year Reich" could last longer than four or five years, the duration of World War I. Soon the realization was forced upon us that the German people would hardly find the strength to liberate themselves and that the brown terror regime would lead to a second World War.

It was clear to us that we refugees could not stop the course of history. But we refused to be discouraged. We were not going to stand idly by. Alas, our whole activity spent itself in planning and speculation. And we wrote—articles and reports, memoranda and resolutions.

Letter writing kept me at my desk long hours every day. Friends and comrades were scattered all over Europe and America. The urge to keep our former personal relationship alive was as great as the need we felt to exchange our opinions and experiences. Never again have I written so many letters as in the first years of my exile.

Gertrud helped me. She had arrived in Oslo a few months after me and put some order into my rather disorderly life of being permanently on the move from one furnished room to another, with a small suitcase holding all my possessions and the coffeehouses as our meeting places. In the summer of 1939 she left on a business trip to America. She intended to be away for a year. The war came between us—but not the war alone.

In the last few years before the war I traveled extensively. There were frequent conferences with our political friends, especially in Paris. Exciting were the meetings with our comrades from the underground whom we met in the border towns of Germany's neighboring countries.

In February 1934 I attended a conference of different Socialist youth groups in Holland. To be exact, I *should* have attended it For the conference, which was held in a cheap restaurant in the little town of Laaren, was hardly called to order when the police intervened; all foreign delegates were arrested. The mayor, a Nazi sympathizer, was responsible for this scandal.

This was not the only case of cringing servility before the powerful Third Reich on the part of the Western democracies, defenseless refugees were regarded as troublesome peace-breakers—if not worse.

Four German delegates were taken from Laaren to the German border and delivered, handcuffed, to the Gestapo. Among them was my friend Franz Bobzien, a teacher from Hamburg. For years he was dragged through prisons and concentration camps until he met his death during an air raid on Berlin.

I was saved from a similar fate by a piece of good luck. My Norwegian identity paper impressed the Dutch officials;

together with two Norwegian friends and other delegates from Western European nations I was taken to the police headquarters in Amsterdam. From there we were deported to Belgium.

When they were interrogated by the Nazi police my German friends declared me, as the one who was out of reach, as the real culprit, and to save their neck they put all the blame on me. If the Gestapo had ever caught me they would have presented me with a bill of particulars for which I would have had to pay a high price.

Among my many trips abroad was one that had no political purpose. I had it especially at heart.

In the summer of 1935 Gertrud and I, taking all necessary precautions to elude Gestapo agents, met her mother and mine in Copenhagen.

Two years had passed since I had left Germany. I could hardly believe that it was not more than two years. I felt much older. My Lubeck childhood was far, far away, no ties bound me to my native town. Certainly, I took an active interest in the fate of my friends, and the news of the suicide of my grandfather had been a great shock to me, bitter and painful. I was also depressed by the knowledge that my mother and my stepfather had to endure annoying interrogations and all sorts of chicaneries on account of me.

But Mother had not a single word of reproach. I must not worry about her, she simply said, I did what I had to do . . .

We had no profound discussions, there was no need to explain to each other our mutual sentiments. We knew how close we were to each other and this knowledge gave me comfort and strength.

2

In the summer of 1936 I received a letter from our Paris Committee. I was to take charge of our "Organization Metro"—Metro stood for Berlin. To see Germany again—that was, of course, a very exciting prospect I realized the grave danger involved, but it would have never occurred to me to take the risk as an excuse for saying no.

In Oslo we had a friend who was an expert in the manufacture of the necessary travel papers. He did it for the good cause and would have never accepted a single penny for his work.

Usually I traveled with a Norwegian "passport for foreigners," a paper that looked like the real thing, especially if you put it into a nice cover. But it did not impress the German border guards. A fellow student helped me out. He was of my age and lent me his own passport. Our expert exchanged the picture of my friend with mine; I memorized his personal data and practiced his signature until the copy looked exactly like the original.

First I went to Paris to discuss in detail my Berlin assignment. The meeting with my comrades had a sobering effect on me. Here I was ready to risk my life—like my friends in Germany whom I was going to see in a couple of days—but in Paris there was continual quarreling and wrangling, a rather unpleasant refugee atmosphere. How futile were those fights, how depressing this picture of human pettiness. And for that I should risk my head?

I pushed the bitter thought aside. No, it was not "for that," not to please some persons or groups, that I was going to Germany. The cause was more important than the individual. I must not let myself be confused by passing moods. In the sleeper to Berlin I had already eradicated the last days in Paris from my memory. All my thoughts were concentrated on the task ahead.

The day after my arrival I went as agreed upon to the department store of Wertheim where I was to meet the man who would put me in contact with my Berlin comrades. He was there. And immediately I felt no longer strange and lost. To know that in this city, in spite of all the swastika flags and the parading brown shirts, I had many friends who shared my fate and stood behind me gave me a nice feeling of comfort and security. My party still had a couple of hundred members in Berlin. They were organized in groups of five. And we were only one of many resistance groups in the German underground.

I found a furnished room at the corner of Kurfürstendamm and Joachimsthaler Strasse. The landlady, a nice middle-aged woman, did not conceal her contempt for the new masters. Nevertheless, I dared not betray my real sentiments. I was afraid to let myself be drawn into political discussions and tried to give the impression of a naive student, full of admiration for German science and culture; I had known such youngsters in Oslo and was sure I would not find it difficult to play this part convincingly.

I had not counted on meeting in person such a Norwegian here in Berlin. And this one was not only naive but in open sympathy with the Nazis.

When a few days after my arrival I visited the Reichsbank to arrange for the transfer of my "student marks"—foreign currency that was used for studies in Germany was exchanged at a higher rate—the official had "good news" for me: a countryman of mine, a student like myself, had just been to see him in the same matter. "Here he is!" the official interrupted himself, and pointed to a young man who was standing at the next counter. I had to meet the student straightaway.

"My countryman" was very happy to make my acquaintance. I was much less pleased. He immediately bombarded me with questions about my Norwegian home town, about the school I had attended; he wanted to find out if we had mutual friends. I was sure that the Norwegian I spoke was above suspicion but afraid that in answering the questions I might give myself away. And there was no chance to get rid of him without giving him my address He actually came to see me two days later, insisting that I should join a group of Norwegian Nazi students. I promised to do so in a near future; at the moment I was much too busy, I explained.

Every morning I went like a fine student to the library of the university. Systematically I waded through the turgid and muddy Nazi literature—even *Mein Kampf* didn't scare me. Until then I had tasted only certain excerpts. Now I had to swallow the whole indigestible dish: I read the Hitler bible from beginning to end. A heroic accomplishment, I think, even more so since I also had to find my way through the ideological jungle of Rosenberg and other Nazi "ideologists."

This was the fall of 1936. Those were the months when Hitler's foreign policy dumfounded and paralyzed the world at large and forced upon his opponents inside the Reich the feeling that the progress of Nazism was irresistible and resistance, if not senseless, was in any case past all hope.

The reintroduction of universal compulsory military service, the occupation of the demilitarized Rhineland, the bold abrogation of international agreements—every time the opponents of Hitler, among them high officers in the general staff of the *Wehrmacht*, had hoped the Western powers would block the dictator's way and force him to retreat. They had made preparations for such a contingency and wanted to use the expected crisis for an all-out attack against the impudent gamblers who played banque with the fate of the German nation. Instead they had to realize that Hitler won every game because the Western powers hesitated to call his bluff, even though they held all the trumps in their hands.

How could we, under these conditions, keep the spirit of resistance alive? That was the question which occupied us most. In the big factories there were still cadres of trustworthy comrades. We tried to organize a semi-legal opposition.

Berlin mirrored the megalomania of the dictator. The Olympic games had attracted tens of thousands of foreigners. They were duly impressed by the might of the regime, by the enthusiasm of the youth, by the propaganda of Goebbels. It was difficult not to be overwhelmed by it, for wherever you looked you saw the successes of Nazism confirmed in the smiling faces of the young people, in the new monumental buildings, in the economic boom. Berlin offered magnificent scenery for a spectacle that took the breath of the world away.

To be sure, whoever had a chance to look behind the façade realized that the young could easily laugh because the great Pied Piper had liberated them from the pain of thinking for themselves; they could not notice how the gay play with flags and parades prepared the scene for the bloody drama that was to follow.

Not a single dissenting voice disturbed the jubilation, for the cries from the concentration camps and the death rattle of the tortured victims did not reach the stadium—not even the Kurfurstendamm. In the Wedding, in the suburbs where the workers lived, we heard at least their faint echo. Out there was "the other Berlin."

Soon I had adapted myself to the life of an "illegal" person: it was a perpetual pretense and disguise, the necessity of always hiding your true feelings, the mistrust that makes you fear in every chance acquaintance an informer and in every former comrade a traitor, the organization of "contacts" and secret meetings—my head was full of figures and code words, and they pursued me into my sleep.

One day my landlady greeted me with the information I should appear at once at the next police station and bring my passport with me. Was I suspected? Had anyone denounced me? I decided that any hesitation to comply with this request, any sign of fear could only aggravate my situation. I went to the police.

It was a false alarm. My passport was returned to me a few days later.

Another day I was sitting in a café in the Friedrichstrasse when I recognized an old friend of mine from Lübeck at the next table. He too had seen me. A faint smile passed quickly over his face. I wanted to greet him but I did not dare. I knew he had spent some time in a concentration camp. Was he still being shadowed? And what if he should now come over to me . . . ?

By that time his face had again assumed an indifferent expression; he turned his head away. I understood, paid quickly, and left the café in a hurry.

There were many such little incidents. They kept my nerves under steady tension. The only relaxation I found was on my long excursions through the beautiful surroundings of Berlin and—in music.

Music was a new discovery for me. Until then I had rarely visited operas, concerts practically never. I was convinced music left me cold, I had no appreciation of it. To my great surprise the few concerts I attended meant more to me each time. Music let me forget my worries and depressions. The feeling of an inner liberation that until then I had experienced only on my walks through forests and pastures, I found again in music. It was especially classical music which moved me most. Even today I cannot fully appreciate modern music. Soon every concert evening became a great experience for me. Most people felt the same in those years, when they fled to Beethoven and Mozart, not only to forget the worries of the day but to gain new strength from the realization that in the end the eternal values and the true ideals must triumph over barbarism. This sentiment made of the audience a community in the true sense of the word. Thus the Philharmony became a place of almost religious exultation. Here too, in the Philharmony, was the real Berlin, "the other Germany."

It was a friend of mine, a comrade from the Berlin youth movement, who showed me the road to music. We had been very close to each other in our exile in Oslo. Frequently he had accepted important missions into the Reich. When, once more, he was stationed in Berlin, he too disguised himself as a Norwegian student. He became—and not out of the necessity to play that part convincingly—an outstanding student at the Academy of Music.

My friend was a very sensitive man. He lived in a permanent fear of being found out but never hesitated to accept the most dangerous assignments. The words of Anatole France, "Courage is nothing but the flight forward," could be applied to him. "They will never take me alive," he said to me at our last meeting in the spring of 1938. I tried to convince him—as I told others under similar circumstances—that one must never escape from seemingly hopeless situations into suicide. One never knows if in the end there might not still be a way out; at the last moment a miracle might happen.

He remained unconvinced. But he prepared himself systematically for the eventuality of an arrest. His arrangements were very unusual.

Sverre—as my friend called himself—began with the writing of a diary. The entries gave every appearance of honestly expressing a grave spiritual and moral crisis of the author. From entry to entry, from week to week, the doubts became greater, the admiration for the accomplishments of the Third Reich more pronounced. It was an amazing document that Sverre concocted. It showed how a political enemy, a Social Democratic "outcast," had been converted through his love for the German fatherland. And the sincerity of this conversion was confirmed by the fact that the confession was obviously not intended for the public; it seemed the intimate confrontation of a man with his tortured soul.

Sverre was arrested. The Gestapo discovered his true identity. The diary was found in his apartment. And sure enough, it produced exactly the effect Sverre had hoped for. He explained that he had returned from Norway because he could not live anywhere but in his beloved Germany, he had used the false Norwegian passport only so that he could cross the border. Once in Berlin, he had become, in a few months, a firm believer in Nazism. His diary proved it. He even asked to be presented to Hitler so that he may in person tell the Führer of his amazing conversion.

And in fact Sverre was brought to Hitler. My friend must have played his part very convincingly. No, he did not have to take poison. He was given only a slight prison sentence. In spite of week-long interrogations, in spite of all the indignities and beatings he had to endure before he was "cleared," he did not betray a single one of our comrades.

Unfortunately I have never seen him again. When I visited his parents after the war in the eastern sector of Berlin, they were waiting for him in vain—he was one of the millions of missing war victims, lost in the vastness of Russia.

3

In the last days of 1936 a conference of my political friends from Germany and different emigration centers was to be held in Brno, Czechoslovakia. I went there to report on the situation in Germany. A few of my Berlin coworkers participated.

The conference could not be held in Brno; it was transferred to one of the little towns in the Sudetic part of Czechoslovakia. There I met for the first time Otto Bauer. He was a sort of adviser behind the scenes.

In our youth the books and articles of Bauer had been for us an excellent introduction into the Socialist theory. He had been the leader of the Austrian Social Democrats who in February 1934 rose up in arms against the fascism of Chancellor Engelbert Dollfuss and fought so bravely, though without success, for the defense of democracy. I was especially impressed by Bauer's conduct during the period of his exile. The old leadership, so he said and wrote, ought to step aside as a result of its defeat and limit itself to the study and analysis of the past experiences; the best they could do was to transmit their findings to the younger generation.

Otto Bauer earnestly tried to explore the reasons for the catastrophe and yet remained a prisoner of the Marxian philosophy which always leads to the conclusion that everything happens the way it does—because it has to.

I reported about my Berlin experiences—I had little that was good to report. The reports of the other speakers were not more encouraging. But in the center of our discussions were the terrible Moscow trials.

The accusations, the confessions, the executions horrified us all the more since they meant the end of our hopes that the Communists might become our allies and that the Soviet Union might sincerely support our fight for peace.

The dictatorship of the proletariat had become the dictatorship of Stalin *over* the proletariat—and over all the other classes of the Russian people . . . that was nothing new to me. The Red czar had decreed the rehabilitation of "Ivan the Terrible" not out of a whim but because they both were so similar in character—the terror of the GPU had proven it for years. What shocked me most in the Moscow trials was, aside of the human tragedies, the conclusion I had to draw from them in regard to the imminent future of Europe.

In spite of everything—against logic and reason—we "Leftists" had seen in Stalin a trustworthy ally against fascism.

When he sacrificed in cold blood the German workers, including the Communists, we could explain it—though not excuse it—with the weakness of the Soviet Union, which was afraid of a military conflict and wanted to gain time. The brutal murder of famous Soviet generals and old Bolsheviks who in spite of their grave political mistakes deserved our respect for their revolutionary past, proved conclusively, however, that Stalin had no idealistic or political goals besides and above his lust for personal power.

We still hesitated to admit to ourselves the whole bitter truth. A few months before—in May 1936—the French Popular Front with Léon Blum as its leader had taken over the French government. In that beautiful spring I had felt a new fresh wind in the streets of Paris. A new era seemed in the making. The European Left hoped for a new beginning, a social rejuvenation, for the powerful deployment of a worldwide resistance against the danger of Nazism. After the entry of the Soviet Union into the League of Nations the Popular Front seemed to have great possibilities. Indeed, it did not take long until much water was poured into the wine of our hopes and we had much cause for concern and disappointment.

Three years later the Stalin-Hitler pact confirmed our worst fears. I, however, established during the next few months an intimate acquaintance with the mechanics and intentions of Stalin's foreign policy. This opportunity was given to me during a prolonged stay in Spain.

4

When I went to Spain in February 1937 the Civil War was eight months old. In a few months the revolution had turned into a war of foreign powers against the Spanish people.

As a Socialist I felt my heart beat louder at the news about the heroic resistance of the Spanish workers against the reactionary forces; as an anti-Fascist I longed for the defeat of the rebels and their masters Mussolini and Hitler; as a democrat I could not suppress very painful doubts: I saw the great dangers that confronted the revolution, and these dangers threatened freedom not only from the side of Franco and his German and Italian allies but from the ranks of the Loyalists. As a member of the terribly beaten German labor movement I thought it my duty not to flatter my Spanish comrades but to speak to them frankly and, on the other hand, to draw the proper lessons from the Spanish events for our own future struggle. "We have to help our Spanish comrades," I wrote to Oslo, "but in order to help we must have the courage to criticize."

With this task before my eyes I had gone to Spain as a correspondent for Scandinavian newspapers and as a trusted delegate of my political friends in exile.

The five months I spent in Spain were full of the most contradictory impressions and of important experiences which later largely determined my political actions and thinking.

The confusion and the propinquity of human grandeur and human pettiness—under the existing circumstances I could not expect much else. Revolutions are not the solemn spectacle their official bards make them out to be. The reality is different: less romantic, cruel and confused.

Over and over again I was deeply moved by the examples of heroic self-sacrifice and by an idealism which forced even a cynic to admire the dignity and magnanimity of the common man, of a little peasant, of a poor working woman. The Spanish people won my illimitable love.

On the other hand, the confusion in the republican camp, the naïveté and political ignorance of the revolutionary leaders drove me to despair.

I spent most of the time in Catalonia, the northern part

of Spain. Here the Anarcho-Syndicalists played of old an important role; they represented the majority of the workers. I found among them wonderful men, true idealists who had overcome their dogmas and understood the demands of practical politics. But there were also those naïve visionaries who wanted to abolish all money and insisted on introducing the eight-hour day for the military units at the front.

Together with the Syndicalists the Left Socialists—in Barcelona primarily the POUM, Workers Party for Marxian Unity—raised the banner of the social revolution. The Communists recommended themselves as guardians of the established order. Their main interest was to gain decisive influence on the police and on the leadership of the republican army. As early as December 1930 they enforced a change in the Catalonian government as a price for Russian arms. And the central government in Madrid also had to pay for the Soviet military help with the surrender of certain positions of power to the Communists. The Western powers adhered faithfully to the policy of non-intervention. Mussolini and Hitler felt in no way bound by this policy. In view of such conditions the future of the Spanish democracy looked anything but bright.

The crisis in the republican camp reached its climax in that fateful first week of May 1937. The bloody clashes between the Communists and Socialists were followed by a Communist crusade of vengeance against their opponents among the revolutionary workers.

In a pamphlet written under the fresh impression of those tragic events I tried to explain the double character of the war: "On the one hand it was a struggle for a new social order, on the other hand a national insurrection against the Fascist invaders. The left-wing Socialists had as their main—if not the only goal—the social revolution, the Communists acted exclusively as auxiliaries of Moscow. And Stalin was, no doubt, interested in defeating Franco, but he was not at all willing to let the Spanish people decide for themselves about their own future."

I wrote: "What was needed was a government with only one aim in mind: to win the war and to create the necessary conditions for victory through the organization of a central army, through the centralization of the national economy." I explained that this policy had foundered on the peculiarities and weaknesses of the different labor organizations. The Communists had certainly contributed greatly to the efficiency of the military organization. However: "In order to monopolize the leadership, the Communists do not hesitate to use the most vicious means. In a situation when everything depends on the unity of all anti-Franco forces, the methods of the Communist party, the methods of slander and blind terror against their socialist opponents is terribly dangerous to the anti-Fascist war. These methods undermine the morale of the soldiers, they poison the whole international labor movement, they make a mockery of the Popular Front."

I saw clearly the mistakes and errors of the Socialists, the POUM, the Syndicalists, who often lost their sense of reality. "But," I wrote, "nobody must say that this justifies the persecution of the POUM. The truth of the matter is: the Comintern is determined to destroy all forces that refuse to obey its orders. It is for this reason that the whole international labor movement must rise against it."

When I formulated these accusations, I had in mind not only the arrests of the Socialists and Anarchists, carried out by the Communist police behind the back of the republican government, but also a special case in which I was directly involved.

Mark Rein was a young man, the son of the well-known Russian Socialist Abramowitsch. The father had been one of the most prominent opponents of Lenin, had been expelled from Russia soon after the Bolshevik revolution, and continued all through the years his fight against the Communists with an indefatigable tenacity. First, he lived in Berlin, after Hitler's rise to power he found asylum in Paris. As a close friend of Léon Blum, he exerted a considerable influence on the policy of the French Popular Front. The son, who had been educated in Berlin, belonged to the left wing of the Socialist party. Immediately after the outbreak of the Spanish Civil War he joined the Loyalists and served as a volunteer at the Catalonian front. I met him in Barcelona, and we saw each other a couple of times. He was a very pleasant and intelligent young man.

One night Mark Rein disappeared from his hotel. He had left all his belongings behind. A few days later we heard the mysterious news that Mark had accompanied some friends to Madrid. They had driven away in a car. The news did not make sense, you don't go on a trip without taking even an overnight bag. Besides, nobody had seen him in Madrid. We had reason to believe that the Communists had kidnaped him.

Mark's friends were very much alarmed. I tried to learn the truth, hoping that pressure and strong protests might bring about the young man's release. I went to the Casa Carlos Marx and finally forced my way into the office of the German representative of the Comintern. He pretended to know nothing at all. I told him the abduction of Mark Rein would have grave repercussions—not only in France but also in other democratic countries; since the Communists were so much interested in the preservation of the Popular Front they had every reason to prove their innocence in this case; they must find Mark Rein.

Rein could not be found.

When Abramowitsch, driven by the fear for his only son's life, appeared in Barcelona we had to tell him that all our efforts had been in vain. The old revolutionary, who in his long life had suffered so much and had endured all reverses with a stoical courage, was a broken man. He listened to our reports and our political discussions but always came back to the simple question: "Where is my son? Where is my son?"

As we found out later, the son had been kidnaped, imprisoned, and tortured. When the case made too great a stir, the Communists decided to liquidate it by "liquidating" Mark Rein.

As a result of my intervention the Communists denounced me no longer merely as a "social-fascist" but also as a "Franco agent" and a "spy of the Gestapo." Comrades and friends from many countries, who had followed my activity in Spain, had to vouch for me and to testify that I had "always worked in the interest of a sincere collaboration of all anti-Fascist groups—regardless of the accusations that were hurled against Brandt from different sides."

In Norway before the war I explained in two pamphlets which I wrote for the Labor party what we had to expect from the political strategy of Stalin and from his foreign policy. Many, to be sure, before they understood the true meaning of "Socialist unity" and "Popular Front" had first to live through the experiences in the undergrounds of different European countries; they had to witness Stalin's nefarious role during the Warsaw revolt, when he stopped the advance of the Red Army at the gates of the city to let the Polish freedom fighters bleed to death and thus eliminated the most active opposition against his Communist stooges; they had first to see for themselves with what kind of methods the Communists tried to gain power in postwar Europe.

I have just mentioned attacks against me from *different* sides. Among the critics were some who denounced me for "not always being guided by principles in my policy." I remember a noted Marxian theorist who in a lecture in Paris presented his thesis on the future political developments. He predicted the course which, according to his theories, the world in general and Spain in particular would *have* to take. When I asked him what we ought to do if the reality would not conform to his theories he answered with a superior smile: "All the worse for the reality."

In Berlin, many years later, a political opponent asserted that I had participated in the Spanish Civil War as a "Red Front Fighter," as a member of the "International Brigade." Well, I would not be ashamed if I—like some of my friends at the Aragon front—had defended with arms the cause of the legal Spanish Republic and European democracy. However, my activity was limited to political and literary work; later, after my return to Oslo, I was engaged in humanitarian efforts on behalf of the suffering Spanish people.

It is of great importance to me to acknowledge here and now all that I said and did in the year of 1937 on behalf of the Spanish Loyalists; I have never wavered in my sympathy for the great Spanish people, sorely afflicted for centuries. Indeed, the truth was not so simple as we thought in those days; both sides were guilty of many crimes. But there can be no doubt that the resistance against the fascist insurrection was legal and justified. The Western powers would have acted wiser if they had not let the Spanish Republic fall under the influence of the Soviets and if they had not allowed democracy to bleed to death. A different outcome of the Spanish Civil War would have certainly weakened the position of Hitler and Mussolini, and maybe prevented World War II.

In Oslo, I became one of the secretaries of the Norwegian Spanish Committee which, supported by the trade unions, made considerable effort to aid the Spanish people with medical supplies and food. Little Norway stood—in proportion to its population—at the head of this international philanthropic enterprise. Norway has always reacted strongly to humanitarian appeals; it did so, too, when Finland in the winter 1939–40 became a victim of the Soviet aggression. And as we had previously helped the fighters against fascism, our committee, which now was called People's Aid, helped the fighters against the Soviet invasion.

This was no contradiction. Whoever fought for liberty and was in need, deserved our support—whether in Barcelona or Helsingfors.

5

The presentiment of the coming war could not be banished; therefore the people in the West abandoned themselves to the joys of peace and the democratic statesmen to a hollow activity, like children who in a dark forest try to overcome their fear by singing and shouting. The world had plunged into the *first war* because nobody really foresaw its horrors and its terrible consequences; the *second war* became inevitable because the democracies realized all too clearly the enormity of the catastrophe. The fear of this horror paralyzed them.

I saw both sides of the European situation.

Paris in the summer of 1937 was more beautiful, gayer than I had ever seen it, exuberant in its love of life. The world exhibition was not only a fascinating spectacle but also an impressive manifestation of everything that makes life in free Europe worth living: the genuineness of human relations, the intellectual epicurism, the richness and splendor of its artistic and literary activity.

A few months later Hitler invaded Austria. But that did not adversely affect the tourist season of 1938. The summer resorts on the French coast and in the Alps enjoyed a veritable boom since, thanks to the social laws of the Léon Blum government, the employees and workers were granted paid vacations and took full advantage of this opportunity.

The other side of the picture: I could study it at the many conferences at which I participated not only as a newspaperman but also as an interpreter for Norwegian trade-union leaders, and at my meetings with European politicians and statesmen At nearly every conference and meeting I could see how much power fear and self-deception had gained over the hearts and brains of so many political leaders.

The British Labor party adhered to an extreme pacifism. Influential representatives of the "radical" wing of the French Socialist party had completely unrealistic notions not only about the foreign policy of France but also about economic and social problems in general.

Worse was the case of the ex-Communist and mayor of Saint-Denis, Jacques Doriot. In 1934 he was expelled from the party because he had prematurely advocated the Popular Front. Later he was asked to come to Moscow. He declined the invitation since he was afraid he would have to share the fate of so many other comrades who had deviated from the right path. As a matter of fact, the Comintern intended to offer him the leadership of the French Communist party. For in the meantime the defamed Popular Front had been declared the only true and correct Communist policy.

In the course of a few years Doriot was driven by his hate of Bolshevism into the camp of the fascists. Later on I witnessed in Norway and Sweden a few similar—though not so drastic—cases. I have drawn from them the lesson that it is not good enough to be just an anti-Bolshevik.

In the midst of all the confusion there were still a few labor and trade-union leaders who did not lose their common sense and had a clear understanding of the political situation. Of the better known labor leaders of those years I met Léon Jouhaux, the eloquent chief of the French Trade Unions, and

Sir Walter Citrine, a typical representative of the English fair play which must be granted even your most vicious enemy. A closer personal relationship I enjoyed with Edo Fimmen, the uncontested leader of the International Transport Federation. This former officer of the Salvation Army was a Socialist of sterling worth, an indefatigable defender of the poor and weak. He helped the German resistance and the German refugees to the best of his ability. In Belgium, Paul-Henri Spaak seemed to me the strongest personality among the Socialists. In 1935 he occupied the extreme left position in his party. In 1938, when I met him again in Brussels, he was already Prime Minister and a rather controversial figure because of his complaisance—especially in his foreign policy.

I had many contacts with politicians in the Scandinavian countries. In Sweden I first met the Left Socialists around Karl Kilbom, who soon thereafter returned to the fold of the Social Democratic party. Kilbom himself was a metal worker who had immigrated to Sweden from his native Belgium. Notwithstanding his strong interest in politics, his real aim in life was "to bring art to the people." In Scandinavia there were many good painters and sculptors; Kilbom was indefatigable in his efforts to educate the masses in the appreciation of these artists.

In Denmark my sympathy belonged to the two politicians who had risen from the ranks of the youth movement, and after the war became prime ministers of their country: the cheery Hans Hedtoft Hansen and the purposeful H. C. Hansen. In Finland I became acquainted with the trade-union leader E. Vuori, who after the war was appointed ambassador to London and Moscow.

In the fall of 1938, after the Munich Conference, I once more attended a congress which tried to revive the idea of a "people's front" against the ever growing menace of the Nazi war. The conference was held in the Hotel Lutetia in Paris.

The noted author Heinrich Mann, Thomas Mann's older brother, served as a figurehead for this enterprise. I had read some of his novels and short stories, but with the exception of his *Der Untertan* (*The Subject*) a great satirical, even prophetic novel that had a great influence on my generation, his books left me rather cold. That was probably my fault. I found Heinrich Mann's novels too "artificial," masterful in style and language but without relation to the problems in which I was interested. This, however, did not diminish my admiration for his sincerity and humaneness.

I was all the more depressed when I saw how the Communist wire-pullers of the congress abused the political naïveté of the novelist for their own aims. Many of the "independent" and "democratic" speakers were known to me as Communist functionaries.

I had the occasion for only a very short private talk with Heinrich Mann. I was deeply touched by the sincere and genuine grief of the writer for his beloved Germany. A citizen of the world, world-famous, rooted in the culture and the spirit of France, one of the keenest critics of the German people, he was probably the most German among the German refugees. He too hailed from Lübeck. That brought us close together. Hitler, the war danger, the rising tide of barbarism—he summarized his sorrow in one sentence: "We will never see our Lübeck again." In his case that was unfortunately true.

The debacle of Munich, the surrender of the Western governments, the ardent wish to unite all anti-fascist forces against Hitler and the coming war made the appeals for unity very attractive even to those who could not believe at all in the Soviet Union's selfless love for peace. Willy Muenzenberg, the noted Communist, was the driving force behind the efforts to bring about a close collaboration between the different groups of refugees. And again the Communists did more than their most bitter enemies could ever do to make that collaboration impossible.

Willy Muenzenberg, who in spite of his long membership in the party had kept a certain measure of intellectual independence and whose unusual gift for organization and political acumen even his opponents recognized, losт the confidence of the Comintern. He had been a friend of most of the executed old Bolsheviks, therefore especially suspect to Stalin. Walter Ulbricht, the perfect type of the narrowminded party hack, took over. He was always ready and willing to obey faithfully every order from Moscow. With him no human or political relationship was possible.

Muenzenberg, a strange combination of an old revolutionary and a modern businessman, broke openly with the Communists. Two years later he paid, like many others, with his life for this act of independence. On his flight from a French concentration camp he met his death near the Spanish border. How he was murdered and by whom was never established.

6

Each time I returned to Oslo from my travels abroad I realized more clearly how much Norway had become my second home. The greater my dissatisfaction with a socialist policy that wavered between sterile sectarianism and futile opposition, all the better could I appreciate the program of social reforms and economic planning which the Scandinavian labor parties tried to realize and for which they had also gained the support of a large segment of the middle classes and of the farming population.

Here socialism was felt more and more strongly as a force that strengthened and broadened democracy.

I had overcome my former left-socialist position, not my revolutionary élan but the dogmatic narrowness. I tried to take into account the findings of modern economic and social science. Thus I became a liberal Socialist, a social democrat of the Scandinavian type.

Aside from the political tenets which had an important influence on my future life, I regard as the greatest asset of my years in Scandinavia the human relationships which I established there. I became a close friend of many Norwegian Socialists and trade unionists, also of liberals and conservatives, of poets like Arnulf Oeverland and Sigurd Hoel, of many young men in all parts of the country. That these friendships outlived all the troubles and the chaotic confusion of the past twenty years, and that our respective political careers did not dim our mutual trust—that I count among the happiest experiences of my whole life.

*

CHAPTER FIVE

Prisoner of the Nazis

1

The first months of the war had an aura of unreality. They were like the white nights of the late summer high up in the north: the nerves are tense, you are in a strange state of agitation, the restlessness is like a poison in your blood, and at the same time you feel paralyzed, helpless in the grip of a dull fatalism.

Every morning I went to a small office that I had set up, I gave lectures, wrote articles—and still many letters. I also worked on a book, a dissertation on the war aims. It was based on the certain assumption that the democracies would be victorious, and I tried to penetrate through the fog of slogans to the real problems which would confront Europe after the downfall of the dictators.

My confidence in the future was not the result of mere intellectual speculation. I was in love. Carlota was about to become my wife. She was an assistant at a scientific institute connected with the Nobel foundation.

The founding of a family, a home of our own—that was a piece of reality, a certain foothold in the headlong flight of events.

Unreal was the war in the west, this *drôle de guerre*, not at all droll, but almost grotesque in its paradox. Real was Hitler's victory over Poland, the partition of the unfortunate country between the brown and the red dictators. Real was the Soviet invasion of Finland.

Unreal was the Christmas party with Norwegian friends, radical intellectuals, in a ski hut high up in the mountains, unreal the pacifist ideas they expounded—a few months later the same men were fighters of the resistance.

Real was the harmony, the great quiet and perfect peace which we experienced amidst ice and snow during our Easter vacation of 1940; how far away, here in the mountain retreat of our friends the Lange family, seemed the war, how petty the pretense and the quarreling of human beings. Yet, this thought—was it not self-deceptive, unreal, this feeling of solitude and rapture?

We had been back from our vacation only a few days when on April 8 the reality hit Norway like a hurricane.

The first news in the afternoon papers seemed more mysterious than alarming.

One hundred warships had passed through the Danish straits heading north. What was the meaning of it?

In the afternoon we were told that the Hamburg liner *Rio de Janeiro* had been sunk off the Norwegian south coast by a Polish U-boat. The ship had carried soldiers and horses. A few soldiers were rescued and brought to shore. At their interrogation they declared that Bergen had been their port of destination.

Disturbing news poured down on us like a torrential rain, still the people did not believe in any danger. They could not understand how serious the situation was. The government, too, did not know what to do and how to act. Should it take defensive measures? The same day the ministers of England and France delivered a note to the Foreign Minister Koht, the Norwegian government was informed that the Allies were forced to blockade the Norwegian coast with mines in order to prevent the further misuse of the Norwegian territorial waters by the German Navy.

The Oslo government was determined to do everything to maintain Norway's neutrality and not to give Germany a cause for intervention. Professor Koht and the majority of the members of the government were convinced such a policy was in the best interest of Germany, in their opinion the neutrality was not threatened by Hitler but by the Allies. A German attack could only be the result of Allied "provocations." To exclude such a contingency the government decided to raise a firm protest against the British and French notes.

The same evening, and in spite of the alarming news, the command of the Norwegian Army clung stubbornly to the opinion that the German naval action was directed against Denmark, the Shetland Islands or the Faeroe, certainly not against Norway. The contrary statements of the shipwrecked soldiers from the *Rio de Janeiro* were disposed of as a mere ruse. The government, moreover, did not order the mobilization of the weak military forces. Only the shore defenses were put on the alert. In the evening the beacon fires were extinguished.

That evening of April 8 I addressed a meeting of German friends and declared we might expect an attack on Oslo probably the next day. Yet I did not know that the Norwegian legation in London had already transmitted a warning of the British admiralty against an imminent German landing attempt in northern Norway. Warnings of the German opposition in Berlin did not reach Oslo.

However, I did not draw any practical conclusions from my foresight. I did not take any measures against the threatening danger. The instinctive wish to minimize it was stronger.

I had just received the first author's copy of my new book. I took it home proudly. I did not imagine that a few weeks later my publisher on orders of the Gestapo would have to destroy the whole edition. Incidentally, when they found out that he had published books by Maxim Gorky, the Gestapo demanded to know the address of the Russian novelist in order to arrest him. My copy survived the war and served me well; later in Sweden I used it as a basis for a revised edition.

We had an air-raid alarm that night, but it did not disturb us greatly. Carlota was with child—we took comfort in assuring each other that nothing would happen.

The next morning I was awakened by the insistent ringing of my telephone. A friend told me in great excitement that for two hours he had tried to reach me without success; the line had been out of order. German warships had penetrated the Oslo fjord; German invasion troops had landed at different places along the coast.

A few minutes later we were on our way. First, we went to the Sewerins', a doctor's family, good friends of ours. There I was told to drive immediately to a certain place in a suburb of Oslo.

Carlota had to stay behind. Norwegian relatives and friends would take care of her; but this assurance did not dispel my worries, nor ease the pain of our parting. Carlota was very courageous—besides, we clung to the hope that our separation would be of short duration: in a few days the Allies would intervene and then the tables would be turned quickly.

At our meeting place Martin Tranmael and the two secretaries of the Labor party were waiting for me. Together we drove north, via Gjoevik to Hamar, where the government and the Storting had preceded us.

Thousands like us left the city—escaping from harsh reality into an uncertain future.

2

The Norway that was attacked on April 9, 1940, was one of the oldest constitutional states of Europe. For centuries it had lived by the principle that the nation, built on law, must never be destroyed by lawlessness. Justice was one of the fundamental pillars of the state. Nothing enraged the Norwegian people more than the arbitrary manner in which justice and law were trampled on during the occupation. Among the sources that fed the Norwegian resistance, the highly developed sense of justice was probably the most important.

The second driving force was the Norwegian people's love for liberty. This country had never been a victim of foreign invaders. In 1905 when the union with Sweden was abolished, Norway gained her full independence. She gained it peacefully, no bitterness remained. The three Scandinavian nations felt like members of the same family.

For a hundred and twenty-five years Norway had lived in complete peace. She had no military tradition. She hated war. She concentrated all her energies on her efforts to raise the standard of living, to develop an exemplary social legislation, to expand public education. National unity was no empty slogan. Norway had much to defend, and the knowledge of the magnitude and the value of her accomplishments was the third and not the least motive of her resistance.

After World War I, in which she had maintained her neutrality, Norway supported the policy of collective security and advocated it energetically in the League of Nations.

When this policy foundered in the blackmail of the "Axis," in British-French complaisance, and in American isolationism, the Scandinavian states and Finland, in accord with Holland, Belgium, and Luxembourg, retreated to a position of absolute neutrality. In the spring of 1939, Hitler proposed a non-aggression pact. Denmark signed the agreement; Norway, pointing to her neutrality, refused to enter into negotiations with Germany. Both nations met with the same fate.

Hitler officially recognized Scandinavian neutrality, but on his orders from the first day on the U-boat war was ruthlessly conducted against neutral shipping, too. In the months prior to the invasion Norway lost 54 ships and 380 sailors. Almost all ships were torpedoed without warning. Protests were ignored in Berlin.

Norway's neutrality did not please the Western powers; Churchill, at that time First Lord of the Admiralty, declared in January 1940 that neutrality in the conflict with the Nazis was "immoral." He pointed out that quite a few Allied ships had been sunk by German U-boats operating in the Norwegian territorial waters. The Oslo government, however, remained firm, and the Allies had to bow, though reluctantly, to this decision.

Nevertheless, Hitler asserted that with his action against Denmark and Norway he had merely stolen a march on an attack of the Western powers. This assertion was the main point in the note which the German minister handed Professor Koht in the early morning hours of April 9. In fact, there existed certain Allied plans for the establishment of military bases in Norway. But neither these plans nor the Allied mine fields along the Norwegian coast could influence Hitler's decision—because he had come to it already, six months before, in October 1939.

Immediately after the outbreak of the war German admirals recommended the conquest of Norwegian bases. When in the first week of December, the Norwegian Major Quisling, whose name has become a synonym for traitors, was called to Berlin and served up the convenient lie that Norway had secretly agreed to an English occupation, the invasion was resolved. That was on December 12. The date of the attack was left open. On March 7, 1940, all preparations had been concluded. On April 2 came Hitler's order. On April 3 the first invasion boats put to sea.

3

The German attack was a daring enterprise. Through a combined maneuver of navy, air force, and army Oslo and the most important ports were occupied in the early morning hours and during the day of April 9. The airports in southern Norway and most of the military depots fell in a few hours into German hands. Careful preparation and energetic and audacious action played a decisive role.

The German success was greatly facilitated by the lack of Norway's military preparedness and the general weakness of her defense. The existent weapons were deficient. There were no tanks nor anti-tank weapons

At the outbreak of the war Norway was just beginning to build up her armed forces to meet the requirements of an active defense. The military budget had been raised. The Labor party recognized more clearly than others the Nazi danger. Yet it found it hard to give up its pacifist attitude, which was rooted both in a national and socialist tradition.

Nobody can prove that a little country like Norway, even with a stronger and better organized defense, could have prevented the German attack. When certain German plans for the invasion of Sweden and Switzerland were put aside the military preparedness of these two small nations had something to do with Hitler's hesitation.

Yet it is also possible that in the case of Norway, Hitler in

April 1940 would have not recoiled from the greater risk, and the result would have been nothing but a prolonged, yet equally hopeless fight, greater sacrifices, more destruction and more dead. The fact remains that the Norwegian people, precisely because it was free of any militaristic spirit and not weakened by inner dissensions, could give the solemn example of a nation which in complete unity rose in the defense of her most cherished values.

On the night of April 9 the German minister delivered a "memorandum" to the Norwegian government, assuring them that the German troops had come as friends; Germany did not intend to infringe upon the territorial integrity and political independence of Norway. If, on the other hand, Norway did not accept this generous offer, any resistance would be mercilessly wiped out and would only lead to senseless bloodshed. To the memorandum was attached a list of demands which had to be fulfilled at once. The Oslo government was ordered to direct the population and the military forces to desist from any active opposition. Military installations had to be handed over, all means of communication had to be placed at the German disposal, press and radio had to operate under the German censorship.

Foreign Minister Koht conferred briefly with his colleagues. They all agreed that no independent state could accept the German demands. The ultimatum was rejected. The King and the government left the capital. Only a few ministers remained in Oslo for a few more days. Theirs was the task to save the gold reserve of the Norwegian state bank. Trucks transported it out of the city just at the moment when the first German units marched in. Later the gold was smuggled in fishing boats out of Norway and brought to the United States after a long and adventurous journey.

4

On April 9 the members of the Storting assembled in Hamar, approximately eighty miles north of Oslo. The Foreign Minister informed them of the latest developments. In the midst of his report the news arrived that a German unit was approaching the town. The deputies had to continue their flight. They moved to the town of Elverum, closer to the Swedish border.

Our small party of four—Martin Tranmael, the two secretaries of the Labor party, and myself—arrived there late in the evening. We were told that a few hours before, the Storting in its last session had decided to cast a special vote of confidence for the government. To strengthen the national unity representatives of the non-socialist parties entered the cabinet.

Since the German minister suggested further negotiations, the Storting appointed a delegation which consisted of the Foreign Minister and three deputies. It was felt that no attempt ought to be left untried in order to arrive at a last-minute, peaceful solution of the conflict. The government was voted extraordinary powers. Until the Parliament could meet again, it was empowered to take all measures that it thought necessary in the interest of the country. The last and most important motion was put before the assembly by Mr. Hambro, the president of the Storting and leader of the Conservative party: under no circumstance must the King and the government let themselves be taken prisoners. If necessary, the constitutional government should be established outside the borders of Norway. The motion was carried unanimously.

In the night from the ninth to the tenth of April a German unit tried to reach Elverum. The intention was probably to prevent further deliberations of the Storting, to take the King and the members of government prisoners, or to chase them at least across the border into Sweden.

This attempt was thwarted by Colonel Otto Ruge, who in a great hurry improvised a line of defense with officers and volunteers. We ourselves had passed that position; we had to leave our car there, and drove then in a truck toward Nybergsund, a little town near the Swedish border, where the King and the government had already established themselves.

On our way we were passed by a car with the then Minister of Supplies and later UN Secretary-General Trygve Lie; he advised us at what spot we could, if necessary, cross the Swedish border. After the German advance had been checked the necessity did not arise.

On April 10, King Haakon drove to Elverum and received the German minister. The latter stated that the Führer not only insisted on the acceptance of his demands of the previous day but had added a few more "requests." It was Hitler's will that a new government be formed in which he could have confidence. Vidkun Quisling was to become the new Prime Minister.

The King replied that he had to conform to the Constitution and the law. He could not appoint a government which did not have the confidence of the people. However, as a constitutional monarch he was willing to put Hitler's demands before his ministers.

In a session with the government and the members of the Storting the King explained his position: he saw clearly the terrible dangers that threatened Norway. The government ought to make a decision without regard to his person. In case they wanted to accept the German demands, he for his part would take the consequences and resign.

Again the government decided to reject Germany's ultimatum The next day came Hitler's answer. It was given by the Luftwaffe. Elverum and Nybergsund were subjected to a heavy bombardment. As if by miracle the King and the government escaped with their lives.

The confusion was terrible. That evening, after the bombardment, I found in a hotel room a few forgotten valises with important government papers. I helped to secure them.

The spiritual chaos was no less frightening. That night, together with a high official, I was quartered with a peasant. A few months before I had had a rather lively political discussion with the gentleman, since he declared we ought to appreciate Hitler's accomplishments and meet him halfway. Now he put all the blame on the Versailles Treaty—it had not been harsh enough and was, therefore, responsible for our present misery. And the man was, no doubt, an intelligent and politically experienced man.

The realization of how difficult it was in times like those to make oneself understood even by men of good will, kept me awake for long hours. Not till dawn did I fall asleep.

Since the war could no longer be stopped my friends sought refuge in the interior of the country. And what should I do? Escape to Sweden? But did I have the right to abandon my Norwegian friends? And besides, was it so certain that Sweden would not be attacked and occupied also? I decided to stay, and drove back to Hamar and from there north to Lillehammer, where I knew my colleagues from the People's Aid had gone. We immediately went to work.

First we decided to collect woolen blankets and bandaging material and thus help to alleviate the most urgent need behind the front.

But where was the front?

Colonel Ruge, who had been promoted to general and Supreme Commander of the Army, was confronted with a unique task. An orderly mobilization was impossible, since in the southern part of Norway not only many military depots had fallen into German hands, but also all documents and lists concerning the mobilization. Because in the meantime the Oslo radio and other radio stations in southern Norway had been taken over by the Germans, many army units could not even receive their orders. Telegraph and telephone were under censorship. Vidkun Quisling, who had appointed himself head of the "national government," issued immediately a proclamation to all military commanders and all men liable to military service, canceling all orders of the constitutional government. Soldiers and officers on the way to their units were to return home immediately. And two days later, on April 12, the German commander of Oslo announced that "the first saboteurs had been arrested, condemned to death according to international law, and instantly shot."

General Ruge described later "the army" with which he was supposed to stop the advance of the invasion troops:

"From Oslo flocked hundreds of men who could not be mobilized there, since the Germans had occupied the city. They rallied around one or another commander and formed a company. They united with other similar groups from other places and formed a battalion. Some officer assumed command. The accident brought together in the same company infantrymen, artillerymen, sailors, and airmen. By good fortune we even had cars and drivers whom we found, God knows how. These units gradually grew into combat troops. The commissariat was improvised and took care of feeding the small army. The women on the farms cooked and helped the soldiers. We had no medical corps. Thanks to the initiative of energetic doctors it was created from scratch."

Ruge's plan was based on the following consideration: to carry out offensive operations with the forces just described was out of question. On the other hand, one could count on a quick and effective Allied assistance; Paris and London had firmly promised it. The intervention would be best effected from the vicinity of Troendelag. The first objective was the reconquest of Trondheim by combined operations of British naval forces and Norwegian and Allied troops. Therefore, the German columns, advancing from Oslo, had to be prevented at all costs from joining the German garrison at Trondheim. According to this plan the Norwegians retreated from Hamar and Lillehammer through the valley of Gudbrand northward in the direction of Dovre. At the same time at many points a not very effective, more or less symbolic resistance was offered.

Ruge's opponent was the German Supreme Commander, General Nikolaus von Falkenhorst. He was an excellent staff officer, and as a commander of an army corps in the Polish campaign he had also gathered practical front experience. He immediately saw through the Norwegian plan. The relatively weak and isolated German garrison in Trondheim was ordered to form a "hedgehog" and not to let itself be provoked to any offensive action. Simultaneously superior German forces were to push forward from Hamar in northerly direction, to break through the Norwegian lines, and to relieve Trondheim.

Thus a race against time began.

On April 15 the Allies landed at Namsos, north of Trondheim, a few days later at Aandalsness south of Trondheim. But already on the twenty-second the German troops had conquered Lillehammer and pushed northward.

On May first the race was over.

On April 28, England had notified the Norwegian Supreme Commander that the Allies had abandoned their plan to reconquer Trondheim and were forced to retreat from southern Norway. Once more, France and England had underestimated the power of their enemy. Too little and too late—that was all that the Norwegian people could say about the Allied help.

To be sure, one must not underestimate the great difficulties that confronted an Allied expeditionary corps. Troops could land at Aandalsness, but even there it was almost impossible to land heavy war matériel. The Germans were in command of the air. All Norwegian airports were in their hands. The British had no choice. On May 1 they evacuated Aandalsness, a few days later Namsos.

The fate of the Norwegian forces operating in southern Norway was sealed. They had to lay down arms.

In northern Norway the fight continued until June 9. Two days before, the King, some of his close advisers, and the government had fled to England. In the meantime Narvik was reconquered by the Norwegians and the Allies. But the fate of Norway was decided on the western front, for Holland and Belgium had fallen, and in France military resistance broke down quickly.

Hitler's complete control of the continent was an accomplished fact.

The cause of liberty seemed lost. Its flame was about to be extinguished. In those anxious days it was Churchill who kindled that flame and did more than any other man to restore the faith in victory—although he could promise his countrymen nothing but "blood, sweat and tears."

5

I was a civilian. In the Norwegian war I had carried no arms. But that could not save me from the vengeance of the Gestapo. In 1938, Hitler had taken away my citizenship. The following year I had applied for my naturalization in Norway. Trygve Lie, then Minister of Justice, had informed me that I could expect my papers in half a year.

Then, after May 1, I found myself in a valley north of Aandalsness—an expatriate German and a stateless Norwegian. The valley had only one access. And this was blocked.

My friends and I deliberated whether we should try to escape on skis over the mountains, but we had to abandon the plan because it promised no chance of success. Instead it was decided to put me into a Norwegian uniform. As one of thousands of Norwegian soldiers I could hope to be treated as a prisoner of war, and probably I would soon be released. As a civilian, on the other hand, I had to expect the worst, once my true identity was established.

I threw all my papers away and put on the uniform. It did not fit too well, the pants were too short, the jacket was much too wide, but nobody could find fault with my Norwegian pronunciation. Together with a few hundred other soldiers I was taken to Dovre, where the former school served as a prisoner of war camp.

Those were depressing days and weeks. The debacle, Hitler's victories in east, north, and west seemed to secure his power for many years to come. The future was without hope. What could I expect? I let my life pass before my eyes and decided with all the superiority of my twenty-six years that it had been a failure.

But over and over again the wonderful comradeship of the young Norwegians among whom I lived restored my spirit.

And then there was something else that gave me confidence in my darkest hours: soon our child would be born. I was to become a father. No, I must not despair. Even if I should not see the end of this road—my child would remain. Life went on. This thought gave me calm and comfort. I would not give up!

The four weeks in the camp of Dovre offered me an opportunity for personal contact with German youth that had reached manhood under the Nazis.

The guards were mainly Rhinelanders. It had been impressed upon the German soldiers to treat the Norwegians with respect; since the latter were "pure-bred Aryans" it should be very easy to win them over to Nazism. Nothing but blindness and vicious propaganda had turned them into enemies of the new Germany. How tragic that many of the "liberators" did not realize that the real blind were they themselves.

I could also easily see that to many of the young German soldiers Nazism was still something extraneous—an elementary force which one did better not to resist. If you wanted to have nothing to do with it, the best way was to retreat into a private world and concentrate thoughts and hopes on the marriage you planned after victory was won, on the new furniture you had promised your fiancée.

To show his good will the commander of the camp granted us privileges which ordinary prisoners of war usually are not entitled to. We were allowed to visit, in the company of our guard, the nearby farms to buy some food. And while in a backroom we listened to the London radio and enjoyed a free chat with the farmer, our guard sat outside on the doorstep and enjoyed the milk and a piece of sausage which the farmer's wife served him at our request.

This superficial harmony was broken on May 17.

For already, the week before, an incident had occurred. During a discussion in the schoolyard the flight of the King was mentioned, and a non-commissioned officer accused the King of cowardice. I replied calmly, "If King Haakon is a coward, then Hitler is a coward too."

The sergeant stared at me more terrified than outraged. He could not comprehend how somebody—on top of it, a prisoner—dared offend the Führer in public. He turned red; for a moment he was speechless. His helplessness was almost comical. The next moment he exploded: "You dare call our Führer a coward!"

I remained calm. "I have said: if the King of Norway should

be considered a coward, then Hitler is one too. If you take back your insult, we are even."

An officer appeared. He had just caught my last words, frowned, took the sergeant aside, and advised him to leave the "hysterical youngster" alone. From then on I was regarded as a student who could speak German quite well but who otherwise was a little mad. This label was not a bad protection for me.

May 17 is Norway's national holiday, the day on which the Constitution was proclaimed. We decided to ask the commander to allow us on this special day to set the Norwegian flag at half-mast. Our request was denied.

We were not willing to give in.

Every morning, as soon as a signal was given, we had to assemble in the schoolyard. The morning of the seventeenth we did not wait for the signal. Three minutes before, we were ready. We drew up in military formation and stood at attention.

Complete silence. Nobody moved. Then one of us stepped forward and said loudly and clearly: "Never forget! Never forget this seventeenth of May on which we were not even allowed to fly our flag at half-mast."

The little demonstration was already over when the guards came running.

We did not escape punishment. Presently we were led to the railroad station of Dovre and ordered to unload bombs from an ammunition train.

Johan Capellen, one of our elected spokesmen, stepped forward and declared that according to international law prisoners of war must not be employed in any military work. The protest was in vain. A very furious first lieutenant gave us two minutes' time for reflection. Either we obeyed the order or he would "make an example of us." We had to give in.

As soon as we returned to our camp, Capellen insisted on

being taken to the commander. The request was granted. Capellen, a good friend of mine, who after the war entered the diplomatic service and at present is attached as a counselor to the embassy at Geneva, is, like his two brothers, an excellent lawyer. He knew what to say in the interest of his comrades.

The commander, a captain, did not fly into a rage. He did not threaten. He adopted a conciliatory attitude: "If I forward your protest to the division," he said with a faint smile, "we all will run into trouble. The prisoners will be punished for their insubordination and I for my complaisance. Therefore, it is wiser to drop the protest. In return I promise you that the prisoners will never again be ordered to do this kind of work."

And he kept his promise. In the German Army there were Nazis—and Germans.

CHAPTER SIX

A Twofold Immigrant

1

In the beginning of June we were released from the camp. I was permitted to return to my "home town." As soon as I was in the train to Oslo I went to the lavatory, put on my trench coat, and put the military cap in my knapsack. Now I looked again like a civilian. Without difficulty I arrived in Oslo.

Of course I could not go home, nor was it advisable to show up in the city, for the Gestapo would be all too glad to catch me.

At the camp, friends had given me the address of an apartment in a suburb of Oslo where I would be safe. I was heading there now.

My friends had a wonderful surprise in store for me. When I rang the bell it was Carlota who opened the door. Instantly all the pain and the sorrows of the past weeks were forgotten.

A few days later our happy reunion was over. I had to go on. I dared not endanger my friend more than necessary.

In the following weeks I lived the life of a hermit in a secluded summer house on the Oslo fjord which a colleague from the People's Aid had placed at my disposal. Besides, this friend had succeeded in drawing from the bank the arrears of my salary, so that for the moment I need not worry about money. There remained my concern about our future. What was I to do? I tried to put my thoughts and feelings in order—it was not lack of time that made it so difficult for me to make plans for the future.

A few friends knew where I was hiding; they and Carlota sometimes visited me. Every visit involved grave risks.

As a result of our long talks and deliberations it was decided that I should leave Norway. I could not hope to find a safe hiding place anywhere but in a remote corner of the country. Since I was well known, I could easily be recognized and thus jeopardize my collaborators. And I surely did not like the idea of remaining idle. My friends suggested that I go to Sweden, where I could work as a journalist—also for the cause of a free Norway.

In July I started on my flight. A good piece of the way I traveled by car, then I took a train, the last distance I covered on foot. The third day I reached a farm near the Swedish border. The farmer, a Norwegian reserve officer, knew the surroundings intimately and was well acquainted with the conditions at the border; he put me on the right path, and after a long march, eluding the German patrols, I crossed the border without being noticed.

On Swedish soil I reported to the first military post. The next morning I was taken over by the police and brought to Charlottenberg, where I was interned in a house near the railway station August Spangberg, a deputy of the Riksdag, whom I had met during the street battles in Barcelona in 1937, came to see me and bailed me out. Via a rather comfortable refugee camp—an old castle where Ernst Paul, the secretary of the Sudetic-German Socialist party, took care of us—I reached Stockholm as a free man.

There I learned shortly afterward that the Norwegian government-in-exile had approved my citizenship. Now I was a twofold immigrant: a German who had fled to Norway and a Norwegian who had escaped to Sweden.

In Stockholm, Martin Tranmael had established a public relations center of the Norwegian Socialist Movement. Here I found many an old friend. However, for years I did not see Halvard Lange, later the Foreign Minister. He went back to Norway, although he must have expected to be soon arrested, as his two brothers were; all three of them landed in a German concentration camp.

I became a good friend of the secretary of the center, Inge Scheflo, whom I had known for a long time, just as I had known his father. The elder Scheflo, Olav, had won my particular affection for two reasons. first, because he described to me the Socialist movement as the "natural child of liberalism," and in the second place, because he awakened in me the passion for fishing. He had been a leader of the Left, and in the field of domestic policy he was a bitter opponent of Tranmael, but that did not disturb in the least the co-operation between Tranmael and the young Scheflo. In 1944, Inge went back to Oslo as an "illegal" editor and later on became secretary of the parliamentary group of the Socialist party.

It took me some time to get used to the political atmosphere in the Swedish capital. To be sure, the Swedish people were in full sympathy with their Norwegian brothers, the overwhelming majority of them wanted to have nothing to do with Hitler-Germany. But the government followed a strictly neutral policy, and at first had been quite willing to make some concessions, in order to keep the country out of that horrible war. And this policy was in full accord with the general feeling of the population; of course, one complained about the rationing of food, but after all, one was quite satisfied with the way the government acted.

I quickly made contact with the German refugee circles in Stockholm and was heartily welcomed by my friends.

I lived in a predominantly Norwegian environment; that did not exclude my friendly relations with the Stockholm Labor party and its youth organization. I also maintained close contacts with the anti-Nazi circles around the Stockholm author Ture Nerman and Torgny Segerstedt, an editor in chief of a Göteborg paper. I was in contact with still another group, the editors and sponsors of the magazine *Nordens Frihet,* among them the poet Eyvind Johnson and Bo Enander, a noted columnist on foreign affairs.

My journalistic activity in Sweden began with a series of articles about the Norwegian campaign. These articles later formed the basis of a book—published in German in Switzerland—which was followed by three others. Shortly after the war I published a two-volume study of wartime Norway; it had many shortcomings, I must admit. I wrote a study on guerrilla warfare, prepared a revised edition of the already mentioned book about the peace aims—*After the War*—edited some other books, contributed to a treatise on the history of World War II, which was published by the Institute of Foreign Affairs in Stockholm, and wrote several booklets for the same institute.

And yet I did not neglect the daily work of a journalist. I felt bound in honor and duty to keep the Swedish and foreign press informed about the events in Norway. My one-man business expanded into a "Swedish-Norwegian Press Agency," which furnished news about these countries to many papers.

My journalistic and political activity soon made it necessary for me to take a personal look again at the latest developments in Norway. In December 1944 I went back to Oslo temporarily.

Not only political considerations prompted me to undertake this journey. I was also longing to see my daughter Ninja, who had been born in October.

My friend Inge and I had good connections with certain circles in the Swedish Army. We got a special permit to visit the border zone. There a "pilot" awaited us; under his guidance we by-passed some frozen waters and arrived safely in Halden. From there we simply took a train to Oslo.

Illegal border crossings were nothing new to me. Nor was I any longer the amateur conspirator of the early days of the Nazi regime. But nonetheless, it was much easier for me to travel in Norway than it had been in Germany. There at every step I had the feeling of being in an enemy country—in occupied Norway I felt much safer. I knew that almost everybody, worker or shopkeeper, the stationmaster and the taxi driver, were friends whom I could trust.

2

When I arrived in Oslo a new phase of the Norwegian resistance had just begun. At the outset of the occupation it had by no means been unified. In the first months the Hitler government, as a result of its moderate and somewhat conciliatory policy, seemed to succeed in inducing the Norwegians to adopt a neutral attitude toward the occupation forces.

The first Quisling government had not lasted very long, it had been followed by an administrative council. The members of the Quisling party remained in the background—in reserve, as it were—and were winning new followers, particularly among the better-off farmers.

In the summer of 1940, after the surrender of France, there was a strong feeling that further resistance was useless. Even in September the majority of the members of the Storting, assembled in Oslo, were ready to vote for a "suspension" of the King for the duration of the war. They demanded in return that the Reichskommissar (German civilian governor) and the German police not interfere with the civilian affairs, that censorship and the harsh economic measures of the occupation forces be abolished. But Reichskommissar Terboven rejected any and all compromises. He declared the King deposed, dissolved all political parties, confiscated their property. Activities "in the spirit of the forbidden parties," in favor of the Royal Family or the government, were to be punished with hard labor.

This attempt to conquer the nation from within united the people in a firm resistance. The measures of Nazification at first resulted only in spontaneous protests of small and isolated groups. But these individual actions soon led to a general uprising. The resistance rested on three strong pillars: church, schools, and courts.

When I arrived in Oslo, shortly before Christmas 1940, all the supreme judges had just resigned their posts. They declared that the decrees issued by the Reichskommissar were violating Norwegian law. And this demonstration decisively influenced the whole resistance movement, gave it direction, and determined its character. It was not by accident that the Supreme Judge, Paol Berg, became the central figure of the "Home Front."

The Supreme Court had always played an important role in Norway. Similar to the Supreme Court in the United States, it is the third power beside the Executive and the Legislative. It has to decide whether laws passed by the Parliament conform to the Constitution, and its decisions are binding on Parliament and government.

Prior to the resignation of the Supreme Court, the opposition had, in fact, not been directed against the occupation forces as such. The military regime was regarded as an unalterable fact. But the attempt to impose on Norway a new political, spiritual, and cultural order was generally felt to be contrary to the rights of an occupation force, according to international law. With their resignation the members of the Supreme Court fully accomplished what they had intended: the fight against the conquerors was to be fought in the name of justice and law.

In the end of 1940, Norwegian teachers were asked to expound in class "actively and positively" the ideas of Nazism. More than ninety per cent declared they were determined to remain faithful to their conscience and their vocation as educators of youth. In the spring of 1942, on orders of Quisling, more than one thousand teachers were arrested. German authorities deported most of them to the shores of the Polar Sea, but they could not break their will of resistance. Many died from forced labor and exposure.

In 1943 came the climax in the struggle for the University of Oslo. Rather than give up their rights to free research and free teaching, members of the faculty preferred to suspend their lectures. Didrik Arup Seip, the chancellor of the university, was deported to Germany. His example kindled the spirit of the students. Hundreds of them were arrested and deported to German camps. There they were to be "reeducated in the Germanic spirit." But even Buchenwald, where many of them survived the war, could not make Nazis out of them.

Writers and publishers stopped their work in protest against the censorship. Actors and dramatists refused to take part in any Nazi performance, or to appear on the Nazi-controlled radio. Against the Nazification of theaters and cinemas the public reacted with a general boycott.

Bishop Eivind Berggrav, head of the Norwegian Church, had at first been willing to come to an agreement with the

Nazi overlords and had been rebuked by many of his countrymen for his compliance. But the Church, though ready to make some political concessions, was not in the least willing to recognize the totalitarian claims of the National Socialist regime. The clergy insisted on fulfilling its mission as a guardian of national and moral values As Bishop Berggrav was under no circumstance going to desist from the defense of the freedom of conscience, as he stood up for the traditional administration of justice, for family, school, and the protection of the individual against the arbitrariness of the authorities, the open conflict was unavoidable.

In the beginning of 1942 all the bishops issued a pastoral letter, in which they announced that after careful consideration they had decided to resign from their worldly posts; but they did not think of giving up their clerical functions. Ninety-five per cent of the clergy declared their solidarity with them.

Berggrav was arrested. Terboven wanted to put him before the "People's Court," and only an intervention of some influential moderate Germans saved him from the concentration camp. He was interned in a country house near Oslo, but was not allowed to have any contact with the outside world. As a prisoner of the Nazis, the bishop gained a greater influence with the Norwegian people than he had ever had. He became a symbol of the resistance.

As I have already mentioned, the first Quisling government had lasted only for a few days. But Norwegian National Socialists were soon given important posts in the administration, and in February 1942, Quisling reached his most coveted goal: he was made Prime Minister by the grace of Hitler.

Meanwhile matters were becoming critical. There were bloody clashes; a major one occurred in the fall of 1942, after the workers of Oslo had been placed under a state of emergency. Then, as well as later, I lost good friends, and I followed with great sympathy the actions of the Norwegian resistance groups in the last years of the war. And yet the tactics and methods of civilian and unarmed resistance impressed me most.

Moral integrity distinguished the men and women who led this fight without arms. Politics were not their forte. Only slowly did they acquire the necessary experiences of underground activity, and sometimes their decisions may have put the patience of the active fighters to a hard test. This they took in stride, for they wanted to prevent a split between a small, resolute vanguard, and an indifferent majority. In their opinion, the defense of the Constitution and of international law was not the prerogative of the Supreme Court; whether freedom of science prevailed or perished was not of concern only to the professors; it was not up to the teachers alone to repulse the Nazi attacks against the schools—those were questions of life and death for the nation as a whole.

If one takes freedom seriously—this was the message of the Norwegian Home Front—it is not enough to defend it with material means only. True enough, the military power of the Nazis could only be destroyed with stronger military forces. But fascism as the result of a social process, of a decaying society, could only be overcome by eliminating its social sources. This pestilence of immorality could only be abolished by setting law against arbitrariness, freedom against tyranny, conviction based on knowledge against slogans, personal responsibility against the *Führerprinzip*—and if one stood up for those principles. This knowledge, acquired in the Norwegian resistance, is today as pertinent as it was twenty years ago. It has an extremely important bearing upon the struggle of the Berliners.

3

One evening during my "illegal" stay in Oslo I met a prominent personality of the civilian resistance. It was Einar Gerhardsen, the former mayor of Oslo. The Germans had dismissed him, and he was now employed as a municipal worker.

"You are the comrade from Sweden about whom my friends have written me?" was the astonished question of this huge man with his kind eyes and his warm voice.

"You of all people are the one who is in command here?" I asked in return.

In the course of 1941, Gerhardsen was arrested. Before he became head of the government in 1945 he had to spend long years in different concentration camps.

The journalist in whose house we used to meet in the evenings—we could only leave our quarters after dark—was arrested when he attempted to escape from the west coast in a fishing boat. His comrades, among them a close friend of mine, were shot. He himself was saved through the desperate efforts of his wife.

In Stockholm my expedition had consequences which I had not foreseen. Apparently the police did not know that our journey had been undertaken with the consent of the military authorities, nor did I tell them. When I applied for an extension of my residence permit I was kept in custody. Meanwhile the police tried to find out whether I had been working illegally on behalf of a "belligerent" power—the Norwegian government-in-exile. The police could have treated me better, but after a few days I was set free. Members of the government bailed me out.

Personally I had no further troubles with the Swedish authorities during the war. But there has been many a case when Norwegian or German refugees were called to account for their "illegal intelligence activities," even though what they did had nothing to do with military intelligence, or spying For instance, after a visit to occupied Norway, one of my friends was sentenced to prison, because a letter had been found which he had written to the government-in-exile in London.

My contacts with the Norwegian Home Front remained close. My journalistic work was primarily devoted to Norway; my wife was working in the press section of the Norwegian embassy.

Carlota had come to Stockholm with our little daughter in the spring of 1941. We moved into a small, but comfortable home. For the first time I could devote myself to my family. Members of the Norwegian resistance, especially from the Socialist movement and intellectual circles, were often our guests; Torolf Elster, a young author, was then an intimate friend of mine.

The Swedish Social Democratic party counted many noteworthy personalities among its leaders; there was the head of the government, Per Albin Hansson, a statesman of quite an individual stamp; Gustav Möller, whom one could call the father of Sweden's exemplary Social Reform program and who was always ready to help the refugees from all over the world in the very spirit of international solidarity; Ernst Wigforss, the Minister of Finance, whose work in the field of political economics would have secured him an even greater international reputation, if he had published his ideas in a language better known to students. There were the solid leaders of the trade unions, numerous politicians of the younger generation. Some of them, like Torsten Nilsson and Sven Andersson, entered the government, others chose the diplomatic service. Ole Jödal, who as editor in chief published many of my articles, I met again as ambassador in Bonn.

I often gave lectures on Norway and on international affairs, met interesting personalities of other parties, representatives of the press and literature, teachers of colleges and universities. My relations with many of these men were closer than they would have been if only professional or political interests had brought us together. One of my closer friends was Professor Gunnar Myrdal, who through his studies on the Negro problem has become widely known in the United States and whose effective work for the UN in Geneva has carved him a world-wide reputation. He, his wife Alva—later Swedish ambassador in India—and his assistant, Richard Sterner, took a vivid interest in the work of an international study group, about which I shall speak later.

We were all moved by the same concern about the future. Every one of us believed that he could best serve his mother country by working in union with the others for a Europe and a world free of an arrogant and self-righteous nationalism. Personally I did not see any contradiction between my status as a Norwegian citizen and my fight for a free, democratic Germany.

Trygve Lie, the Foreign Minister of the Norwegian government in London and later Secretary-General of the UN, was, however, of the opinion that I was too "pro-German." He misunderstood my sharp opposition to Vansittartism and was afraid that I was influencing the Norwegians in a wrong way. In his memoirs he wrote:

"Meanwhile I had become rather fed up with the attitude adopted by leading Norwegians in Sweden. At first they had tried—since they were forced to stay in Sweden—to defend Sweden's neutrality as best as possible; later they had given the kindest explanation that one could possibly give of Finland's participation in Hitler's war against our allies. But in my opinion it was going too far when they now seemed to be more concerned about Germany than about Norway's interests and about how to win the war."

A pamphlet which I wrote in collaboration with some exiled German Social Democrats who shared my convictions explained the political point of view which I advocated at that time, in the midst of war. Today I still adhere to the basic ideas which were guiding us when we wrote that booklet. Therefore, I should like to quote some of its essential points:

"One may reproach the old German labor movement with its lack of a constructive policy and with a not too heroic attitude in 1933. It is a fact, however, that the Social Democrats—contrary to all bourgeois parties—have not let themselves be cajoled or forced into a collaboration with Hitler. It is also a fact that especially the members of the younger generation of Socialists have played the most active part in the underground struggle against the Hitler regime.

"It should be clear that there exists no underground movement strong and effective enough to assume, alone, power the day after Hitler's defeat. On the other hand, we can hope that the resurgent forces of German labor and democracy will be strong enough to establish and preserve a new order through a coalition of all progressive groups and parties.

"Of course, we do not oppose Vansittartism because it exposes the crimes of the German Nazis, militarists, and imperialists We oppose it because it is, if consistently executed, nothing but Nazi race policy in reverse.

"German Democrats and Socialists will have to start from the fact that with the end of this war the international balance of power will have completely changed. Germany will play the part of a second-rate power in Europe. It will be the task of German Democrats and Socialists to defend the right of self-determination of the German people in the framework of an international organization, and to secure for the nation the means of existence. It cannot be their task to fight for the re-establishment of a German supremacy on the continent.

"We believe that the international situation urgently demands a restriction of national sovereignty in favor of a true collective security We firmly uphold the principle of the right of self-determination for all people, although we realize that there are border cases in which common European interests must take precedence. At the same time we disapprove of the plans of those who want to push Germany far back behind the borders of the Weimar Republic, or even to dismember her and cut her up into different states"

In the same pamphlet we expressed the opinion that the war would be won by a coalition not at all uniform in itself, but that an intelligent German foreign policy must not be based upon the differences between the victors: "We believe that a foreign policy trying to play off the victorious powers one against the other is fatal, because it would endanger the reconstruction of a new Germany and arouse nationalistic aberrations." We even advocated the most friendly relations possible with the Soviet Union, and rejected the idea that a European federation could be formed in opposition against either Russia or England.

We paid particular attention to the question of restitution, especially in favor of persecuted Jews: "Great is the responsibility of a large segment of the German nation for what their fellow citizens of Jewish origin had to endure One may hope that the Nazis themselves have reduced anti-Semitism to the nonsense it actually is. Yet anti-Semitism and other forms of race hatred must be eradicated by laws. Beyond this, economic support is necessary."

We believed the Socialists should, right from the beginning, take an active part in the reconstruction of Germany and assume their share of responsibility. We put a special emphasis on the need for a renovation of the German educational system in the spirit of democratic pedagogics and humanism. But we concluded, "The democratic re-education of the German people must essentially be the work of the Germans themselves."

4

It was not only after El Alamein and Stalingrad that we Social Democrats and our democratic friends in Sweden were convinced that Hitler's defeat was inevitable. We knew it, at the latest, after the German attack on Russia and America's entry into the war.

We were increasingly occupied with the questions of the future organization of Europe, with the problems which the nations and the governments of the democratic powers would have to solve, once the Hitler-regime broke down. From 1942 on we met at regular sessions of an "International Circle of Democratic Socialists"—not because we thought that we in Stockholm could exert an effective influence on the course of events, but rather because we wanted to clarify our own thinking. In fact, more than once did we stimulate the international exchange of ideas. Our opinions on the German question, well balanced and free of any feelings of hatred or revenge, found, for instance, an echo in the underground press of Norway and France.

The circle, which met in the building of the Swedish trade unions, had hardly more than two dozen members. Most of them were, of course, Swedes and Norwegians. Danish and occasionally Finnish friends took part in our sessions. Fritz Tarnow was the spokesman for the Germans. This former member of the Reichstag and a prominent union leader was not only an intelligent and stimulating speaker, but thanks to his tact and sincerity he also enjoyed the confidence of the representatives of the nations under the Nazi heel.

Bruno Kreisky, at present Foreign Minister, represented the Austrians, Ernst Paul the Sudetic Germans.

There was Wilhelm Böhm from Hungary, France was represented by a grandson of the famous Socialist leader Jules Guèsde. Members of our group were also Stefan Szende, Dr. M. Karniol, ambassador of the Polish government-in-exile, representatives of the Czech, Spanish, and Baltic Social Democrats; furthermore, there were a number of young socialist Zionists, whom I also visited at their places of employment, where they prepared themselves for the emigration to Israel as farm hands or artisans. Occasionally we received visits from English unionists and from the members of the Belgian or Polish government-in-exile who for the time being were staying in Sweden. Also representatives of the American trade unions, who were stationed in Stockholm, kept closely in touch with us.

Ernst Paul was the chairman of the council, Richard Sterner his deputy, I worked as an honorary secretary. Aside from our private sessions we organized a few public meetings and tried to inform the press about some results of our work. We received horrible reports from the occupied countries . . . for instance, the first detailed information about the gas chambers in Poland. I shall never forget how Tarnow refused to believe in the truth of those reports. It could not, it simply must not be true. Personally I never doubted them. The song of the youth movement, "Man is good," has, I am afraid, no more validity than the saying, "Man is a swine"; the truth lies somewhere in between.

Some of our ideas of that time did not quite correspond to the reality. We hoped, for instance, that the war experiences and the co-operation with the Anglo-American powers would bring about a gradual democratization of the Soviet regime. We also hoped that it would be comparatively easy to establish a system of international law and order. As far as the German question was concerned, our ideas have been proven correct. Correct, but disregarded also, were our suggestions for an international co-operation between the European Social Democrats and similar movements in other parts of the world. And last but not least, we were right in stressing the importance of a joint and common effort in the interests of the reconstruction of Europe, and advocating most strongly an extensive aid for the underdeveloped countries.

5

The year 1944 brought me to a turning point of my life. My marriage broke up.

In a large measure the pressure of external circumstances —the outside world—may have hastened our mutual alienation. Life in exile puts every human relation to a severe test. Finally we had to admit that there was a wall between us and we could not break it down.

I had a feeling of guilt. Was it not all my fault? Should I have married at all? Politics is a stern master. I would always find it difficult to lead a normal family life. Had I the right to bind myself to a woman, to ask a woman to put up with the hazards and uncertainties of my existence? I was in conflict with myself: here we were in a most crucial period of history, these last months of the war demanded from each of us a cool head and a strong heart, great were the sacrifices others had to make—how little my personal troubles counted in comparison. This was a logical argument, but sentiments will never be overcome by logic.

We parted without hard feelings. Ninja grew up at her mother's place in Oslo. In these years I did not see my daughter as often as I wished to, but every summer she came for a visit to Berlin. And I was really proud of her when recently she graduated as the best of her class.

There were a few reasons why I decided to return to Berlin and to stay there for good What clinched matters was an event which affected me deeply. It happened on the twentieth of July, 1944.

*

CHAPTER SEVEN

Leber's Last Message

1

To maintain our relations with Germany—with the "other," the true Germany—proved in the course of the years more and more difficult. The contacts with our friends in the other refugee centers suffered from postal and other technical obstacles.

Yet, through Swedish correspondents, businessmen, representatives of the Church, also occasionally through government officials, we were much better informed about Germany than our friends in London or New York. My friend August Enderle, acting as a liaison man of the International Federation of Transport Workers, tried not without success to organize a system of underground communication with German sailors, till the end of the war, for instance, he regularly kept in touch with a group in Bremen. We had not only sources of information inside Germany but could also rely on trusted persons in many cities who were able to help us in our efforts to save friends in need and danger.

In these endeavors we could always count upon the assistance of Swedish organizations—both private and official. Several times we managed to smuggle forged papers, even ration cards into Germany; without them our comrades, always on the move, always hiding, would not have been able to buy their food or to elude the control of the Gestapo. Thanks to Swedish intervention, Léon Blum and the Dutch party leader Koos Vorrink, deported after the occupation of their countries to a German concentration camp, survived this terrible period. During the war Einar Gerhardsen was transferred from Sachsenhausen to the at least less dangerous camp of Grini, near Oslo.

My acquaintance with a German businessman who had his residence in Oslo and later fled to Stockholm was of particular consequence to me. In the second half of the war he put me in contact with outstanding people of the inner German resistance. One evening he introduced me to Theodor Steltzer, who as head of the German military transport office was attached to General von Falkenhorst's staff in Oslo. Steltzer belonged to the "Kreisauer Circle," a group in which Count Helmuth von Moltke was the dominant figure. He, just as von Moltke, did not approve of the plan for the assassination of Hitler which the other members strongly advocated; he supported the resistance, however, with exemplary courage, irrespective of personal danger. From the first he told me that he did not intend to discuss anything that would bring him into conflict with his conscience and honor as an officer—a request which I, of course, respected—but he made no secret of his real feelings and of his close relations with the Norwegian Church. I knew that more than once he had done his best to alleviate some of the hardships and abuses of the occupation.

When after the attempt on Hitler's life, the twentieth of July, he was arrested and sentenced to death, the intervention of influential Scandinavian circles saved him from execution. After the war this noble and upright man became one of the founders of the Christian Democratic Union in Berlin and later the first premier of Schleswig-Holstein.

Steltzer gave me an insight into the thoughts and plans of the leaders of the opposition and of their ideas about the new Germany that were to emerge on "the day after." This was the first time that I heard again about Julius Leber and the important position he held among the conspirators in Berlin. I was very thankful to Steltzer for his information and asked him to give Leber my regards and to tell him about my work.

2

In June I again received news from Julius Leber. I was visited by a man from Berlin who aside from greetings brought me also an urgent request from my former mentor. This man was Adam von Trott zu Solz.

Adam von Trott, although Counselor of the Legation in the Foreign Office, was a convinced enemy of Nazism. As the son of a Prussian Minister of Education, he had spent the years of his early youth in foreign countries; he had studied as a Cecil Rhodes scholar in Oxford and had lived for a long time in Peiping and Washington. His vast knowledge, his intellectual curiosity, and his liberal, in the best sense of the word, European background opened for him everywhere the doors of the outstanding personalities of public life and of leading statesmen.

From the start he foresaw the catastrophe into which Hitler's war would drag Germany and the world, and tried to prevent it. In July 1939 he had a long interview with Neville Chamberlain and Lord Halifax. He urged them to take a firm and unyielding stand against the Third Reich.

After the outbreak of the war he took advantage of a visit to America, where he had been invited to a conference, to submit a memorandum to President Roosevelt. He tried to convince the President that the opposition in Germany deserved confidence and support. The identification of all Germans with the Nazi leaders, the demand for unconditional surrender must have driven great parts of the German people right into Hitler's arms and made the fight of the opposition extremely difficult.

Von Trott's arguments met with no response in Washington. He had to return to Germany empty-handed Yet he refused to be discouraged and continued in his efforts. Because of his personal contacts in England and America, and thanks to his position which permitted him frequent travels abroad, he was an excellent liaison man between the German center of resistance and its friends in the other countries.

He, too, was in close touch with the Kreisauer Circle around Count von Moltke, with Count Stauffenberg, Count York von Wartenburg, and Colonel-General Ludwig Beck. They all agreed that the dictatorship could not be overthrown by a mere officers' revolt and that the resistance had to be organized on the largest basis possible. Therefore, they had formed an alliance with political personalities "from the Right to the Left" and with representatives of the labor movement. Among them the most prominent were Wilhelm Leuschner, the former Minister of Interior of Hesse and Vice Chairman of the Trade Union Federation, and Dr. Julius Leber.

Leber had spent four years in different prisons and concentration camps when he was finally released in 1937. He was still closely watched and frequently summoned to the Gestapo for long and vexatious interrogations. But this did not prevent him from assuming a leading part in the resistance movement. To cover his political activities he established himself as a coal merchant. Later, on the occasion of the fifth anniversary of Leber's death, President Theodor Heuss recalled those years of the underground struggle: "The two small rooms in the shabby little house, near the Schoeneberg railroad station, between coal heaps of the firm Bruno Meier, were a real den of conspirators. From time to time the doorbell would ring, and Leber had to rush into the anteroom to put a customer off. But in the backroom, on wobbly chairs, political passion had its home, scornful hatred, and ardent love."

When Adam von Trott came to see me in Stockholm, the men of the resistance were just making the last preparations for the *coup d'état*. The "coal merchant" was in the center of the action; he was a good friend of Count Stauffenberg, who finally took it upon himself to start the overthrow of the Nazi regime by the assassination of Hitler.

At first I had received the information about the intended action with considerable skepticism. Like most of my friends, I had no great faith in the political and revolutionary determination of the high and highest officers. Ernst Reuter had expressed exactly what I, too, thought and felt, in a talk with his colleague Karl Friedrich Goerdeler, the former mayor of Leipzig.

Goerdeler, chosen to be the Chancellor in the temporary government that was to be formed after the fall of Hitler, had visited Reuter in Ankara to inform him about the plans of the conspirators He could not dispel Reuter's doubts. "I don't know your generals," Reuter said, "but I cannot believe that the generals will overthrow the man who after all is nothing but their own creation."

Von Trott's visit did much to make me change my mind. He told me, for instance, about a recent remark of General Beck. When some generals at the western front declared it did not make sense any longer to overthrow Hitler because the Western Allies in a couple of months would break through the front anyhow, Beck replied: "I want the history books of the future to record: And yet, there still were men!"

In two long conversations we discussed the problems that would have to be solved after Hitler's fall. Von Trott wanted to know whether I would place myself at the disposal of the new government.

It was clear from von Trott's report that Leber had lost neither his courage nor his sense of political reality. The Gestapo had not been able to break him—nor had his views on the world situation been blurred by his intellectual isolation.

It had been Leber's basic conviction that a resistance movement under the conditions of modern dictatorship could not be organized on a large social basis. Therefore, one part of the armed forces had to be played off against the other. Was it possible to break the power of the Nazi military apparatus by the rebellion of a sufficiently great part of the Army? In the interest of such a development Leber was from the start willing to come to terms even with dubious allies. "To accomplish the fall of Hitler I would even make a compact with the devil," he declared.

On the other hand, through a uniformed bloc of the Left he tried to retain a decisive influence on the shape and content of the future. In the government that was to be formed Leuschner was to be Vice Chancellor, Leber was to take over the Ministry of Interior.

The young officers around Stauffenberg and the progressive men of the Kreisauer Circle were rather critical of Goerdeler, who all his life had been an avowed German nationalist To them he seemed too strongly rooted in the conceptions and ideas of the past. They would have preferred Leber as head of the new government. Even Colonel-General Beck, the presumptive head of state, was not unwilling to accept Leber instead of Goerdeler.

But Leber refused. In his opinion the Social Democrats must accept only as a last resort the main responsibility for the liquidation of a war which from the beginning to the end they had tried to prevent at great sacrifices.

Some of my closer political friends regarded Leber's alliance with the officers and conservatives as wrong and dangerous. They were afraid that the "Right Social Democrats" might let themselves be used as a façade for reactionary forces

I contradicted them vehemently. The formulas of the time before Hitler seemed to me out of date. I had full confidence in Leber's judgment and in his political instinct.

This instinct he showed clearly in his estimate of the relationship between the Western powers and their Russian ally.

Like the majority of his comrades, he had hoped at the beginning of the war to win, through a successful *coup d'état*, an honorable peace which would grant Germany's independence within the borders of 1938. But since 1943 he was convinced that an unconditional surrender was inevitable. In contrast to many of his friends, he did not expect any immediate political rewards from the *coup d'état* except the overthrow of Hitler. His main intention was to demonstrate to the world that there were still men in Germany who were ready to risk everything for justice and liberty. This to him was a moral duty.

And furthermore: it was simply inexcusable to let the people continue to suffer from the miseries and horrors of a criminal war. The price of unconditional surrender and loss of German independence was not too high for saving what was still to be saved—hundreds of thousands of human lives.

Leber had no illusions about the chance of splitting the anti-German coalition of the Western powers and the Soviet Union, and thought it wrong to attempt to win, by some clever maneuver, the support of one side against the other.

The repeated attempts to gain, in London and Washington, appreciation of and sympathy for the German resistance movement had failed time and again. Adam von Trott knew it best. "Hard peace," Vansittartism, and Morgenthau Plan —these slogans had understandably a strong hold on the hearts and heads of the Western peoples.

Now, after the successful landing of the Allies in France, Stauffenberg had raised the question of whether it might not be possible to arrest the collapse of the eastern front by a voluntary withdrawal from the western front and by a co-operation with the democracies. Leber regarded this hope as illusory. His intention was to establish contacts with the Western democracies as well as with the Soviet Union, in order to win assurances from both sides that in the case of a successful revolution the new government would be recognized as a real partner in the ensuing negotiations, though he had no hope that it would be able to exert any appreciable influence on the decisions of the Allies.

Would the new government at least be given a short breathing space to consolidate its power? Were the Allies ready to stop the advance of their troops into the interior of the country, as soon as Germany had surrendered?

I promised to contact several personages in the Western camp with whom I was well acquainted. Martin Tranmael was ready to speak to Mrs. Alexandra Kollontay, the Soviet ambassador in Stockholm. But then Adam von Trott countermanded his orders. The conspirators were afraid the Soviet embassy was not "safe"; they had reason to suspect that it had been infiltrated by Nazi agents. One decided to choose another way.

Von Trott was hardly back in Berlin, when the conspirators were hit by a terrible blow On the Fourth of July, Leber was arrested!

It was a bad omen for the planned action. "It signaled the tragic turning point of the drama whose climax came on the twentieth of July," as Theodor Heuss later described this blow

Paris was freed, the Allies were advancing against the Rhine and the Russians against the Oder, Hitler's war machine was breaking to pieces, the doom of the Third Reich was sealed.

With commotion, moved to tears, I looked forward to Europe's deliverance from the scourge of war and slavery; yet my joy was overshadowed by a deep anxiety and grief: by the knowledge that Hitler and his fellow gangsters until the end—even now, when they must see that their fall was inevitable—were dragging thousands of human beings—foreigners and Germans—into the ruin. The only thing they were after was the destruction of everyone who stood in their way. The list of horrors increased from day to day; the concentration camps continued to be filled with ever new victims, around the gas chambers the mountains of bones and ashes rose, the executioner was not allowed to rest.

The tortures Leber and his friends had to endure were horrible, the martyrdom of their execution was the more tragic, as it was utterly senseless. On January 5, 1945, Leber was executed. Not quite four months later he could have been a free man.

As senseless as his end was, his death, the sacrifice of the men of the twentieth of July had a deep and lasting sense. In his last greetings to his friends Leber summed up the reasons for his action in these very modest words:

"The sacrifice of one's life is the appropriate price for such a good and just cause. We have done all that was in our power. It was not our fault that everything ended this way and not otherwise."

Winston Churchill attributed much greater significance to the sacrifices of the men of the twentieth of July. In 1946 he said in the House of Commons:

"In Germany there lived an opposition which was weakened by their losses and an enervating international policy, but which belongs to the noblest and greatest that the political history of any nation has ever produced. These men fought without help from within nor from abroad—driven forward only by the restlessness of their conscience. As long as they lived they were invisible and unrecognizable for us, because they had to camouflage themselves. But their death made the resistance visible."

In the first weeks and months after the tragic event I had not yet gained the necessary distance to evaluate its importance correctly. Another failure—Leber was dead and Hitler was alive . . . this thought was like a dreadful physical pain. It befell me in the midst of the jubilation of my Norwegian and Allied friends.

If the *coup d'état* had been successful, if this one or the other one had not failed, if my German countrymen had shown the same courage on the home front which they had proven on the battlefield, if the Western Allies had followed a more farseeing policy, if the Communists—if the Social Democrats—if . . .

The "ifs" increased my pain.

The commission which Julius Leber had asked me to undertake was now without object. The example of his deed and of his end spoke to me in the course of the next months with ever growing clarity and urgency.

This message of the deceased, more than anything else, prompted me to dedicate my life to the reconstruction of a new Germany: in the spirit of the men of the twentieth of July.

The decision was not made easy for me.

3

In the evening of May 1, 1945, our International Workers Council, together with various groups of refugees and the Stockholm Social Democrats, organized a mass meeting. The chief speakers were Professor Myrdal and the Norwegian author Sigurd Hoel.

When I was walking up to the platform to deliver a short address, I received a note which had just arrived; it contained the news of Hitler's suicide. When I announced it to the audience a deep silence was the answer—no applause, no joyful shouts. It was as if the people simply could not believe that the end had actually come. And at the same time a question was almost physically present in the room: Hitler's dreadful challenge to all mankind—had it really ended in this way?

Only a few days passed, and then with the liberation of Denmark began the ecstasy which in the following weeks shook Stockholm like a fever and reached its climax on the seventh of May. At the news of the official end of the European war the Swedes, allegedly cool and reserved, burst into a veritable frenzy of enthusiasm. Perhaps the rejoicing was so exuberant because many of them wanted to deafen the pangs of their conscience: the Norwegian and Danish brothers had suffered very much, they themselves had kept aloof from the struggle. They had been lucky, but shouldn't they have made some sacrifices too? Now one was rid of the dilemma once and for all; one could breathe freely again, in the truest sense of the word.

In the last weeks of the war our greatest concern was for the prisoners in the concentration camps. For months Count Folke Bernadotte, the Vice President of the Swedish Red Cross, had been negotiating with Himmler to rescue those men and women who were in danger of falling victims in these last hours to the Nazis running amuck.

In February the count had tried to have the deported Danes and Norwegians transferred from the German concentration camps to Sweden. Himmler refused, but agreed to have the prisoners assembled in the camp of Neuengramme near Hamburg, where they were placed under the care of the Swedish Red Cross. After further negotiations Bernadotte in April prevailed upon the Nazi authorities to release the prisoners of this camp, the interned civilians and the female prisoners of Camp Ravensbrueck, and to let them go to Sweden. In the end of April about 3500 of the Norwegian prisoners came back. Now, at the end of the war, the number of those who had been saved by Swedish intervention had increased to a total of 15,000 to 20,000.

I shall never forget my first encounter with the friends who came back from Germany worn-out, sick. Their bitterness was almost terrifying. The more impressive and touching was my encounter with others who, in spite of all that they had suffered, were free of hatred. There was a brother of Foreign Minister Lange who right after his arrival in Sweden declared that now was the time to co-operate with the better elements in Germany. There was another friend who had been imprisoned at hard labor in Hamburg and yet did not want to hear anything of indiscriminate vengeance and retaliation. Those who had suffered much were the first to hold their hands out to the Germans in the spirit of reconciliation.

An outstanding chapter of Swedish humanity was written in Hungary. There thousands of Jews owed it to the efforts of Raoul Wallenberg that they were not carried off to the extermination camps. To help unfortunate people, that was the only aim of this young Swede, whom his King had sent to Budapest as secretary of the embassy. Those Jews were saved by Wallenberg's personal courage and the ready devotion of Jewish-American organizations which were willing

In front of his City Hall

Telegraf Bankhardt

The mother *B Schnoor*

A boy called Karl Frahm

War correspondent in Spain

Norwegian officer

1944 Adam von Trott zu Solz The attempt against Hitler's life has failed

1933 The people of Lubeck demonstrate against the Nazis The fight was lost

Julius Leber before the "People's Court"

Hildstelle Telegraf

At a congress of the Social Democratic party Brandt, Allenhauer, chairman of the party, Reuter, Louise Schroeder, the predecessor of Reuter

Ernst Reuter, a symbol of Berlin's resistance

Dr Kurt Schumacher, a symbol of Germany's resurrection
Rhein-Bild-Verlag

Rubble turned into playgrounds
Photo by Leon Muller

FACING THE RUSSIANS

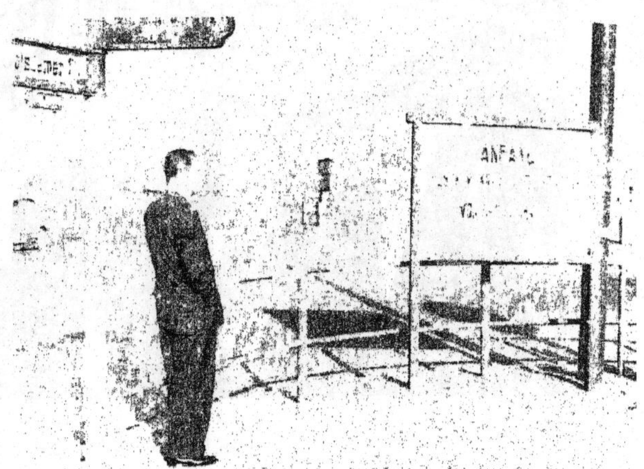

The border between East and West

The Berliners defy the Soviet threat

Schirner

Foto Wimmer

"The Economic Miracle" To the left, Minister Ludwig Erhard

THE NEW MAYOR, THE OLD MAYOR

Berlin mourns the death of Ernst Reuter

Kindermann & Co

REPRESENTING THE NEW GERMANY

Heinz Koster

At the opening of the Berlin Film Festival, with Mrs Brandt

Host to Chancellor Konrad Adenauer *Georg Holly*

Addressing the Council of Europe, Strasbourg, January 1959

Pressebild Schubert

The members of the "Atlantic Bridge" visit Berlin. At the mayor's right former Secretary of State Dean Acheson at his left Governor Meyner of New Jersey.

Nehru advised patience

Gopal Chitra Kuteer

Aneurin Bevan recommended firmness

Schirner

In New York

American-built "The pregnant oyster"

Wide World Photo

Louis Armstrong—one of Berlin's most popular visitors

Mr. Eric Johnston being decorated for his work on behalf of Germany's film industry. To the right, Van Heflin

Harry Croner

Ninja

Fotograf Ornelund

On vacation with Ruth, Lars, and Peter

to pay every price the monsters demanded for the freedom of their brothers.

Personally Raoul Wallenberg paid with his life for his mission in the service of humanity and charity. Where and how he died has never been ascertained. After the Russian occupation of Budapest he vanished. Among the heroes of World War II this Swedish civilian holds a place of honor.

Aside from the concern for our friends in the concentration camps, we were vexed by the uncertainty as to whether Norway could be spared a devastating final battle. Forty thousand mostly poorly armed members of the Home Front were opposed by 380,000 German soldiers with first-rate equipment. A terrible catastrophe was inevitable, if the German Army staff in Oslo decided to continue the war.

Various attempts were made from the Norwegian and the Swedish side to avert such a catastrophe. I too contributed my humble share.

Shortly after I had heard of the meeting between Himmler and Count Bernadotte in Lübeck on April 24, I rang up Oslo —it was a Sunday afternoon—and asked to be put through to Terboven, the Reichskommissar himself. My very energetic demand must have made some impression; the Reichskommissariat connected me immediately with Skaugum, the palace of the Crown Prince, which was now Terboven's private residence. He personally answered the call. I asked him what consequences he intended to draw from the meeting of Count Bernadotte with the Reichsführer SS; as he surely knew, Himmler had declared that he was ready to surrender to the British and Americans. Terboven gave no answer, he handed the receiver on to somebody else, and to my great surprise it was Wilhelm Rediess, commander of the SS and chief of the police in Norway. He was taciturn and only pointed out that we would be informed of all further measures "through official channels." The same answer he gave to the question as to what would become of the six thousand prisoners in the concentration camp in Grini.

As vague as this answer was, one could yet conclude from this conversation that Terboven and Rediess had given up the thought of continuing the war in Norway on their own.

Some prisoners were released from Grini. This was another favorable indication. Therefore, on May 3 the leaders of the Home Front issued a proclamation warning the people of any rash actions. All provocations had to be avoided; the surrender of the German forces was not to be made unnecessarily difficult. Only thus could violent clashes and bloodshed be averted. The slogan of the day: calm—dignity—discipline was obeyed unanimously and in exemplary order.

On May 8, General Boehme signed the capitulation. In the same hour Rediess killed himself with a bullet through his head. Terboven had the corpse brought to his bunker, and the same evening blew up the bunker, the dead Gestapo chief, and himself.

4

With the end of the war the refugees had to face the question of whether they should stay in their countries of asylum or return to their old homes. Those who in the intermediate years had been able to find in exile a new position, whose boys and girls were going to school there and understood the foreign language better than that of their parents, now realized that the country of their children had greater claims on them than the country of their parents. Others felt that the horrible persecutions which they had endured were a fathomless abyss, separating them from Germany forever. The memories of the past were stronger than their hope for the future.

But to the politically conscious the return to the liberated mother country seemed a point of duty as well as of political opportuneness—though some Allied authorities seemed not to understand this. Due to some peculiar regulations many who felt urged to take part in the reconstruction of Germany had to wait for months until they got their travel permit.

My case was different. My Norwegian passport was to me more than just a useful travel document; my Norwegian citizenship was to me more than a mere formality. Consequently, I felt certain obligations which I could not simply shake off.

Norway, though by far not as much ruined as Germany, was yet a country of grief and misery There were "only" ten thousand victims to deplore, but after all Norway numbers only three million people. The economy was bled white, in the cities famine went from house to house. And then: the legitimate pride in the moral strength, which the Norwegian people had shown in the war, must not make one blind to the deplorable fact that the war had, also in Norway, left an evil heritage. The resistance had been necessary, there had been many solemn examples of idealism and self-sacrifice, but war, even the most justified one, does not ennoble people but makes them brutal and cruel, even those who fight for progress and freedom. The Nazis were beaten, but their depraved spirit had infected many of their opponents.

A weary work of reconstruction had to be done, in all fields of public life. My Norwegian friends had to master very difficult tasks. Could I leave them? Just now?

Two days after the end of the war I departed from Stockholm—for Oslo.

*

CHAPTER EIGHT

Return to Germany

1

There was no "night of the long knives"—the Norwegian people in its overwhelming majority wanted no lynchings. Traitors were to be tried legally and lawfully. Only in a very few cases emotions, suppressed for five years, erupted in violent acts of primitive revenge, and such incidents always aroused sharp protests.

The Home Front regarded a radical purge from the Quislings and their jackals as a preliminary condition for the rebirth of the nation. Many thousands of them were arrested.

Fifty thousand legal cases in a country of only three million people represented a hard task for the judicature—and affected the life of almost everyone. But this was by far not the only difficulty my Norwegian friends had to master. The economic situation was desperate. The whole nation took an active part in the efforts to balance the political accounts of the past and to lay the groundwork for a better future. Great were the tensions, great the hopes.

As far as I was concerned, for the time being I merely rejoiced in meeting my old friends. Each day was a holiday for me. I also met a number of Germans who had not been interned and during daytime were permitted to move about freely in the city: some guards of Grini, for instance, who had secretly co-operated with the Norwegian prisoners, some officials of the Reichskommissariat, a brother of Count Moltke. All of them could hardly wait to return home. We made plans, but the news from Germany was discouraging.

I was a correspondent for Swedish newspapers, and during the whole summer I traveled to and fro between Stockholm and Oslo. For the Institute of Foreign Affairs I wrote a pamphlet about the trial of Vidkun Quisling, for the Norwegian Labor party another against the unity swindle of the Communists.

In the flush of victory one had hoped that the national unity, which had stood the test so well in the years of the resistance, could also be preserved in the time of peace. After its return from exile the government had resigned in June; in October elections for the new Parliament were to be held. Meanwhile a coalition government of all parties was formed, headed by Einar Gerhardsen, the leader of the Labor party.

Gerhardsen's courage, which he had proven on the front of the resistance and in concentration camps, his sincerity and the tolerance he showed toward his opponents had won him the confidence of all circles from Left to Right.

The Communists, who too were represented in the interim government, tried to take unfair advantage of the situation. They wanted first of all to bring the labor movement under their control. This was a problem which all nations in Europe had to struggle with—at least in the first year of peace.

The Communists had played a part in the underground movement. Many of them had distinguished themselves by their determination and their self-sacrifice. Common sufferings, the common enemy had brought together Socialists and Communists; many of the old ideological conflicts seemed definitely out of date; this was the time for co-operation. The call for a "unity party" found a strong response.

In Sweden during the war the same question had occupied us greatly. I myself had not excluded the possibility of a certain co-operation, although the Communists' party apparatus had attacked me in the most disgusting manner. I was of the opinion that we ought to turn the tables and try to free the honest members of the Communist movement from Moscow's tutelage. In August 1942, I wrote in a private letter to America that the old conflict between a "democratic" and a "revolutionary" wing of the labor movement need not come up again. Of decisive importance, however, would be the question of whether the Russians would be willing—in their own interest also—to demobilize their parties, which had certainly done enough damage already.

Now, after the end of the war, one had to say openly and clearly that the Communists, as laudable as the war record of some of them was, were separated from the Socialists not by a different interpretation of economic or ideological questions, but by principles and ideas with which a liberal Socialist must have nothing in common. It was not a question of different ways to a common goal. The Communists started from the premise that the end justified the means; power meant everything to them, the individual nothing. They regarded Russia as their actual fatherland; the party was in fact nothing but a kind of foreign legion of Moscow.

At that time many people could not share these fundamental reservations. The Soviet Union was an ally of the Western powers; one felt great admiration for the heroic deeds of the Red Army, for the immense achievements of the Russian people. In Norway the trade unions saw themselves compelled to convene a "unity congress," which was to prepare a common program, to nominate common candidates on joint lists, and lay the groundwork for the formal unification of both parties. But hardly had the delegates left the conference table, when the Communists started a campaign of vilification against the leaders of the Labor party, and proved clearly that they put their party interests above those of the working class. By their attempts to "unmask" the "rightist" labor leaders they actually unmasked themselves.

This was the end of the Socialist-Communist honeymoon. It had lasted less than three months. In the elections the Labor party gained 76 of the 150 seats in the Storting, the Communists 11. And ever since, the number of their followers has steadily decreased.

In other countries—I am primarily thinking of France and Italy—the labor movement and democracy did not pass this test as quickly and successfully. In Eastern Europe the Communists, supported by the Red Army, won their game In the West Zones of Germany and Austria the Social Democrats, by their uncompromising fight for freedom, won in those dark years of hunger the trust of the workers; they broke the Communist influence. The fight for Berlin has demonstrated this success to the whole world.

2

In October 1945, I came back to Germany for the first time. The Norwegian Social Democratic party press sent me to Nuremberg to report on the trials of the war criminals.

I flew in an American plane from Oslo to Copenhagen, and from there on to Bremen.

Prostrate Germany was like one of those horrible visions that sometimes overcomes us on the verge between sleep and waking: more real than any reality, and at the same time there nests in a remote nook of the brain the conviction that one is but dreaming, and instantly the ghastly dream will disappear.

But the surrealistic vision of the destroyed cities, the bombed and burnt-out houses, up and down the streets, the debris-covered fields, the mountains of rubble and rubbish, between which human beings crawled about in the dark like hungry rats, the merciless cold, the unspeakable misery—no, one could not shake off this vision; with every minute it became more urgent, there was nothing beside it, it encompassed heaven and earth.

Of course, I had been prepared for such a sight; of course, I had many arguments ready which conclusively proved why it had to be so and not otherwise. Yet the sore nerves, the throbbing heart could not be quieted.

August and Irmgard Enderle had managed to be repatriated immediately after the war; in Bremen they were colleagues of Felix von Eckardt, later the press secretary of the Federal government in Bonn, and worked as editors of the *Weser-Kurier*, a paper licensed by the Americans. What they and mutual friends, who had courageously survived all the years of the underground struggle, had to tell was enough to drive one to despair.

I heard of the fatal effects of the directives which determined the occupation policy of the Allies. The prohibition of "fraternization" was politically shortsighted and practically impossible to enforce; the suspension of all political activity affected primarily those people whose active contribution to the reconstruction of the new Germany was vitally important. Almost everywhere in those first months resistance groups tried to prepare the ground for a new democratic order; they were abruptly dismissed and pushed aside by the Allied authorities.

But in Bremen some rays of light penetrated the general

gloom. Wilhelm Kaisen, then mayor, simply radiated faith and confidence. That men such as Kaisen and Senator Adolf Ehlers, a distinguished member of the resistance, were holding responsible posts, was a hopeful sign.

The countryside, the small villages, the farms right and left of the *Autobahn* should have restored my balance. In comparison to the cities here was peace, normal life. But this sharp contrast only deepened my depression. How many of the hungry dockers in Bremen had actively opposed Hitler, how many of those who had safely and without sacrifices survived the catastrophe had been partly enthusiastic, partly willing followers of Nazism! Where, then, was justice?

At home my unexpected return was greeted with great enthusiasm. My half-brother, who had been five years old when I fled, had meanwhile become a young man. In the last months of the war, like so many youths, he had been called up for military service. Perplexed and lost, he was a typical representative of the new generation. How terribly they had been wronged. It would be hard to make up to them for the sins of the recent past.

From conversations with my political friends I learned little that I did not know, but the stories of those immediately concerned put the things one had heard and read about in a new and even more dreadful light. I could not have said what depressed me more. the indifference with which each of them spoke of his horrible experiences—without raising his voice . . . in parenthesis, so to say—or the bitter complaints about the occupation and about new acts of injustice, more acts of violence

Nobody reproached me, nobody brought up the argument that abroad I had had a better life. Yet, I had to admit to myself that my lot had been a much easier one. Certainly, in exile I had not rested on a bed of roses, but through my own work I had made my living, I had had the chance to learn and to widen my horizon, I had overcome these years of terror sound in body and mind.

I was most deeply affected by our conversations about the extermination camps and the mass executions behind the front. Some of my friends pretended to know less about it than they actually did. But why? They were above suspicion, they themselves had been victims of the tyranny. Now one could see the fatal psychological effects of the thesis of the collective guilt. Horrified at the charge that "every German was a murderer" and conscious of the fact that they would not have been able to prevent these foul deeds even at the risk of their lives, these friends took refuge behind paltry excuses and tried to minimize before themselves the actual extent of the crimes.

I stayed only for one day in Lübeck, which was no longer "the town of the seven spires"; the churches and the historic buildings of the city had suffered much. And yet the war damage in Lübeck was much less serious than the damage in Bremen or Hamburg, or in Frankfort or Nuremberg, where I was going.

I was not one of those who on principle criticized the decision to put the chief culprits of the Hitler regime on trial in an international court of justice and to call them to account for their crimes against humanity. As inadequate as the attempt was, the proceedings at least allowed us a clear insight into the brown gangsterism that had been elevated to a national policy, during the war and before it.

The factual reports on what had happened in the occupied countries and in Germany, in the concentration and extermination camps made one's flesh creep. The men in the dock had ordered and instigated those horrors. One could not feel pity for them. One could only hope that all mankind would learn from these experiences, for fascism was not a mere German phenomenon. But it had received a special German stamp and demonstrated in a terrible way to what evil purpose power can be abused in a highly developed country ruled by totalitarianism.

At that time I did not meet anybody in Germany who would have declared his solidarity with the chief defendants in Nuremberg. But I met many who asked why one had not "cut it short" and hanged the criminals without much ado. There were others who would have preferred to see the Nazi leaders tried by a German court, the representatives of the "other Germany" should have been authorized to prosecute and administer justice themselves. But even among those hundreds of correspondents who were permitted to attend the sessions there were only a few Germans. As if among all the Nazi crimes the gravest had not been the one against the German people; as if it did not matter how the Germans would accept the evidence presented at Nuremberg.

More serious was the complaint that the International Tribunal did not administer justice impartially. This objection could not be dismissed out of hand, because the Soviets were sitting in judgment, too, and pretended to represent the perfect constitutional state. This hypocrisy was grist to the mill of the cynics, who could declare the Nazi leaders had not been executed because they had started a criminal war, but because they had lost it.

From many an observation, from talks with many people, and the reports I gathered, it became obvious to me that it would be more than difficult to build a new German democracy on ruins, on hate and military-bureaucratic folly. I witnessed many an incident that filled me with shame and bitterness, I saw acts of brutality, the victim of which was some poor devil, who thus was made to "expiate" the Hitler regime. In fact, such vengeance only proved that the war had brutalized people everywhere and that Nazis could be found not only in German uniforms.

In February 1946, I met Kurt Schumacher. We met near Frankfort, although his home was in Hanover, where for months he had been busy with the reorganization of the Social Democratic party. At that time he was more than a party leader, he was a symbol of the suffering and sorely afflicted Germany and the representative of a new national consciousness.

3

If one wanted to reduce Kurt Schumacher's personality to a short formula one had to say: the dominating feature of his character and the strongest impulse of his life and work was his extraordinary will power. I have met many a man in my life who possessed great energy; in extraordinary times such as ours, statesmen need this quality in a high degree; yet I could hardly name another man who had Kurt Schumacher's strength of will.

He came back from a concentration camp as a cripple, doomed to death. He had lost his right arm in World War I; soon his left leg, too, had to be amputated. His life in these last years was a slow way of dying. His body was dying piece by piece, he was dying alive, as it were.

But Schumacher seemed not to take notice of his physical decline. Preachers and poets praise the spirit which triumphs over the body. In Schumacher's case this phrase, often all too easily used, was living reality.

He had proposed to himself one task, and he was possessed with it. The Social Democratic party, which Hitler had destroyed, whose leaders had either been executed or forced to flee, the property of which—houses, newspapers, libraries, funds—had been stolen by the Nazis, whose members, provided they had not fallen on the fronts of war or resistance, could keep up their political contacts only in small groups and circles—this party was to be revived, greater and more powerful than before Hitler; it was to become the party of national deliverance and assume leadership; and it was to use its power to blot out the mistakes of the past. He knew that only a few years were left to him to complete this task; he realized clearer than others that especially the first years of the occupation would make the reorganization of an independent party twice as difficult, but he did not shrink back: he would just have to work twice as fast and twice as hard and drive his colleagues and himself thrice as hard.

Whereas in Berlin as early as June 1945 a Central Committee of the Social Democratic party—with Otto Grotewohl, a former deputy of the Parliament as chairman—had been authorized, it was not until October that Schumacher was able to arrange near Hanover the first party conference in the British Zone. Even with this step he was infringing upon the Allied directives, since for the time being the Western powers wanted new parties to be organized only on the level of towns and districts. Nevertheless, the "Bureau Dr. Schumacher" became a center of the non-communist Left.

The reorganization of the party could, of course, not be the work of a single man. Many others shared this task with Schumacher. But they will be the first to admit that without him, without his leadership and will power the results of the first postwar period would not have been achieved.

Schumacher had already become a national figure, when Mr. Konrad Adenauer, the mayor of Cologne, was still little known. Schumacher's party seemed to have the best chance to become the moving force behind the reconstruction of Germany. Its men and women could indeed be proud of their accomplishments, of the many lives they saved, of getting, in cities and hamlets, things out of the mess—for which others were responsible. Schumacher had a much more ambitious goal. He proclaimed the thesis of a basic democratic and socialistic renovation of Germany.

It shall not be denied that Kurt Schumacher was a rather difficult person. Like many others, I, too, did not find it easy to work with him. His authoritarian attitude, the almost fanatical tenacity with which he clung to his decisions, his way of overemphasizing national points of view—no, I could not say that we were kindred souls. But this did not impair my deep respect for him.

Schumacher was in a precarious position. To the Russians he was the No. 1 enemy, for by rejecting any compromise with the Communists he thwarted their "united front" strategy, barred their way to the west of Germany, and laid the foundation for their defeat in Berlin. The Western authorities disapproved of Schumacher for other reasons. For the Americans he was "too socialistic," for the English he was "too aggressive," for the French "too German." They all found that he was "too independent." At first they even reprimanded him severely for his criticism of their Soviet ally. And they did not at all appreciate it, when he wanted to deal with the occupation authorities as with his equals. "Who did he think he was?"

Well, Schumacher was indeed of the opinion that he and those represented by him—workers, employees, and intellectuals—were as much entitled to participate in the decisions about the organization of a new, free Germany as, say, American industrialists, English diplomats, and French generals. After all, had they not earned this right by the sacrifices they had made for democracy from 1933 on?

Schumacher refused to orient his party according to the views of Washington, London, or Paris. He had only one guiding star: a free Social Democratic movement in a free democratic Germany. He was convinced that sooner or later the West would recognize that such a policy was in its own best interests.

To some extent he was right in this opinion. After a few

short years the attitude of the Western powers toward Germany had to be changed considerably, and quite a few of Schumacher's ideas were adopted. Thus, much was saved, but the consequences of many a wrong decision could not be undone, for the Soviets had had a clearer political concept and had meanwhile created accomplished facts in their zone of occupation.

When I met Schumacher the turning point of the Allied policy was still far off. It was the time when anti-Nazis and honest democrats began more and more to doubt whether the economic chaos could be overcome at all, and whether those who profited most from the liberation were not the men of yesterday. They had only to be shrewd enough to choose a place of residence where, because of their profession or their connections, they could count on the right support. According to a bitter joke of those days a follower of Hitler, if he was an aristocrat, ought to settle in the British Zone, where his manners and his fluent English would save him from any prosecution; if he had good connections in Catholic circles, he should make his home in the French Zone, a banker in the American Zone, a scholar or writer in the East—he only had to join the Communist party, and all his former sins and crimes would be forgiven. True and upright democrats, however, who had no connections and no particular talents, were worse off: they were eyed with suspicion in all three western zones, and in the Soviet Zone they were put in concentration camps.

As is usually the case, such a generalization was false. Yet this joke had a grain of truth in it. The measures taken by the Allied authorities in their respective zones were indeed not uniform. Especially in the American Zone one found beside stolid and often politically inexperienced officials and officers, also men of great human quality and professional skill.

In the English Zone the legal and constitutional right of

the population were, comparatively, best protected. On the other hand, one could meet there officers like the colonel with whom I had a conversation, which I still recall vividly. Personally he was a very nice man with long experiences in the colonies. But when he was given the control over the police he promptly dismissed all Social Democrats and reappointed all those officials who had faithfully served the dictator to the last "They know their job," he said, "and will obey orders promptly." This was the only point that mattered to him.

My first meeting with Schumacher impressed me very much, conferences with various party friends who had just come back from their London exile and were now assuming leading positions in the party were instructive. In May, I met them again in Hanover, at the first congress of the newly established German Social Democratic party.

The deliberations in Hanover were overshadowed by a bitter disappointment. Only the three western zones were represented at the congress, from the "East" only the delegates of Berlin had come For a short time before, in the Soviet Zone the unification of the Social Democrats and the Communists had been enforced under the pressure of the occupation force. The Central committee of the Social Democrats, which led the organization in Berlin and in the Soviet Zone, had declared itself for a union. Otto Grotewohl gave as the reason for this step that otherwise the party would be forbidden by the Russian authorities.

Schumacher had personally flown to Berlin in a British plane, had warned and protested, had demanded that the party be dissolved instead, that it must not surrender to the Communists. Grotewohl and his circle were in favor of surrender. The enforced union of both parties in the Soviet Zone was to be sealed on the first of May.

Then a small group of mostly younger Social Democrats in Berlin intervened. They refused to accept Grotewohl's policy and pushed through a plebiscite against the opposition of their leaders.

In the Soviet sector of Berlin the plebiscite was forbidden in the last moment, when the Russians realized that their intensive campaign had come to nothing. Only 33,000 of the 60,000 members of the Social Democratic party in Berlin could, since they were living in the western sectors, participate in the voting, 23,755 cast their ballots, 19,529 of them—more than eighty per cent—voted against the enforced union.

When Grotewohl's Central Committee then declared that the union would be carried through despite the voting, the opposition broke with him, and on the seventh of April the Social Democratic party of Greater Berlin was constituted anew.

This fight within the party about the preparation and execution of the plebiscite was in truth the first political battle for the future of Berlin. Berlin was then still undivided; the Nazification of the Social Democrats would have made it much easier to incorporate the city into the Soviet Zone, and most probably the *Anschluss* would have been an immediate consequence. It was for this reason that the whole population of Berlin had watched the progress of this fight with utmost attention and with great concern.

The Western powers at first did not understand the implications of this fight; frequently they regarded the advance of communism as far as to the Rhine as "unavoidable." Correspondents of the democratic world press and a number of American and British officials, political liaison officers, who were well versed in the problems of the labor movement, realized what the opposition in Berlin meant for the future of Germany as a whole. They saw to it that the plebiscite took place without disturbances, they provided the opposition with paper for pamphlets; in the West—especially in America

—they prepared the ground for a better appraisal of the role Berlin—the already given-up Berlin—was destined to play.

At the party congress in Hanover the Berliners were the heroes of the day. After thirteen years Germans had had the opportunity to make a political decision freely, and they had voted for freedom, in spite of all the allurements and threats from the East, in spite of many a disappointment about the lack of understanding of the West.

Now one ought to be in Berlin, I thought. With "one," I meant myself.

4

But for that, the time had not yet come. There still were several intermediate stations on my way.

In May I once again went to Nuremberg. My reports for Scandinavian newspapers became the basis of a book which I published that spring *The Criminals and the "Other" Germans* was not only meant to be a summary of the evidence presented in Nuremberg, but also a first attempt to take stock of the intricate situation of Germany at that time. As strong as my intention to enlighten my readers was, the book also stemmed, I think, from the—at least subconscious—wish to clarify my own thinking. I felt skeptical and moderately optimistic at the same time.

In May 1946, I was back in Lübeck, also in Kiel. There Theodor Steltzer, the provisional Prime Minister, told me that the mayor of Lübeck was going to be transferred to another post. He asked me whether I did not want to take the vacant place in the city hall of Lübeck.

This was not the last call I received to return to my birthplace. And it was not easy to say no.

In Lübeck I had started my political career. There the position which Julius Leber had held was not yet filled. But on the other hand, I had been away for long years, and the city seemed to me a bit provincial.

A few months earlier—just before the end of the war—I had met Ruth. She was a refugee from Norway, still almost a girl. We met again. We continued to see each other.

In the summer I went with Ruth and friends on a holiday trip, first to the Sogne fjord, then to the Hardanger fjord. Those are two of the most beautiful spots of Norway, most appropriate to make one forget one's troubles and cares. But my thoughts were occupied with Germany. What happened there—or did not happen—was keeping me in permanent tension. Was I right to limit myself to the role of an observer—interested, sympathizing—but always a mere observer?

When in early fall I resumed my work as a correspondent in Germany, I first traveled to Bielefeld to attend the congress of the trade unions for the British Zone. There also appeared Max Brauer, still an American citizen, who soon was to become head of the free city of Hamburg. In Lübeck I met Julius Leber's widow, who had come on a visit from Berlin; in Travemünde I shook hands with the fisherman who thirteen years before had taken me to Denmark. In Hanover they had an offer for me. Would I like to become the political editor of a German news service controlled by the Allies? And a few weeks later, back in Oslo, I indeed received a telegram asking me to come to Hamburg and start with my work.

But meanwhile Halvard Lange had asked me whether I would like to go to the Norwegian embassy in Paris as a press attaché. This assignment would open the door to a diplomatic career which, as Lange said, would offer me an opportunity to serve usefully my second home—Norway. Such an idea had never occurred to me, but I did not dislike it.

When I looked up Lange to discuss with him the details of my assignment, he surprised me with the news that he and Gerhardsen had changed their minds; I was not to go to

Paris but—to Berlin. The Norwegian government wanted a man there who was thoroughly familiar with the conditions in Germany and could keep them correctly informed about the political development. I would get the title of a press attaché, and, since I would be attached to the Military Mission at the Allied Control Council, the rank of a major.

Berlin—this decided the issue. Without hesitation I accepted the offer.

In a letter to my German friends I gave the reasons for my decision in the following words:

"To some of you it may perhaps look a bit peculiar that I go to Berlin as a 'member of the Allied forces.' Formalities cannot be decisive. The important question is: where can each of us best serve the rehabilitation of Europe and German democracy? As you know, I have for years stood up for 'German' as well as for 'Scandinavian' interests. These were and are not contrary to each other.

"I will continue to act as an intermediary between both sides, in the interest of mutual understanding . . . It is my first aim to work for peace, for the development and stabilization of European and international co-operation."

So after many detours fate had yet brought me back to Berlin. In December, I made the necessary practical preparations; at Christmas I set off, with a Norwegian diplomatic passport in my pocket.

Almost at the same time—only a few weeks before—another emigrant returned to Berlin. I came from the north, he from the southeast, from Turkey: Ernst Reuter. Here in Berlin our paths of life were soon to meet.

CHAPTER NINE

The Nightmare That Was Berlin

1

Berlin in winter, 1946: craters, caves, mountains of rubble, debris-covered fields, ruins which hardly allowed one to imagine that once they had been houses; cables and water pipes projecting from the ground like the mangled bowels of antediluvian monsters, no fuel, no light, every little garden a graveyard, and above this all, like an immovable cloud, the stink of putrefaction.

In this no man's land on the edge of the world there lived human beings. Their life was a daily struggle for a handful of potatoes, a loaf of bread, a few lumps of coal, some cigarettes. Many only went to work to earn more food, or to get somewhat higher—though still completely insufficient—rations.

Berlin had ceased to be the capital and therefore one half of the population had lost their means of existence. The other half lost their jobs, when seventy-five per cent of the still undamaged machines and industrial plants were dismantled by

*

CHAPTER NINE

The Nightmare That Was Berlin

1

Berlin in winter, 1946: craters, caves, mountains of rubble, debris-covered fields, ruins which hardly allowed one to imagine that once they had been houses, cables and water pipes projecting from the ground like the mangled bowels of antediluvian monsters, no fuel, no light, every little garden a graveyard, and above this all, like an immovable cloud, the stink of putrefaction.

In this no man's land on the edge of the world there lived human beings. Their life was a daily struggle for a handful of potatoes, a loaf of bread, a few lumps of coal, some cigarettes. Many only went to work from sheer habit, or to get somewhat higher—though still completely insufficient—rations.

Berlin had ceased to be the capital, and therefore one half of the population had lost their means of existence. The other half lost their jobs, when seventy-five per cent of the still undamaged machines and industrial plants were dismantled by the Russians and carried off to the Soviet Union. In the beginning of January many of the factories which slowly had resumed production had to shut down again. For want of coal they had worked on a part-time basis—now there was not even enough coal for that. There was no material to repair even the slightest war damages; the clearing of the roads from rubble and debris had to be suspended also. Many women were employed in this work. Since machines were lacking, they removed the ruins with their bare hands, stone by stone Presently their arms and hands failed them.

For a new terror gripped the city: an icy cold. In the streets it attacked the people like a wild beast, drove them into their houses, but they found no protection there either. The windows had no panes, they were nailed up with boards and pasteboard. The walls and ceilings were full of cracks and holes—one covered them with paper and rags. People heated their rooms with benches from the public parks, cut down the trees in the Grunewald, even burned up their own furniture. The cold receded, but two hours later it broke into the room with double fierceness, the fire had burned down, and the wind defiantly whistled through all the cracks and leaks. The old and sick froze to death in their beds by the hundreds. Within living memory Berlin had not experienced such a severe winter.

It was a good time for black marketeers, informers, prostitutes. It did not bother them that the mark was worthless, for they accepted payment only in the new currency: cigarettes. For cigarettes everything could be bought: coffee and warm water, military secrets and love.

If in that winter someone came to Berlin he could hardly see anything other than these pictures of material and moral decay, so overwhelming and unique were they. He might share the opinion of those Allied officers who at the end of the war had given up Berlin as completely destroyed—

"strategically and politically uninteresting." They overlooked something essential: Berlin was still situated on the river Spree, not in Siberia. And they overlooked the decisive point: Berlin still had a population of nearly three million people—compared to four and a half million before the war.

The black marketeers, informers, and criminals, though they dominated the scene, were still a very small minority. Hundreds of thousands had found refuge in the less devastated suburbs; with incredible tenacity and inventiveness they built themselves a "home" in half-destroyed houses, even in ruins. They all were cold and hungry, but they lived: filthy, but with a clean conscience. Mothers and women took the heaviest and most unusual jobs, but they did not sell themselves. Men, underfed and deadly pale, staggered across the streets like drunkards—but they did not give up their self-respect. They were the true heroes. They were the pledge of future victory. They—the overwhelming majority of three million people.

This was the city to which Ernst Reuter returned. Before Hitler and before he became mayor of Magdeburg he had—as city councilor for transport—exerted a strong influence on the life of Berlin. Now he was called upon to use his experience in municipal affairs and his statesmanship to save Berlin from death.

Several months before, in October 1946, the first postwar elections had been held in as yet undivided Berlin; they have been the last ones up to this day. The Social Democrats gained nearly half the votes and sixty-three of the seats in the city parliament. The Communist Unity party received as little as twenty per cent. The provisional constitution, enacted by the four occupation powers, prescribed that all four parties—apart from those already mentioned there were the Christian Democrats and the Liberal Democrats—should be represented in the Municipal Council.

On his way back from Turkey, Reuter had hoped that he would be offered the post of lord mayor. But he had been in exile for many years, and many of his younger party friends could hardly remember him. The Communists, on the other hand, regarded him with understandable hostility; he had broken with them in 1922 and had given them no quarter since, they described him as a "Turk." Reuter was elected city councilor. Beside his former transport department—the gas, water, and electricity works were under his direction—a heavy load of duties, which under the circumstances required great energy and even greater patience and diplomatic skill.

Energy was necessary to overcome the obstacles of a hostile nature, patience, to hold his own in the no less exhausting fight against the frequent whims of Allied bureaucracy; diplomatic skill, to assert his viewpoints against the Four Power Headquarters. It was Reuter's greatest asset that he had all three qualities in a high degree.

I first met him in Annedore Leber's little house in Zehlendorf. Amidst an icy desert of destruction this was an oasis of kindness and warmheartedness; here German and Allied friends would meet; here reigned an atmosphere of solidarity and humanism.

It was not by chance that Reuter was the center of our circle. The heavy man with his big skull gave one the impression of an old tree which had braved many storms, and under which one would like to seek protection, and rest. He looked tired, his hair was thin, his face lined with deep wrinkles, but his eyes were young, and a half-wise, half-roguish smile was constantly dancing in them.

He was full of admiration for this city, called it "remarkably thrilling, the people more openminded than anywhere in Germany." His praise was unpathetic, but he spoke with great seriousness, even when a slight undertone of irony was discernible in his reflections on the weary negotiations with the occupation powers.

Like Kurt Schumacher, whom only recently he had come to know somewhat better and with whom he hoped to establish a fruitful co-operation, Ernst Reuter desired a renewed democracy, not a mere restoration of the Social Democratic party. Stronger than Schumacher he emphasized that the power of the party bureaucracy must never be put above the intellectual and moral aspirations of the individual. The party must do more than defend the workers' material interests, it must become a popular movement, must speak for the middle class and especially for the intellectuals, who were longing for a revival of the social order.

Each time he spoke of freedom and democracy his words had no hint of the common sound of clichés and rally speeches. He did not bray them out, he used them carefully, pensively. To the objection, particularly frequent in hard times, that people cannot live on freedom, he used to answer:

"Well, the fish do not live on water either, but *in* it. Man does not live on freedom, but he can only live in freedom. Without freedom people eventually suffocate in a soulless technological machinery, they become ants in a huge mass of ants. The spiritual death will be followed by physical death, will be followed by the destruction of everything that makes life worth living."

One could hardly imagine two men of greater contrast than Kurt Schumacher and Ernst Reuter. On one side the man of fanatical will, completely absorbed in his ideas, on the other side the prototype of a humanist, who, though he never compromises in the pursuit of his ideals, also never forgets that all human toil is ephemeral.

The one was rather suspicious of anyone who contradicted him, the other much more willing to refute wrong opinions with patience and by better arguments. While, for instance,

Schumacher's protests against the occupation often sounded as if he thought the Allies were motivated only by hate and prejudice, Reuter warned the Berliners to beware of self-pity as well as of illusions; they had to accommodate themselves to the circumstances, Berlin was not the navel of the world, and not the Allies but Hitler, not the present but the past were responsible for the terrible hardships the German people had to endure.

Where Schumacher stormed and protested, Reuter sought to win the confidence of his Allied partners and to make them better understand the situation of Berlin and Germany Both were resolute in the defense of their political independence, but one felt that Reuter had gathered experience in foreign countries, whereas Schumacher was all the time tormented by the thought that the German Left could once more be accused of weakness and lack of patriotism. Both combined their strict rejection of communism with the conviction that Germany had nothing to gain from playing the four great powers off against each other. Reuter, who loved the Russian people as much as he detested the Stalin regime, wanted no conflict with the Soviets; neither side should have the feeling that the Berliners wanted to fish in troubled waters.

It was not that Schumacher was a "nationalist" and Reuter an "internationalist." Both were—both. But whereas Schumacher concentrated all his thoughts and desires on making his party the ruling power of the new Germany and a fundamental pillar of the reconstructed free Europe, Reuter would look beyond the frontiers of his own country. He believed in a united Europe, in a world of material and intellectual cooperation. The realization of this goal was for him, beyond the immediate tasks of reconstruction, the true mission of the German Social Democracy.

It was not that the one was "harder" or "stronger" than the other, the one more detached, the other more impetuous—

here the man of thought, there a man of action. What most distinguished Reuter from Schumacher was the complexity of his character: he was an intellectual in the good sense of the last century, which had sought a synthesis of thought and action. As a follower of Kant he rejected the idea that man is but a product of his environment; as a socialist he knew that, nevertheless, man can only fully develop his personality if conditions that infringe upon the right and dignity of man are abolished.

At a party meeting in Berlin, in the beginning of 1947, he summed up his creed in the following words:

"Since our daily struggle is often and primarily concerned with rather earthly objects, with better living conditions, which we want to make available to everyone, there arises the impression that this is our only aim. But the well-clad, well-fed, well-housed, and well-nursed robot is not what we are striving for. Our aim is the free man, conscious of his dignity and his rights."

Reuter belonged to a generation which, from mine, was not only separated by the usual twenty-five to thirty years. In these twenty-five years there was the shattering experience of World War I and the great social earthquake in which not only property, money and possessions, cities and countries were destroyed, but also nearly all the values had broken apart which for decades had been regarded as invulnerable and incorruptible.

Freedom, Democracy, Socialism, Pacifism, Humanism—for those born in the nineties these ideas were more or less of eternal truth We of the younger generation saw these ideals go bust, one after the other. Our fathers had still been able to preserve their faith past all crises and doubts—the sons were robbed of it. They seemed to be cynical, when in reality they were only lost and suspicious of bombastic programs and promises, after so many of these had eventually proved to be nothing but empty slogans.

No doubt, I did not always share Reuter's views of Germany and the political tasks of the day. But from the first moment, I felt that Reuter and I understood each other very well. When I was a young man I never felt that the difference of twenty years in our age alienated me from Julius Leber; that difference did not matter in my relationship with Ernst Reuter either.

No, he was not an "old man." Though he always turned to the classics when he was in need of courage and faith, and in the gravest crises sought comfort in Homer and Goethe —or rather just because he was accustomed to adopting a lofty standpoint toward life—he remained young at heart and young in spirit. This made him a comrade of the seekers and strugglers. We came from completely different social environments, but we did not only have the same aim, we also traveled the same road, for we had in the political firmament and in the world of the spirit the same stars after which we steered our course.

2

With the Norwegians in Berlin I felt at once at home; there was a pleasant, friendly atmosphere. I also met members of the Allied missions, a number of Scandinavian and Allied correspondents, various representatives of the political life in Berlin. Erich Brost, who originally came from Danzig, was a tactful interpreter between Germans and their foreign guests. Ernst Lemmer, the former left-democratic member of Parliament and later Federal Minister, was one of the founders of the Christian Democratic Union. The first time we met was shortly after my arrival; then we did not know that some years later we would be the heads of the two big parties in Berlin.

In April, Ruth arrived.

Though Germany was strange to her, the chaotic atmosphere frightened her as little as the hardships of daily life among the ruins. From childhood she was used to being on her own. She was three years old when she lost her father. At fifteen she had to earn her livelihood; first, she worked in a bakery, then, as a needlewoman. Like her sisters, she joined the Youth Movement at an early age. During the occupation of Norway she belonged to a group of the underground, she was arrested, spent some time in prison; after an adventurous and perilous flight she finally landed in Sweden. In Stockholm she worked at the Norwegian embassy, after the end of the war on an illustrated weekly in Oslo. Not without success she had taken up writing. Now she was transferred to the military mission in Berlin. So we were united by our work also. She was a great help to me.

This first year of my diplomatic career was marked by the change in the attitude of the Western powers toward their Soviet ally. It was the beginning of the Cold War. Germany was one of its centers, Berlin a front, where the Russians tried their strategy and their tactics, all the weapons of their political and psychological arsenal, which they planned to use immediately thereafter in Czechoslovakia and in Yugoslavia, in the Near East and in Korea.

The Cold War, too, was in its beginnings a *drôle de guerre* —more paradoxical than frightening. James Byrnes in his speech in Stuttgart, in the early fall of 1947, announced a new policy in regard to Germany. The British and the Americans, and some time later also the French, began to coordinate the economy of their occupation zones and to confer more responsibilities upon the German authorities. Reparations to Russia were suspended.

At the Four Power conferences and in the Allied Control Council it became more and more apparent how difficult it would be to adjust the views of the victors to each other. In Berlin, however, the Allied headquarters for the present still gave the impression that the West was willing to compromise the differences by making large concessions to the Russians. Time and again the representatives of America, England, and France allowed themselves to be outmaneuvered by the Soviet side.

It was the time that a spokesman of Berlin expressed the mood of many of his fellow citizens in these words "The worst is not that we have to fight with our backs to the wall —but that the Western powers are no wall to lean against"

The first lord mayor proved unequal to his difficult task and in the middle of April was asked by his own party to resign. Everybody expected that Reuter would be his successor. But the Russians came out against him and the Western representatives gave in.

Some of them were rather cross with Reuter, anyhow; they accused him of having sabotaged, during the hardest months of winter, the measures ordered by the Allied headquarters to economize on the use of electricity. A sub-committee of headquarters had even demanded Reuter's dismissal from his post as city councilor. In reality many of the measures were completely impracticable.

In the middle of June, Reuter was at last elected lord mayor by the Municipal Council. Now the Russian commandant, General Alexander Kotikow, insisted that Reuter could only assume his post if all the four occupation powers formally approved of him; as for himself, he vetoed the election.

A correct interpretation of the provisional constitution would have shown that only a majority veto had any validity. The dispute was transferred from headquarters to the Control Council, and again for the sake of peace the Western representatives gave in. As Frank Howley, the American commandant of the city, declared later: "At that time the

Western powers did nearly everything to win the sympathy of the Russians, to dispel their suspicions and convince them that we were their friends."

Louise Schroeder, until then one of the deputy mayors, was made acting lord mayor. A brave, upright woman, she invited Reuter, of whose ability she had a high opinion, to co-operate very closely with her. He, on the other hand, was much more interested in constructive and practical work than in formalities. Officially he acted as Frau Schroeder's assistant. Together they steered Berlin through a very hard time. When Louise Schroeder fell ill, Ferdinand Friedensburg became head of the Municipal Council.

The "mayor crisis," with its ups and downs, with its many shifts and changes, dominated the Berlin scene. I was busy making the Norwegian government, the Scandinavian press, and influential Western circles not only see the importance and the background of this conflict, but also to inform them of the general development in Germany and of the conflict between the East and the West that became apparent at that time.

Here and there, at Allied parties, there was still a chance to have a friendly conversation with a Russian official. Here and there I also met a few German communists. Among them was my former party friend Jacob Walcher, who had spent the war years in America and had arrived in Berlin almost the same day I had. In exile he seemed to share the basic opinions of our Stockholm circle. But when we met again in Berlin, I at once became aware that—despite our friendly feelings for each other—we were advocating diametrically opposed political convictions. Walcher expounded his political creed to me: no matter what had happened, one could not but realize that the Soviet Union was representing historical progress. Personally he acted according to his conclusion and joined the Unity party. The Communists appointed him chief editor of a unionist newspaper. And he gave me to understand that even the highest positions were within my grasp, if I followed his example.

If Walcher had not been my friend, and if I had not been able to see beforehand how deplorably his debut in the Soviet Zone would end, I could have laughed at his blindness and naïveté. And indeed, it took only a few years until he was pushed aside and vanished from the political scene. He was not pliant, not unscrupulous enough to make a career among the comrades.

Once, in my capacity as the Norwegian press attaché, I accompanied a conservative Norwegian editor to see Wilhelm Pieck, then chairman of the Unity party and later President of the Soviet-German state, the so-called German Democratic Republic. The old man, who stolidly and without imagination had followed every twist and turn of the party line without so much as a murmur, and thus for thirty years had survived war, revolutions, crises, and purges, gave the impression of a communist Hindenburg. Obviously he had reached a high degree of senility, but since his outward appearance corresponded to the primitive conception of a workmen's leader "turned gray honorably"—with red cheeks and white hair—he was exhibited as a monument of himself. It was an embarrassing rather than a sad spectacle.

Only once an original, unrehearsed remark turned up in this otherwise empty conversation. The Norwegian had broached the subject of the concentration camps, which in the Russian Zone had been reopened again. And in many cases the same people were again put in the camps: two years ago "heroes of freedom"—today "traitors against freedom."

Pieck did not understand at all the bitter irony, and quite guilelessly he remarked: "Oh yes, if you knew what letters I receive—from comrades whose sons have vanished—but we have no say in this matter—this is solely the business of the Soviet authorities."

Eventually he even asked the conservative journalist to give his love to "the comrades in Norway." Which the other, with appropriate irony, promised to do.

I have never personally met the other chairman of the Unity party and later "Prime Minister," Otto Grotewohl, but I once heard him speak in Wilmersdorf. He did not impress me particularly.

In June 1947, I attended a second congress of the German Social Democrats in Nuremberg. Thereafter Ruth and I went to Prague.

For the first time I had the opportunity to see with my own eyes how things were progressing in the most western of the satellite states. There the co-operation with the Communists seemed not to endanger personal freedom, and gave one hope that the conflict between the West and East could be settled amicably. As is well known, the government in Prague had then declared its willingness to accept Marshall Plan aid.

Nine months later in a speech to the Berlin members of the Social Democratic party, I reported on my experiences in Czechoslovakia.

"One felt that the people were working for the reconstruction of their country with energy and vigor.

"To tell the truth—there was no open terror at that time. In the press, in Parliament, in meetings and nightly gatherings on the Wenzel Square the problems of the day were discussed with vivacity. It is true, the Communists had been able to obtain advantages, especially in the field of propaganda, not at all proportionate to their actual strength, but people could openly declare themselves against the Communists and criticize the policy of the government, headed by the Communist leader Gottwald. Many Czechs believed in the new national revolution, which at the same time was to lay the foundations for a socialist republic. They all agreed that a foreign policy directed against the Soviet Union was out of question. And this they proved not only by pointing to the geographical situation, to Slavic solidarity, and the relations of power in postwar Europe, but first of all by reminding one of their experiences in 1938.

"The experience of Munich is deeply rooted in the memory of the Czech people They felt utterly abandoned by the West and therefore saw their only salvation in a close cooperation with Russia Time and again they emphasized, nevertheless, their determination not to exclude themselves from the cultural community of the West, nor from its commerce. They hoped to be in the position to act as an intermediary between the East and the West."

If these hopes in Czechoslovakia should come true, one was also allowed to look forward with some confidence to the future of Berlin, to the reunification of Germany. If the Czech experiment was successful, could one not then draw positive conclusions in regard to the German problem?

Nine months later we received the unequivocal answer to this question. In the above-mentioned speech, on March 12, 1948, I summed up the results of the Czechoslovakian catastrophe:

"The hope to act as an intermediary, to be a bridge between the East and the West, has collapsed. Nothing is left of this theory. We say this without malicious joy. For how much easier would have been our own situation, if it had been possible to build such bridges But let's face the truth. Whether we like it or not, nowadays bridges are not built, but blown up It will be up to a later time to re-establish honest connections between the Eastern and the Western part of the world. But this will only be possible if we first put our part of Europe and the world in order, if we strengthen our own ranks and do not retreat a single step."

The Communist coup in Czechoslovakia was a rude awakening for many "Leftists" and liberals and an important lesson to the peoples of the West.

I explained: "We have good reasons to approach the Czechoslovakian tragedy with awe. Let us not forget in this hour how much the Czechs have suffered from German fascism Let us not forget either that unfortunately all too many Germans in their blindness have let themselves be instigated to look down on the Czechs, to maltreat and to persecute them. Let us remember what happened immediately after the establishment of the so-called protectorate in 1939. The students in Prague were shot at, and soon thereafter the intellectual elite of Czechoslovakia was put in the concentration camps; a great part of them never returned."

Of course, I also had to mention the fact that a great part of the Sudetic-German population had fallen for Hitler's propaganda. On the other hand, I had to raise the question of whether there had not "previously been committed very serious mistakes by the Czechs, which made it difficult for the three and a half million Germans to establish a positive relationship with the Czechoslovakian Republic." And I spoke of the revenge in 1945, of the cruel excesses, of the expulsion of almost the whole Sudetic-German population, including the socialist fighters for freedom: "We German Social Democrats do not accept double standards in politics. Injustice remains injustice, be it committed in the name of anti-Nazism, democracy, or people's democracy. But we German Social Democrats do not for a moment think of making even the slightest concession to nationalistic feelings of hate and revenge."

Then I continued: "We have been against terror—the others only wish to be the ones who practice the terror. Whoever joins the Communist United Front will perish of it. Two years ago the Social Democrats in Berlin raised their banner of independence. For that the Social Democrats of Germany and the world owe them a debt of gratitude."

When I made this speech, I was no longer a Norwegian diplomat. At the end of the year of 1947, I had taken a step which since the end of the war I had considered again and again and yet put off: to become active again in the politics of my destroyed mother country.

I gave up my Norwegian citizenship—and the advantages, economic and personal, which I derived from my status as a Norwegian diplomat. I applied for my renaturalization in Germany. The immediate cause of this decision was a suggestion of Kurt Schumacher.

3

The suggestion, which had been thoroughly discussed at one of my visits to Hanover, amounted to the proposition that I take over the Berlin liaison office of the Executive Committee of the Social Democrats. It was not alone and not even primarily my task to maintain contacts with the party organization in Berlin and with friends in the Soviet Zone, but first of all I was to deal with the top-ranking officials of the Allied powers who at that time were still in Berlin.

Here a post was offered me in which I could help to win understanding of and support for an intelligent policy toward Germany. The time seemed to have come when I could do more for democracy and peace as a German in Germany than in my last position. But first two questions had to be clarified.

The first question concerned my right to an opinion of my own. I told Schumacher I knew perfectly well that I would have to represent the views of the Executive Committee but that it would make things easier for me if I was given the unrestricted right to present—if I felt it necessary—my own opinion to the party leadership. Schumacher said this was a foregone conclusion and added that "in Hanover they were not omniscient either", my criticism and my suggestions would always be welcome.

The second problem was posed by my intended resignation from my position in the Norwegian Foreign Office. I wrote a letter to my chief and friend Halvard Lange and explained my case to him. It was not necessary to assure him that I had not lightheartedly made the decision to renounce my Norwegian citizenship—he knew my feelings toward Norway too well. Our personal relationship had never been marred by a dissonance. I frankly declared that I accepted the position offered to me without any illusions and that I was prepared for disappointments. As I wrote to Oslo: "Perhaps I shall experience the great failure of my life here in Berlin. But if that should come to pass, I would like to meet this defeat with the feeling that I have done my duty."

In his answer Lange assured me that he understood my motives very well; he found my decision justified. Although he did not have a successor at hand he was willing to release me at the end of the year.

Other friends also found my decision right. Gunnar Myrdal, who shortly before had asked me whether I would like to take a post in the UN Economic Commission in Geneva, wrote me that he and his wife had read my letter with cordial sympathy: "We do not know all the circumstances, but we feel that you are doing the right thing when you resume your work for that of your two countries which is the poorer and needs your help more."

Yet it looked as though the disappointments I feared would come sooner than I thought. It hardly had become known that I was to take over the Berlin secretariat when the intrigues began. The exile gossip was revived with its absurd insinuations. There also were some people who, alluding to

Walcher's occasional visits, tried to depict me in Hanover as "not quite trustworthy."

In a rather long letter to Schumacher I gave him my opinion on these partly open, partly hidden insinuations. I reminded him that "I had on mature consideration resolved to give up my Norwegian position, but that I did not insist on a specific post.

"Let me unequivocally declare," so I concluded my letter, "that I stand by the principles of Democratic Socialism in general, and by the policy of the German Social Democracy in particular Please, let me in the end assure you that I have never been a simple yes man and that I hope I shall never be one. But I have long learned to work in discipline and with all my strength for our cause, whatever my assignment has been.

"If actually, for reasons that I do not know, decisive objections had been raised, then it would be better to drop the subject once and for all. I do not doubt that I could make myself useful in any other field of work.

"I do not want to be obtrusive, I cannot see any reason why I should defend myself, but I stand by the cause and by my word."

This letter cleared the atmosphere. The Executive Committee confirmed my appointment, and on the first of January, 1948, I could take up my new job.

The adjudication of my German citizenship followed some months later. If I had waited a little longer it would not have been necessary to apply for my renaturalization at all, for according to the Constitution of the Federal Republic I would have received it automatically. Since I was born in Lübeck, I was naturalized in Kiel. The document listed both my names—the one which I had borne at my birth and the other which I had used in my political activity since I was nineteen years of age; the formal change of my name was licensed by the president of the police in Berlin. As Willy Brandt I had escaped from the Hitler Reich, as Willy Brandt I had worked in exile and returned to Berlin—therefore I wanted it to be my official name in Germany from now on.

Thus I entered the new—and as I was convinced—decisive phase of my life, but not alone. Ruth stayed in Berlin, at my side.

Berlin in 1948 may have been the last place one would choose for a regular and safe family life. But in spite of the uncertain future, we married, nevertheless, there and then—in Berlin in 1948. A Norwegian parson married us. We moved into a little house in Hallensee.

CHAPTER TEN

The Blockade

The year 1948 was a turning point [illegible] future of Germany and of Europe. It was the year of the Blockade and the airlift, of the decision of the Allies to unite the three western zones not only economically but also politically, and it was the year of the counter-offensive which, at least in Europe, brought the further advance of communism to a halt.

The basis for this change, however, was already laid in [illegible] by the historic address of General George Mar- [illegible]

[illegible]

[illegible] Moscow conference had thus [illegible] forced Stalin to embark on other fronts [illegible] push forward the [illegible] of Germany.

The Foreign Ministers' conference opened the eyes of the representatives of the Western powers. It disclosed Stalin's

*

CHAPTER TEN

The Blockade

1

The year 1948 was a turning point in the history of Berlin, of Germany, and of Europe. It was the year of the blockade and the airlift, of the decision of the Allies to unite the three western zones not only economically but also politically, and it was the year of the democratic counter-offensive which, at least in Europe, brought the further advance of communism to a halt.

The basis for this change, however, was already laid in June 1947 by the historic address of General George Marshall at Harvard, when he stated America's intention to grant large-scale economic aid for the restoration of Europe.

The Truman Doctrine, proclaimed in March 1947, saved Greece by America's determined show of force. This defeat caused Stalin to advance on other "fronts," and above all to push forward the Sovietization of Germany.

The Foreign Ministers' conference opened the eyes of the representatives of the Western powers: it disclosed Stalin's determination not to allow Germany to be reconstructed under a democratic system of government. The Soviet policy was definitely opposed to the economic rehabilitation of Germany and Western Europe.

The Cold War entered a decisive phase. Germany was the prize—but it could not be won by Stalin without the conquest of Berlin.

For the time being it appeared as if the Allies considered Berlin not a key position but a strategically indefensible and politically unimportant outpost While the Russian pressure intensified, the Western Allies seemed to be unable to come to an agreement upon a common action.

The defeat of the Communists in the October elections of 1946 had been a grave disappointment to the Soviets. Not only on the occasion of the election of the chief burgomaster had they systematically tried to cause difficulties to the self-governing municipal organizations; the districts of the eastern sector were subjected to a particularly heavy pressure.

In addition, the ghost of kidnaping stalked the city. And the Communist police president refused to accept orders from the Municipal Council; he felt responsible only to the Soviets.

Protests of the Western commanders were of no avail. There were, of course, official statements on the part of the Western military authorities and of the American and British governments—such as of the British Foreign Secretary Ernest Bevin and of the American Military Governor Lucius Clay—that they had absolutely no intention of abandoning Berlin. However, the indulgence shown so far made many Berliners doubt the seriousness of the declarations.

It was urgently necessary to combat the growing pessimism; it might have become a dangerous epidemic, paralyzing the hearts and brains of men.

In this situation Ernst Reuter's extraordinary gift for political leadership became apparent. He well knew how very important it was to demonstrate an independent will By the example of his own determination and confidence he gave new courage to the skeptics and pessimists.

The anniversary of the March revolution of 1848 was the external occasion. The democratic leaders decided to stage an independent demonstration without—and against—the Communist Unity party, which usually participated in affairs of this kind, in fact, it was still represented in the Municipal Council.

The eighteenth of March was a cold day, it was pouring rain, but sixty to eighty thousand men assembled on the huge square before the ruins of the Reichstag to profess their faith in liberty. After the addresses of the leaders of the Social Democrats, the Christian Democrats, and the Liberal Democrats, Reuter reminded the people of the fate of Prague: "It was Prague's turn, Finland was next, whose turn is it now? It will not be Berlin's turn! The Communist flood will break on our iron will. Then the nations of the world will know that they must not leave us in the lurch, and they certainly will not leave us in the lurch!"

The loud applause, lasting for several minutes, was more than a mere outbreak of enthusiasm—a spark had kindled the will of resistance still glowing under the cold ashes of fright; the signal was given for the mobilization of the people of Berlin.

In the meantime two decisions of far-reaching importance to all of Germany, primarily to Berlin, were in preparation.

The Western powers decided to unite the German territories under their control. The Americans urged this development. The French hesitated; in 1945 they had opposed any attempt to constitute all-German administrations. The Soviets maintained that the plans for a "Western state" would bring militarism and fascism to power again; they walked out of the Allied Control Council.

While the difficult negotiations about the reorganization of the state were still in progress, a decision on the currency reform was imminent. Without it, no economic restoration was possible. Now, with the consent of the German authorities, the Western powers decided in any case to put the economic conditions in order in their zones—in "Trizonesia."

That was done on June 18, 1948 But what should become of Berlin? Since spring the Soviets by ever new "measures" had made traffic from and to Berlin more and more difficult. For the time being, however, nobody thought of a blockade.

For the present, Berlin was to remain excluded from the West German currency reform France, above all, objected to the introduction of the West mark in Berlin The Berliners had to fear that their city by means of the East mark was to be incorporated into the East Zone. Suddenly, a proclamation of Marshal Sokolovsky announced the "temporary" stoppage of all passenger traffic from West Germany to the Soviet Zone and Berlin. The import of the new West money was prohibited under threat of punishment. As a reason for this decree the Russians alleged there was a danger that Berlin might be swamped with the old money that had become invalid in West Germany.

At the same time the Communists also pushed forward. In the Municipal Council their speaker announced the end of the Four Power administration of Berlin; henceforth the whole city would be put under Soviet "protection."

For us, Reuter's friends and co-workers, it was now of primary importance to make clear to the representatives of the Western powers that they would unfailingly lose Berlin if they permitted the city to be included in the sphere of the East mark. But in order to convince the Allies we also had to make clear to the population of Berlin that these were not problems of a technical and financial nature, but that the liberty of the city, its membership in the free part of Germany and in the democratic world was at stake.

The Social Democratic party could and had to speak more openly than it was possible for the Municipal Council. I submitted to the State Committee a statement in which the Soviet policy of the last three years was held responsible for Germany's financial chaos. We declared that Sokolovsky's proclamation had to be rejected as invalid. Liberty and unity for all of Germany could now be achieved only by the economic and political stabilization of the three western zones.

There were many people who shrank back from stating that principle. There were many irresolute, skeptical people, ready for a compromise. The Berlin Social Democrats stood up for clarity and firmness. The power of the Soviets over East Berlin was a fact. Those, however, who in the Western sectors still favored the Eastern currency chose the regime of the Communist dictatorship. With this slogan the Social Democrats assumed the leadership in the fight for the defense of Berlin.

The Allied authorities sincerely tried to come to an agreement with the Soviets; they demanded at least to participate in the control of the East mark circulating in West Berlin. Only after this request, too, was rejected by the Soviets, they brought West German marks to West Berlin. The settlement was a half solution. The East mark continued to be valid currency in many walks of daily life, also in West Berlin. Only in March 1949, at about the end of the blockade, Ernst Reuter succeeded in making the West mark the exclusive currency for West Berlin, and many months later he had still to struggle against West German plans which might have canceled this decision, so vital for the reconstruction and the security of the city.

In June 1948 the Berliners lived between fear and hope. They learned that the Western powers didn't intend to abandon Berlin but they learned also that the Soviets were posed for a trial of strength.

2

The Soviets proclaimed the blockade of Berlin on the pretext that the streets were temporarily impassable and that near Magdeburg a bridge had to be repaired. Railway traffic, *Autobahn*, highways, and waterways from and to the West were blocked. Only the three air corridors, each thirty kilometers wide, remained open. The magazines of the Municipal Council, located in the East sector, could no longer be used for the supply of the West sectors. Even the supply of medicine for sick persons and milk for little babies was stopped. Two million West Berliners were to be starved into capitulation.

Among the chiefs of the Western Military Administration, General Clay realized most clearly the danger of retreat and pleaded in a most determined manner for energetic countermeasures. He suggested in Washington that the blockade should be broken by an American military train. He thought it unlikely that the Russians would use force to stop the train. He was convinced that the Soviet Union didn't want a war but that they hoped the Western powers, from fear of a war, would abandon their positions. It is less known that Aneurin Bevan, then a member of the British cabinet, pleaded also for the same determined action.

Washington and London, however, considered the risk too great. It was decided to hold Berlin and to supply by air the occupation troops—and as far as possible the Berlin population—with the most urgent necessities of life.

Nobody knew how long and to what extent the city could be supplied in this manner. Clay himself at first counted on a daily capacity of five hundred to seven hundred tons, and hoped to be able to carry on the operation for three to six weeks "until the situation would have somehow been clarified." Thus, on June 26, thirty-two twin-engined Dakotas were put into action for the flight to Berlin. They brought medicine, some important foodstuffs, and mail for the civilian population.

Four weeks later Clay reported to Washington that Berlin could be held for an unlimited time if sufficient airplanes were available. At that time the American and British planes flew daily an average of fifteen hundred tons to Berlin. An extraordinary achievement, though not at all sufficient to secure the existence of the civilian population. And what would happen in the coming winter when people not only needed foodstuffs, raw material, and fuel for the industry, but when they would also have somehow to cope with the cold? Could one subject the Berliners to such a severe test? Would they be willing to take upon themselves still greater privations? The decision of the Western occupation powers depended in the last resort on the answer to this question.

The answer of the Berliners was given to the Americans by Ernst Reuter.

At the end of June, I accompanied him to a conference with some gentlemen of the American administration. They tried to "encourage" us—perhaps it would yet be possible to supply Berlin. Reuter smiled skeptically. He couldn't quite believe it. But he told them—and he spoke without any sharpness—"We shall in any case continue on our way. Do what you are able to do; we shall do what we feel to be our duty." Berlin would make all necessary sacrifices and offer resistance—come what may.

The gentlemen were visibly impressed. They had perhaps expected to hear complaints, reproaches, conditions; instead they heard quite another sound. A European politician declared that he was ready to assume a hard task without making its achievement dependent on equivalent American services—not even on a financial support.

Reuter's frankness and his firm unshakable attitude won Clay's sympathy. At first the general had clearly given him the cold shoulder. By the way, this was mutual. Reuter too had at first a rather critical attitude toward Clay. The southerner, grown up in the ideas of American federalism, thought Reuter too authoritarian, too centralistic; it may not have been easy for Clay to free himself of the prejudice to see a "Red" in every Social Democrat. Reuter, on the other hand, believed that an American general could hardly understand the European conditions, and the position of the German democrats in particular He definitely refused to be considered an instrument of American policy, or of any other foreign government. Nevertheless, in the course of this crucial year the two men formed a close partnership which secured the victory in the struggle for Berlin.

The efficiency of the airlift surpassed the highest expectations. The organization of the operation, the technical achievements of the flyers and the ground crew, the exact co-operation of all nine air bases in western Germany with the airports in Berlin—all that bordered upon the fantastic. The transport capacity increased from week to week. One had counted on a minimum requirement of 3400 to 4500 tons; in September, on a single day, approximately 7000 tons were flown into Berlin. And on the sixteenth of April of the following year 1400 planes landed in Berlin's airports—an airplane every 63 seconds. They transported 5300 tons of coal, 1850 tons of foodstuffs, 1000 tons of raw material of different kinds—i.e., on a single day 8000 tons of freight. That was the same quantity which prior to the blockade was brought to Berlin on all highways and waterways.

Not only semi-manufactured products and bales of newsprint were flown in, but even bulky pieces of generating equipment, among them installations for the Power Station West which was in construction and which was to make West Berlin independent of the power supply from the East sector. Before being loaded on the planes the machines were cut to pieces with a cutting torch, and afterward in Berlin they were welded together again.

Beside the organizers and the flyers of the airlift, the workers which were employed in the unloading of the airplanes also achieved real miracles. They worked ten and twelve hours daily, without break, and succeeded in unloading ten tons of freight within five to six minutes.

When the blockade was lifted by the Russians on May 12, 1949, it had lasted exactly 322 days. In these eleven months more than two million tons had been flown into Berlin—a gigantic achievement which revolutionized all ideas regarding air transport, prevalent up to that time.

Over these figures, these miracles of technique, organization, and machines, we must not forget the victims. Thirty-nine Englishmen, thirty-one Americans, and nine Germans lost their lives on the front of the blockade.

And behind all these rightly honored heroes stood two million nameless men and women who endured all privations and sufferings of this year unhonored and unsung. The manner in which they endured all hardships was to me perhaps even more remarkable than the achievements of the flyers.

The Berliners couldn't have held their ground without the airlift—but the airlift would have been senseless without the courage of the Berliners, without the determination shown by the civilian population.

3

At the beginning of the blockade the supplies in the West sectors were sufficient to guarantee the barely sufficient rations for approximately four weeks at maximum.

In the first months just enough food was brought in by air to secure the further issue of the rations and to save the Berliners from starving to death—but hunger they could not be spared.

The stock of coal was supposed to last for thirty days, but it was impossible to replenish it to the same extent as the urgently needed food. Apartments and the greater part of offices—even the administration buildings—could no longer be heated. Every family got for the whole winter an allotment of twenty-five pounds of coal and three boxes of wood. Some fuel was smuggled in by black-marketeers. Most of the families were glad when they could keep one room of their apartment moderately warm for a few hours of the day. Fortunately, the winter was not particularly severe.

Cooking in Berlin was done ninety per cent by gas. During the first five months of the blockade consumers were limited to half of their previous gas consumption. Electric current was only available for four hours daily, usually in two periods of two hours each. These periods came at different times of day in different sections of the city, and people had to rise at odd hours in order to take advantage of the available current. The preparation of a cup of hot ersatz coffee or of a bowl of soup put the housewife before a nearly insoluble problem.

In the long winter evenings people would sit in their kitchen by candlelight, hungry and shivering from cold. Then they dressed as warmly as possible. . . . No, they didn't go out, they only went to bed.

One factory after the other had to shut down. Small businesses that required electric current for their operations had no choice but to operate when this was available, even at four o'clock in the morning. Most often their employees had to get to work on foot. The subway operated only from six o'clock in the morning to six o'clock in the evening; the streetcar service was greatly curtailed; the buses ran only at rare intervals because of limited gasoline stocks. Although 25,000 unemployed were occupied with the removal of the ruins, the figure of people out of work increased to more than 150,000.

In the meantime the Communists had changed their tactics: after threats and intimidations they all of a sudden made a tempting offer to the West Berliners They asserted that the Soviet government had brought large quantities of foodstuffs into the East sector. All the West Berliners had to do if they wanted to get that food was to register with ration offices in the East sector. The answer was very impressive. The ration office in Treptow had sent out invitations to 285,000 persons. At first only twenty persons from the West sectors registered. Sixteen persons registered in Prenzlauer Berg, and nineteen in Pankow. By the end of the year 85,000 of two million Berliners had accepted the Communist offer—four per cent of the population. And most of them were people who lived in the West sectors, but who worked in the East sector and continued to buy their rations there as they had always done.

The Berliners did not waver, though in addition to hunger and cold—particularly in the first months of the blockade—they were subjected to a vicious fear propaganda. The Soviets had declared that all of Berlin was theirs, and their newspapers in German language didn't cease to foretell the realization of that claim. They spread rumors of different kinds, they didn't spare threats and intimidations. Thus, here and there, doubts arose as to whether one would be able to resist the Russian pressure in the long run. The retaliation and vengeance in case of a defeat would be terrible.

In spite of Reuter's rousing appeals and in spite of General Clay's assurances, one couldn't close one's mind to the plain fact that, from the military point of view, Berlin's situation was hopeless. The United States had 3000 troops in the city, the British 2000, and the French 1500, while the Soviets had 18,000 soldiers in East Berlin, and a further 300,000 in the East Zone. They could at any time overrun Berlin. And what would happen then? Would the Western democracies risk a world war in the interest of a few million Berliners?

The secret doubts were continuously nourished by means of a sometimes skillful Communist propaganda. Their press and their radio brought up every day new "revelations" regarding the imminent withdrawal of the Western powers; the Communist Unity party swamped Berlin with pamphlets; at the borders of the sectors propaganda cars were placed, their loud-speakers announced the hopelessness of any further resistance. The "front-porch politicians" asked the Berliners to sacrifice their savings in favor of the West mark; the workers were asked to leave the Communist Trade Union Federation, and thus lose their relief contributions; hunger and unemployment were their certain fate—and all that for what? For the defense of a system the collapse of which was only a question of weeks.

The Communists didn't limit themselves to mere propaganda by word and writing. The sessions of the Municipal Council were broken up by a Communist mob, Social Democratic city councilors and members of the Municipal Council were assaulted when they were leaving the hall, policemen who tried to come to their aid were arrested.

Dr. Otto Suhr, the chairman of the City Assembly, demanded a guarantee from General Kotikov that the regularly elected municipal bodies could hold their meetings without being disturbed. But his demand was as unsuccessful as the protests of the Western military governors against the riots plotted by the Communists.

The city parliament and the Municipal Council were forced to transfer their sessions to West Berlin. The split of the Municipal Council became more and more evident.

The cases of kidnaping and arbitrary arrests increased from month to month. Russian soldiers repeatedly invaded the American sector. Once they kidnaped five policemen and confiscated their police car. That same day a city councilor was arrested in his office by the East sector police. The next day Soviet military police assaulted two Berliner policemen in the American sector. When they tried to resist the arrest they were knocked down, stabbed, and dragged into the Russian sector.

The blockade became tighter from week to week. Throughout the summer West Berliners were able to obtain a limited quantity of food and other supplies from the Soviet Zone. Trucks drove out daily into the surrounding countryside and brought back vegetables; individuals went on "hoarding expeditions" to the East Zone and returned by boat, train, subway, or bicycle with wood, coal briquettes, potatoes.

In the fall the Soviets sealed these holes. German travelers were forbidden to bring food and supplies from the surrounding countryside into the West sectors. Controls were extended to the subway lines running between West and East Berlin. The Communist police not only confiscated food and other goods, but extended their searches to pocketbooks and wallets and confiscated West marks. Even the possession of a West Berlin newspaper made a person suspect—the police took his name down, he was a marked man.

The Berliners lived in a besieged fortress. To hunger and cold was added the paralyzing feeling of complete isolation from the outside world.

And yet life went on in this sorely afflicted city. Theaters and cinemas performed as in the time before the blockade, marriages were contracted and children were born—the statistics did not differ from those of former times. It was, however, not the astonishing "normalcy" of those months that impressed me most. It was the simple manner in which the

Berliners demonstrated their allegiance to common basic values; their knowledge that they stood for each other and could rely on each other; the determination they manifested in the defense of justice and freedom of speech and press; their acceptance of individual responsibility. All that reminded me of the admirable resistance the Norwegians had offered nine years before against all attempts to break their will and their spirit. As I felt then that Norway had never been greater than in the time of its hardest distress—just so I experienced now the real greatness of Berlin.

The three democratic parties stood firmly together. The independent trade unionists and the shop councilors fought the Communists without fear and helped to defend the economic basis of the city as much as possible.

The students who had opposed the Nazification of the university, which was located in the East sector, and who had been persecuted on account of their liberal attitude, had at the beginning of the blockade demanded the establishment of a free university in West Berlin. Reuter had their demand particularly at heart. He and Professor Edwin Redslob took the chairmanship of a committee and started immediately with the necessary preliminary organizational work. American authorities supported the project, released buildings, and granted the first subsidy. The lectures started in November. They were attended by two thousand students.

It might have been expected that thieves and burglars would profit from the dark streets and the lack of domestic lighting, but the criminal statistics showed no increase. According to an American investigation there was less crime in West Berlin during the blockade than in any other population group of that size in the Western world. Only the death rate increased—particularly among children and teen-agers.

Ernst Reuter, in his quality as "elected but not confirmed

chief burgomaster" was the soul of the Berlin resistance. He gave the decisive watchword.

At the beginning of the blockade in a mass demonstration before 80,000 men, he had formulated the order of the day: "With all means at our disposal we shall fight those who want to turn us into slaves and helots of a party. We have lived under such a slavery in the days of Adolf Hitler. We have had enough of that. We want no return of such times. We know all too well that we are an unarmed, defeated nation, and in fact, a defenseless nation, too. Our strength doesn't lie in the external power, we are deprived of that. Our strength lies indeed only in the fact that we represent a good and just cause.

"There are always people who, in a critical hour, start talking of the necessity to put up with the realities, with the facts, with the circumstances. Well, we Germans have had our experiences in this respect. The people who put up with the real circumstances were those who, in 1933, decided to make their peace with Hitler. They wanted always to "avoid the worst"—and at the end Germany was in ruins. We had not only lost our freedom, but we were also thrown back for a generation, condemned to a beggar's existence. Today it's the same all over again. Today also Germany can only live if she learns to fight for her freedom and for her right.

"In this crisis we not only ask you to have confidence in us; rather we appeal to you to have confidence in yourself."

Under this watchword Reuter's battle was fought. He spoke for all of us when on September 9—the Western powers were about to discuss with the Russians once again an eventual compromise—he addressed several hundred thousand people, assembled before the ruin of the Reichstag; he passionately appealed to the nations of the world not to leave us in the lurch. At the beginning of 1949 he flew to America,

London, and Paris to prevent the further development of Berlin's being separated from free Germany.

Many other people proved their courage. I, too, tried to make my contribution as organizer and speaker. But I was a newcomer in Berlin and certainly did not yet belong to the "first class." There must be mentioned the members of the Municipal Council, with Louise Schroeder and Ferdinand Friedensburg at the head; the city councilors with their chairman Otto Suhr; the Social Democratic chairmen Franz Neumann and Kurt Mattick, the exiled Christian Democratic chairman and later Federal minister Jakob Kaiser, and the other leaders of the democratic parties; the independent trade unionists around Ernst Scharnovski. They and many others daily gave the example of a civil courage which was seldom evident in Germany during the last decades.

It was also of great importance that there were well-functioning organizations behind the democratic leaders. The different departments of the municipal administration accomplished their tasks generally in an ideal manner. Of course, it would have been impossible to bring the word and the instructions of the leaders to the public without a democratic press. The newspapers of the occupation forces had within a few months developed into combat organs. Among the powers of resistance they must be given an important place.

But no appeal could be so effective and no example could be so convincing as the never ceasing roar of the Allied airplanes in the sky above the city.

A Berliner described in a letter to the editor of a West Berlin newspaper how in a few days he was freed of his doubts and how he regained his faith in victory:

"First day—got to Zehlendorf. Amis still there. Am calmed.

"Tenth day—dried potatoes, dried vegetables, tinned meat, egg powder, I'm still calmer.

"Thirtieth day—coal from the heavens. Planes like clockwork. Earplugs by my bed."

The roar of the airplanes became the recurring motif of the resistance and the pulsation of the life in the besieged city.

In November suddenly the pulsation ceased. On fifteen days out of thirty the weather conditions were so bad that the air traffic nearly had to be stopped completely. The weather forecast for December was not better. The stock of coal was sufficient only for one more week. Fortunately the weather improved before the crisis could lead to a catastrophe.

At the culmination of the crisis—on the thirtieth of November—the split of Berlin became official. The "Democratic Bloc"—a union of Communist organizations and their partisans—declared the still-functioning Municipal Council dissolved and appointed Fritz Ebert, a son of the first president of the Weimar Republic, chief burgomaster. With this coup the Communists intended to prevent the new elections for the City Assembly, which were scheduled for the fifth of December.

In West Berlin the December elections took place anyhow, in spite of Communist disturbances, in spite of the threats of Soviet representatives who gave us to understand that their troops would march into the Western sectors. Of the people who were entitled to vote, 83.9 per cent cast their ballots; 64.5 per cent of them voted for the Social Democrats. Against 60 Socialist deputies, were lined up 20 Christian Democrats and 17 Liberal Democratic deputies.

Nobody could overlook the will of the Berliners, which had been so clearly expressed. We urged that Ernst Reuter two days after the election be elected lord mayor for the second time by the Municipal Assembly. And this time neither he nor the Western military commanders had to worry about whether or not the Soviets approved of his election. He was sworn in and could now fully devote himself to the reconstruction of the municipal administration of West Berlin. The consolidation of the city could now start in earnest because it was independent of the Russian control. But many things had to be improvised, and the future of Berlin was still very much in the dark.

When I visited Copenhagen, at the beginning of April 1949, I predicted in a lecture the early end of the blockade. I did not know about the discussions between American delegate Jessup and Soviet ambassador Malik, but a turn was in the air. Stalin himself had hinted at it.

On May 12 the "traffic restrictions"—as the Soviets called their blockade—were lifted. As Reuter said, the Berliners could celebrate "the most beautiful May since 1945."

They celebrated it in a new spirit. It was more than a mere enthusiasm about the end of pressure and privations—the experience of the resistance had given the Berliners the consciousness of their close solidarity with the democratic nations. The relation between them and the victors of yesterday had fundamentally changed. They now felt like partners and no longer like mere pawns in the hands of the great powers. From this feeling, by realizing the important contribution that they had made to the defense of the West, they derived a new self-confidence and new courage. That had not only a bearing on the situation in Berlin but had also an important influence on the development in West Germany. Berlin was, as Reuter said, the shield behind which the consolidation in the free part of Germany could take place.

4

The year of the blockade was also for my wife and for me a year of great experiences and of serious worries.

The material difficulties which Ruth and I shared with all other Berliners did not depress us too much. I have, to be honest, no disposition for an ascetic; I know how to appreciate good food and other comforts; but when circumstances force me to do without, I don't mind. Fortunately Ruth feels the same way.

Besides, our living conditions were still much better than those of most of our fellow citizens. Our Scandinavian friends didn't forget us. We received parcels of various kinds. We got a highly modern petroleum lamp from Sweden, and from West Germany I brought home a cooking apparatus.

By the way: the feeling of solidarity with thousands of other people who had to endure the same fate and the same privations, the unpathetic courage of the Berliners, their biting and inexhaustible humor always gave us additional strength and confidence. We got a rather large dose of it daily.

Real worries I had only in October when Ruth was in the hospital expecting our first child. The hospital was scarcely heated, deficiently lighted; Ruth was more exhausted from the unaccustomed life than she would admit. Peter came into the world by candlelight, according to style: a real child of the blockade. Our second son Lars was born in early summer, 1951. They both have become genuine Berliners.

Among the heroes of the blockade the young mothers deserve particularly to be mentioned. They indeed had a special right to celebrate the victory of May 1949—because for them it was a triumph of life over death.

*

CHAPTER ELEVEN

The Fight for German Unification

1

Ten years after the end of the blockade—on May 12, 1959—we welcomed in Berlin as our guests some of the men who had saved us from starvation and the whole West from a terrible defeat. General Lucius Clay brought us a message from the United States; Lord Attlee and Sir Brian Robertson represented the British government; Robert Schuman spoke for France. The former occupation chiefs were joyfully received. With them, as our guests of honor, came the relatives of the victims of the airlift. We established the foundation "Airlift Thanks," which grants scholarships to students at the Berlin universities.

In a speech I reviewed the times of ten years before:

"It was a piece of good luck in our misfortune that we found friends who gave us the chance to efface the shame that Germany had brought upon herself. We have tried to learn from the past and not to betray the confidence placed in us. From this road nobody shall divert us. We will not let ourselves be led astray into a spiritual neutralism, we will not let ourselves be separated from our friends.

"We have not forgotten the lessons of the blockade. The perseverance of a starving but self-confident people and the technical organizational miracle of the airlift—those were the two pillars of the resistance."

However, I could not suppress a few critical remarks:

"In this hour we are reminded of the many hopes that in this last decade have come to naught. Ten years ago we thought that we had arrived at a historic climax, and yet, it was just another period in a protracted struggle We have also had to ask ourselves more than once, whether the May of 1949 was wisely used, whether it was not a mistake to regard the lifting of the blockade as a major success and to turn immediately to other matters."

The realization that in 1949 chances had been missed, was not an afterthought. Even under the immediate impression of the events we had the feeling that it was made too easy for the Soviets to cover their retreat and to consolidate their advanced positions in Central Europe.

Those positions had to be pushed back—that was the real task. And that meant: the solution of the German problem. But the Western powers were all too glad to have at last come to an agreement on the basic structure of a West German state. They did not want to start all over again from the beginning.

The same day on which the end of the blockade was celebrated in Berlin, the members of the Parliamentarian Council met with the Allied Military Governors in Frankfort for the final deliberations about the Constitution of the "Federal German Republic." The Council, formed by delegates from the Diets of the West German "Lander," convened in September 1948, in Bonn, and had worked on the Constitution ever since.

Berlin was represented in the Council by five members. I was not one of them, but I held many talks with Allied representatives in order to acquaint them with the opinions and suggestions of my political friends. Twice or three times a month I used to fly to Hanover to participate in the sessions of the Executive Committee of the Social Democratic party. The return flight was not always easy—sometimes there were long and annoying waiting periods.

Other matters were not easy either. Whereas in Berlin we sat with the Allies "in the same boat," while they came to visit us regularly and as good companions partook of our spartan meals, in West Germany there was still a wide gulf between the Allies and us. At the airport in Buckeburg, for instance, we were not even allowed to use the washrooms reserved for the Allies. In Hanover we had to wait outside the door of a British office to get our papers checked. All that was certainly not tragic, but it left you with a bitter feeling.

Together with Ernst Reuter I was of the opinion that the political reorganization of West Germany ought to be accomplished as fast as possible. This seemed to us a preliminary condition also for the liberation of our countrymen in the Soviet-occupied zone. As far as the solution of the German question was concerned, we were too optimistic; but who can prove that everything had to happen the way it did? Maybe if our ideas had prevailed and a sterner course had been followed in regard to the Soviets, things might have turned out differently.

The Social Democrats stressed very much the temporary character of the political reorganization in West Germany. Professor Carlo Schmid, their most prominent spokesman in Bonn, advocated this principle with great erudition and Gallic eloquence. I have always felt a real friendship for this man of culture and international stature, even when sometimes I could not agree with one or the other of his ideas.

Konrad Adenauer was then and later much less interested in emphasizing the temporary character of the West German state. He seemed to support the federalistic ideas which were advocated by the French and the Americans. Only much later did he occasionally admit that, in fact, he owed a debt of gratitude to the Social Democrats and the British for having insisted on a strong and firm structure of the German Republic which was essential for its stability.

While the Social Democrats stressed the provisional arrangement of the Federal Republic, they did not want to weaken the Executive; on the contrary, they were in favor of strengthening the position of the future Chancellor. To avoid the eternal parliamentarian crises of the Weimar Republic the Constitution provided that the Chancellor, once elected, could not be overthrown except by a "constructive" vote of no confidence, at the same time agreeing by majority vote on his successor.

This was the only important point on which Kurt Schumacher and Konrad Adenauer could agree, for both prepared themselves to assume the office of the Chancellor. Adenauer was President of the Parliamentarian Council; he became more and more the leading figure of the Christian Democrats. Who knows if he would ever have reached this position if at the end of 1945 a British general had not dismissed him "on account of his incompetency" as mayor of Cologne.

We Berliners were in a peculiar position. On the one hand, we were the most energetic supporters of a quick and positive conclusion of the deliberations in Bonn. On the other hand, we were the stepchildren of the Constitution. The Allies decreed that we could only have a restricted number of representatives in the Parliament, and those were not to be elected directly and had only a limited vote.

The Western powers argued that this decision was determined by the Four Power agreement on Berlin. The men around Adenauer were all too ready to accept the Allied demands. They were afraid of the Social Democratic votes of Berlin. That's what Allied officials who were in the know told me. And after all, it was not surprising that a man like Konrad Adenauer, with his character and his background, did not feel too strongly about the problems of the German East —and for him the "East" began at the Elbe.

Reuter could never suppress the suspicion that Adenauer's preoccupation with his West German concept did not leave him much interest or sympathy for the restoration of Germany's unity. Reuter felt that the President of the Parliamentarian Council and later Chancellor did little to unite the part of free Germany beyond the Russian Zone as firmly as possible with the Federal Republic—and that part was West Berlin.

In 1949 my work as a liaison man of the Social Democratic Executive underwent a considerable change. Many Allied authorities moved to Frankfort or Bonn. My contacts with high Allied officials, originally my main task, lost their importance. In addition, my relations with Schumacher were not as good as before. He had the impression that I, instead of representing the Executive, had become "Reuter's man." Plotters and schemers, to be found in every party organization, tried to create distrust between us. They hoped to maneuver Reuter and myself into an open conflict with the party leader.

That did not prevent Kurt Schumacher from offering me a safe district in Schleswig-Holstein when the party chose the candidates for the next elections. This would have meant leaving Berlin, and that I did not want to do. Therefore I gladly accepted the chance to be sent to Bonn by the City Assembly as one of the eight Berlin representatives and to act as the spokesman for the city in the first *Bundestag*, the Federal Parliament.

The elections in August 1949 were a bitter disappointment to me and to my party friends. The Christian Democrats won by a narrow margin With a majority of one—probably his own vote—Konrad Adenauer was elected Chancellor.

The disappointment was all the greater because the Social Democrats could not only assert but also prove that throughout the most difficult postwar years they had done a good, a selfless and successful job in the country, in cities and factories. Now they remained excluded from the organization of the federal offices, and due to the authoritarian rule of the Chancellor they were pushed into a ghettolike opposition.

When in September the Parliament convened in Bonn it became evident how deep the gulf between the two big parties was. And it became deeper and deeper.

This was mainly the result of the strained relationship between the two leading politicians. They were as strange to each other as only a man from the Rhineland and a West Prussian could be. Yet, after the death of Schumacher, Adenauer still stuck to the old military rule to pursue relentlessly the defeated enemy and to destroy him if possible.

To a certain extent the Social Democrats had to blame themselves for their plight. A simple and clear program of reconstruction and liberty was needed. My Social Democratic friends tried to do too much and squandered their efforts. The conservative forces which after a short "socialistic" interlude assumed the leadership of the Christian Democrats used mainly three arguments. They identified the plan-mad Left with the loathsome government-controlled economy from which the people had only recently been freed; they presented themselves as trustees of everything respectable—from the Church to the Allied Military Governors; and they associated the democratic Left with the conditions in the Communist realm.

That was unfair and ungrateful, but effective. The distortion of the Socialist idea in the East was grist to the mill of the Rightists—it compromised their opponents, at least in the eyes of many who had not yet started to think for themselves.

In Berlin the Social Democrats had taken the lead in the fight for liberty. In West Germany they were outdistanced and pushed to the wall.

My political activity brought me in ever closer contact with the Berlin organization of the Social Democratic party. In the sessions of its Central Committee I still participated as a non-voting member. Nevertheless, I was charged with many an important task. For instance, at a party congress I was asked to give a report on the programmatic principles of democratic socialism. I said among other things:

"Whoever wants to master the problems of our times ought to leave his collection of quotations at home. A man who always looks back is anything but radical. A party can follow a miserable policy in spite of an excellent program. On the other hand, it often happened that parties without a detailed and scientifically exact program had remarkable accomplishments to their credit.

"We can proudly refer to the start of the Socialist movement. But we cannot stop at the preservation of traditional theories and at the adaptation of tried methods. In politics not only the map but also the compass is, to a certain extent, subject to the law of change.

"Our generation must base its actions on a synthesis of sober knowledge and determined will. We must realize that over a lengthy period of time and in a larger context there is never just one possibility.

"First of all, it is up to us to make certain that the state of the future does not become a prison state. Democracy is for us not a question of expediency but of morality."

At this congress, in May 1949, Ernst Reuter asked me to become a member of his City Council. As far back as 1947 he had suggested that I take over the municipal press office. Now he wanted me to head the transport department which he himself had directed during the Weimar Republic and after his return. He was with heart and soul devoted to municipal affairs. In his opinion practical work in the community was the surest way to the building up and the strengthening of a democratic state. Every "national" politician ought to work his way up through the community, he stated.

Much could and can be said for this opinion I was attracted by the idea to direct an important department of the Berlin administration, but I could not renounce the duties with which the Executive Committee of my party had charged me. I also had made up my mind to enter the Parliament. Reuter was visibly disappointed, maybe even a little angry with me "for letting him down."

At the end of 1949, I was offered the chairmanship of a party local in the district of Wilmersdorf. I also took over the editorship of the party organ *Social Democrat,* which later, no longer under my direction, changed its name to *Berliner Stadtblatt* and became a weekly.

The obstacles I had to overcome in the Berlin party organization were not small. They were, in fact, bigger than I expected.

2

The period after the blockade was for Berlin a time of disappointment. The enthusiasm of victory quickly evaporated; there remained a feeling of lassitude; people were exhausted, a psychological reaction similar to the one the soldier feels when he returns from the front: he had been flattered and honored, but now, when he expects to earn the fruits of his heroic deeds—what does he get? Vain promises. One wants to get rid of me, that's all, he says to himself.

"One" was in this case the Allied authorities on the one hand, the Bonn politicians on the other.

The Allies concentrated their attention on the problems which were related to the Constitution of the Federal government; the politicians were occupied with the preparation—and later the results—of the elections. Most of the foreign correspondents moved to Frankfort and Bonn—Berlin was no longer "interesting."

The struggle for the material existence, for the economic future of Berlin was, although not so colorful and dramatic as the resistance during the blockade, no less hard and exhausting. That the people abroad, especially the countrymen in the West, took so little part in it, made it all the harder.

Berlin, impoverished as it was, could not hope to secure even the most primitive existence for its people out of its own efforts and means, not to speak of the gigantic task of reconstructing the industry which alone could help to alleviate the suffering of the steadily growing army of unemployed. At the beginning of 1950 out of 600,000 workers 300,000 were unemployed. Other hundreds of thousands were dependent on public aid.

At that time many Berliners were convinced the city could regain its vitality only when it became the capital of a united Germany again. Therefore, so they argued, all that could be done was to "make the best of it," live from hand to mouth until Berlin could finally be incorporated into the reconstructed nation. Reuter opposed these sentiments most strongly. Great aims must not be used as pretexts for doing nothing, he told us. Over those aims one must never forget the demands of the day.

In other words: we began with the reconstruction of Berlin

without knowing what its political future would be. We did not accept the worn-out maxim of the policy as the art of the possible, but decided to accomplish the seemingly impossible. We believed that there are not completely hopeless situations —if one is determined that they must not exist.

Berlin had to be reconstructed because of the people who lived there, who loved their city and would never leave it. Berlin also had to be reconstructed because here we could demonstrate our responsibility toward the whole of Germany, prove that we were sure of our cause, and would not allow ourselves to be put out.

But what did that mean: to reconstruct Berlin? It meant to transform a desert of rubble, to create new life out of ruins. People who previously had worked in the administration of the state had to find a different employment. The index of industrial production, however, was down to a fifth of the prewar level.

What mattered most was not to let Berlin be separated from West Germany, both financially and politically. During the blockade we had received, aside from the financial help on the part of the three Western zones, subsidies from Allied sources. The latter did no longer flow as abundantly as before. Instead Berlin had to become a part of the European Recovery Program. That was accomplished not without overcoming certain obstacles in Bonn.

In direct connection with these economic and financial efforts was Reuter's demand to have Berlin recognized as the twelfth of the federal *Länder* (states). I supported him with all my strength. This was not a mere constitutional formality. West Berlin could only live if the Berliners participated in the Federal legislation and thus achieved a standard of living which the city could not provide out of its own means.

But precisely this demand met with a strong opposition—in Berlin itself, in Bonn, and in the Allied capitals. The Allies insisted that the city could not belong to the German Republic since this would be contrary to the Four Power agreement on Berlin. Yet, no one of us had thought of touching, not to speak of curtailing, the occupation rights of the Western powers. Their agreements with the Soviet Union were out of question. All that we wanted was to reduce to a minimum the special status of Berlin.

When a change seemed in the offing, and in 1950 American officials confidentially gave Reuter to understand that Allied reservations to the Constitution might possibly be overcome if Bonn would take the initiative in this direction, it became apparent that the Chancellor was not at all willing to make such a step. The French were the least inclined to change the status of Berlin, and Konrad Adenauer was most anxious not to antagonize them.

In Bonn some people asserted in earnest that Berlin was "foreign country," it was "legally inadmissible" to grant Berlin the functions of a capital of the Federal Republic.

Reuter scoffed at this fainthearted attitude of certain influential people. As far back as the fall of 1949 he had said: "If I were the Chancellor I would go to Berlin and establish the Federal government in this city—and the Russians would certainly not start a war on account of it."

In the beginning of 1953 he remarked bitterly that "the biggest political mistake of these years was to move the temporary capital to the left bank of the Rhine."

When in 1951 suggestions came up to make out of Berlin a kind of UN enclave, Reuter declared in the city parliament:

"These ideas are not new, we have heard them quite often, and we have rejected them over and over again. We are not striving for an imaginary goal, an allegedly autonomous territory. We have said 'no' to the East, we have said 'yes' to the West; something third, a neutrality in between, a kind of principality of Monaco, does not exist. We want to see the

Federal Republic rooted as strongly as possible here in Berlin."

In spite of difficulties and insufficiencies some successes were achieved. The economic situation of our city improved slowly, but it did improve. Again there were well-lighted streets, heated apartments; the subways, trams, and buses ran as in peacetime.

The Federal government promised to contribute toward the deficit of the Berlin budget. The Berlin Central Bank was incorporated into the West German banking system. West Berlin goods were exempted from the sales tax in West Germany. Large sums out of the European Recovery Program were invested in public enterprises and in industry.

West Berlin was also incorporated into the judiciary system and the social legislation of the Federal Republic.

A decisive turning point on our difficult road was reached when in 1952 the third *Uberleitungsgesetz* (transitory law) was passed. The driving force behind this law—and behind all our negotiations with Bonn—was the Senator for Federal Affairs, my good friend Günter Klein. As a young *Landrat* (head of the administration of a Prussian district) he was dismissed by the Nazis in 1933. He took a minor job in an insurance business. From a simple salesman he rose to the position of the director of a big company.

At first the new law did not have the support of the Federal government. Thanks to the co-operation of all parties it was nevertheless passed. Henceforth Berlin's financial status was equal to that of all the other states. We transmitted our federal taxes to the Finance Minister in Bonn and profited, on the other hand, from the effects of the Federal legislation. The Federal subsidy which we received now had a legal basis.

As Reuter repeated over and over again, we wanted no alms. We felt offended by the word of "Berlin as a bottomless barrel." We wanted help to help ourselves in the sense of the

Marshall Plan. But we advanced only with great difficulties. Unemployment was hard to lick. When in 1950—on the basis of a program that had been elaborated in co-operation with American officials—Reuter declared that we would create 200,000 new jobs in the course of four years, many people thought him a visionary.

And yet from year to year progress was made. The Berliners again had some firm ground under their feet. But they were not yet out of the woods by a long shot.

3

During all those years I was absent from Berlin on many days. As a member of the Federal Parliament I had to spend much time in Bonn, I had to attend the plenary sessions or to participate in the deliberations of my party. Most often these obligations took up the major part of the week.

For my trips to and from Bonn I used the airplane, but flying was in those years not so comfortable as it became later on. I could not use the railway, or my car, since the authorities in the Soviet Zone would have arrested me. They considered me as the chief of the eastern office of my party. That function I have never held, although as a liaison man of the Executive Committee I had, of course, to deal with the problems of the Soviet Zone. I have also never made a secret of the repugnance I feel for the methods used in the Communist realm, and I thought it my duty to expose the terror whenever I had a chance to do so. Not until 1955, after I was elected President of the Berlin House of Representatives did I dare—at first against the advice of the "experts"—to drive with my car through the East Zone. The Communist control officials always treated me most politely.

In Bonn I was mainly concerned with the problems of foreign policy and questions related to Germany as a whole. I had to represent the interests of Berlin in a number of cases, both in the assembly and in committee meetings. I introduced, for instance, a motion to have the Federal laws applied to Berlin, too, although the content of some of these laws was neither to my nor to my party friends' liking. But we could not just pick the raisins out of the cake, so to speak; we had to take it as a whole or not have it at all. Wherever conditions in Berlin warranted it, I tried, not without success, to arrive at some special arrangement.

In 1952 we succeeded in having the number of the Berlin representatives increased from eight to nineteen. In the Parliament as well as in the Senate (*Bundestag* and *Bundesrat*) we had now greater influence but when it came to the decisive act—to the passing of laws—the Berlin votes were still not counted.

I made my first speech in a plenary session of the Parliament in November 1950, when I thanked our countrymen in all parts of the Federal Republic for all the material sacrifices they had made and continued to make for the sake of Berlin. But I also emphasized that there was still not enough done. In the following years I had to state many times that Berlin represented not a problem of charity but one of extreme importance to the political future of Germany. With this fact in mind we suggested repeatedly that some of the Federal ministries ought to be transferred to Berlin. I spoke many times on this subject and thus helped, to a certain extent, in winning some partial successes. In 1957, I published a little book *From Bonn to Berlin*, which gave a survey of our efforts in this field.

At the end of 1956, under the influence of the events in Poland and Hungary, what might almost be termed a movement started in West Germany for the transfer of the Federal government from Bonn to Berlin. Noted publicists and leading politicians were in favor. But the obstacles were insurmountable. I, therefore, concentrated my efforts on practical measures. the erection of Federal buildings, including the reconstruction of the Reichstag's ruin, the completion of the universities and of other cultural institutions I tried to get "as much as possible and as fast as possible."

I have asked myself many times whether the Russian attempt to throw the Allies out of Berlin—as it was launched in 1958—was not also the result of the hesitant and weak Berlin policy which West Germany and the Western powers had followed for years. I myself had demanded that this policy should be replaced by a "march back to Berlin." I wrote:

"Our countrymen in the Soviet-occupied zone will gain new strength. But also the people abroad, our neighbors in East and West, and all the others on whom the German future depends will sit up and take notice when they realize that the Germans work with energy and imagination for the systematic reconstruction of their capital and for giving Berlin, even in the period of Germany's division, the function of a capital."

The division between the Federal Republic and West Berlin was made more definite than the international situation or the Four Power agreements warranted or justified. The procrastinators may in most cases have had the best intentions, they may have taken legal threads for steel cables—in any event they did not serve the position of Berlin and its security as a part of the free Germany.

4

Ernst Reuter was a clear and warning example that performance—even recognized and successful performance—is not enough to achieve influence in a big and tightly organized party organization. He spent an excessive part of his strength in a perpetual guerrilla warfare against members of his own party.

Party work was not Reuter's forte. In addition, his relationship with Schumacher was not the best, and the chairman of the Berlin Social Democratic party organization, instead of giving him his loyal support, often adopted the attitude of a hostile rival. This was the result of the conflicting characters of these two men, rather than of differences of opinion about the political problems of the day.

I belonged among Reuter's closest friends. Together with some party functionaries and members of the Executive Committee of the Berlin state organization I fought the negative tendencies which in our opinion endangered Berlin, and also especially our party. Much time was lost in sessions, the sense of which was not often easy to understand. Often I had to report on political and theoretical problems. Gratifying was the relationship with Social Democrats in the East sector of Berlin; they lived in semi-legality, but among them we found men whose simple loyalty to party and idea was really heartwarming.

The latent tensions in the Berlin organization erupted into an open conflict when the party suffered a defeat in December 1950. In the meantime a new Constitution had been adopted. Berlin was now both city and state. The Municipal Assembly became the *Abgeordnetenhaus* (House of Representatives), the Municipal Council was now the Senate. The lord mayor was given the somewhat bombastic title *Regierender Burgermeister* (governing mayor) to indicate that he had not only the duties of the head of a city but also those of the prime minister of a German state.

In the elections for the new House of Representatives the Social Democrats lost—in comparison to December 1948—200,000 votes; the two other parties together had a majority of five seats. The result expressed the attraction which the Federal government and the prosperity in West Germany held for the general public. In addition, the Berliners could not always follow the Social Democratic opposition in the *Bundestag*. But this did not mean that they were turning away from Reuter. Most of the Berliners wanted him to continue to govern the city. In a personal election he would have won a tremendous victory.

It was quite different as far as his own party was concerned. Some blamed Reuter for the defeat and declared it was brought about by the co-operation with the other democratic parties which Reuter advocated. There followed protracted discussions as to whether the new Senate should be formed again on the basis of a coalition. And after that had been decided, there started long and bitter quarrels about our relationship with Bonn and about the incorporation of Berlin into the legislative Federal system. In this question Schumacher and the party Executive Committee unequivocally supported the "Reuter line."

But aside from this question there existed open and hidden conflicts. The Social Democratic leaders in Bonn were in violent opposition to Adenauer, who would have made it difficult for even the most conciliatory and clever antagonist to create an atmosphere conducive to a fruitful co-operation. In Berlin, on the other hand, we had to be interested in amicably settling our differences with Adenauer's party friends.

In Bonn the Social Democrats felt slighted by the Allies, who always sided with the government. They reacted with a certain mistrust against the ambassadors and the governments of the Western powers. In Berlin, under the direct threat of the Communists, we realized the necessity of keeping our position in the Western camp. And last but not least, we knew how important it was to have the United States on our side.

The conflicting points of view became especially apparent when in the spring of 1950 at the party congress in Hamburg the majority of the Berlin delegation openly adopted a position contrary to the one of the Bonn Executive Committee. In question was the entrance of the Federal Republic into the Council of Europe.

Germany was to be an associated member only, and by voting "no" Schumacher hoped to gain a status of equality, and to prevent the definite separation of the Saar territory. The Montan union which the Schuman Plan had as its aim seemed to Schumacher dangerous because in his opinion it might lead to a supranational trust. In general he was afraid that by this development the basis was laid for a catholic conservative Little Europe and that hence the Federal Republic might be diverted from its main task—the reunification of Germany.

One cannot deny that some of these fears later on proved justified. Other objections in the course of time lost their importance. One also cannot deny that the foreign policy of Germany would have been much more effective if the government had shown a greater interest in a fair co-operation with the opposition.

In 1950, I belonged to the critics of the official line of my party, for I thought that in spite of all deficiencies the new forms of a European co-operation were a step forward, a step in the right direction. Together with my Berlin friends I was afraid that an intransigent attitude might isolate us in the Western community and rob us of our influence. Even the arguments of my good and esteemed friend Carlo Schmid, who presented Schumacher's thesis very effectively at a meeting of the Berlin functionaries, could not convince us.

It was different when in the fall of 1950 the question of Germany's rearmament became the central theme of our political discussions. In consideration of the war in Korea, Adenauer had offered a contribution to the defense of the Western community without asking the Parliament or even his own colleagues in the government. In this question—and what has been forgotten by friend and foe—Schumacher took anything but a "negative" line.

He went even further than Adenauer at that time. He asked that first the Allies strengthen their own military position in Germany. The Western defense ought to be established as far eastward as possible. The German defense contribution was to be made dependent on the granting of full equality—equal risks, equal obligations.

Schumacher had his own party only partially behind him. Many heard only his objections, did not understand or did not accept his basic attitude. The Social Democratic position in regard to the defense of the country remained for many years unclear and contradictory.

Together with my friend Fritz Erler, who as member of Parliament had undertaken the thankless job of acting as the Social Democratic spokesman in all military matters, I was labeled an especially "militaristic" Socialist. In fact, we were only concerned about the relationship between labor and the state, including its armed forces; we knew that either you lick the army problem or the army licks you.

It is remarkable—and to a certain extent paradoxical—that Fritz Erler, who rightly is regarded as an expert in military matters and has as such the respect of the highest military figures of the West—has never been a soldier himself. Immediately after being drafted at the beginning of the war, he was arrested by the Gestapo as one of the leaders of the underground. He was condemned to ten years of hard labor. Not only did the prison save him from the certain death which he would no doubt have faced in a concentration camp, but he found also in prison the opportunity for intensive study. He learned languages and acquired an unusually sound military knowledge. When a few weeks before the end of the war his prison was evacuated, he succeeded in jumping from a train and hid out till the day of surrender.

I don't want to deny that the procedure which was followed in regard to the German rearmament startled and alarmed me. Just a few short years before, when the Federal Republic was formed, it had been solemnly proclaimed that the Germans never again would carry arms. And suddenly the new signals! It was good that they evoked no military enthusiasm. Our friends abroad were horrified at the reaction of the Germans who were not eager at all to take up arms again, as they were now expected to do. But it was better than if the opposite reaction had taken place.

In December 1950, I was elected a member of the Berlin House of Representatives. In 1952, I ran against Franz Neumann for the office of the chairman of the Social Democratic party in Berlin; Reuter had asked me to. I knew that I could not win, but I had counted on more than a third of the votes. For six more years the fight for the leadership of the Berlin party organization continued.

In August 1952, Kurt Schumacher died. That was a heavy blow for the party, a grave loss for Germany. Some of his opponents admitted it. In spite of all the criticism that his autocratic leadership and some of his decisions deserved—Schumacher's integrity, his will power, his idealism was a great asset for the Federal Republic, for the German people.

The previous spring Schumacher had again called on me for advice and co-operation. He also had not opposed my candidacy for the Berlin party chairmanship. In August 1952, I was on vacation in the Norwegian mountains; a few weeks before I had had a long conversation with the party leader. Did he have a foreboding of his death? A strange, almost pathetic contradiction showed itself in his statements.

On the one hand, he criticized the stubbornness of a certain type of party functionary and demanded a greater intellectual independence; on the other hand, he defended the yes men, who always agreed with everything he said and did.

I had the impression that he himself was aware of these contradictions and that he suffered from them. All the greater was my grief when I received the news of his death.

5

In the spring of 1952, Stalin made a proposal which at the first glance could be interpreted as the Soviet government's consent to the reunification of Germany—provided she remained "neutral."

There were doubts, certainly not without cause, as to whether that offer of the Soviet Union was genuine. Nevertheless, I and my party friends and also some of my colleagues in the government parties regretted that no attempt was made to put the Russian sincerity to a test. Even in 1955, when Adenauer visited Moscow, no precise question was raised as to what military status of a reunited Germany the Soviet Union was ready to accept.

Indeed, there were many indications that Stalin only for form's sake declared himself in favor of German unity, and never dreamed of retreating from his advanced positions on the Elbe and Werra rivers. At that time the treaty over the European defense community was about to be ratified; that was enough reason for a countermove on the part of the Kremlin.

That was also reason enough for the Western powers to reject everything that might disturb their plans. John Foster Dulles told me some years later the Americans, in spite of all other differences, agreed with the Russians that it was contrary to the interests of both sides to leave Germany outside of any firm alliance. He, therefore, thought it quite possible that in the end the Russians might accept the military control of Germany in the framework of NATO.

My friends and I were not at all against the Western cooperation. We certainly did not want to shirk a German contribution to the common defense effort. The question was not whether the defense was to be set up but how it was to be organized. We were afraid the West might adopt a rigid military position and neglect to fight the Cold War on the no less important political front. In other words· was not the liberation of the Soviet Zone in Germany worth more than a number of divisions? In any case we wanted the West not to give the impression that it had left unused even a slight chance in the struggle for Germany's unity.

A few months later, in July 1952, there was the first reading of the European Defense Community Treaty in the *Bundestag* I mentioned the voices of despair which we heard daily from the East Zone, voices that mirrored a mood of "better an end with horrors than horrors without end." I expressed our full sympathy with the terrible fate of our countrymen behind the Iron Curtain but stated plainly and clearly that "the solution of the problem of German unity must not be sought by military means."

When at the end of 1952, after long deliberations in the Committee of Foreign Affairs, the Parliament had to decide on the European Defense Treaty, I reported on the majority and minority opinions of the Committee. I pointed out that the people of Germany had gladly accepted the disarmament of the Federal Republic. All members of the Committee on Foreign Affairs were in agreement that the German policy must be based on the preservation of peace and that the reunification should only be attempted by peaceful means. However, nobody was of the opinion that Germany must never and under any circumstances rearm or participate in a broad defense organization.

In the following debate I stated that nobody underestimated the difficulties which everyone faces when confronted with developing a German foreign policy. "Of course we don't blame Dr. Adenauer for not having won the war. We know very well that the German policy must be conducted in a very narrow frame." But, I added, it is not easy to reach the right goal from a false start. The Western community will only endure if the essential interests of all the partners in the alliance will be taken into consideration.

I spoke of the danger that the "Cold War might be replaced by a Cold Peace at any price which would perpetuate the division of the continent and of our country."

In general I pointed out that the Germans must not overestimate their influence in the world; nor should they underestimate how decisive their own position is:

"We must awake the satisfied and the tired, the lazy and complacent, and never stop asking ourselves whether the German policy has really done all it could do to concentrate all the forces of our nation on one decisive point and to imbue the people with a boundless will to win the struggle for the reunification of Germany."

*

CHAPTER TWELVE

I Become Mayor of Berlin

1

It has never occurred to us that our only task was to save Berlin and to somehow pull our city through the period of Germany's unnatural division. We have always regarded it as our principal duty to work—at least to speak—also on behalf of our countrymen in Soviet Germany, who had been robbed of the freedom of speech, press, and organization and who are still bereft of it.

It was Berlin's task to form the living link—not between the regimes but between the people, the families that arbitrarily had been separated. We have tried to prevent the political division from developing into an irreparable mutual alienation of the people. The spirit of solidarity has been stronger in our city than it is between the two parts of Germany. Many a Federal Republican seemed to think that he was the better German. And yet some had been as little able to choose the Americans or British, as the others had been in the position to reject the Russians; the latter had only drawn the smaller prize.

But there were grave danger signs in Berlin, too I live not far from the zonal border. Often people from the border areas appeared in our district to sell something or to ask for some help. In former years they were more conspicuous than now by their worn-out clothes. One day my wife told me excitedly of an incident she had witnessed. Some transport workers had chased a visitor from the zone away from our door telling him that "Russians" had no business to be here. Ruth was quite bewildered, remembered her experiences in Norway, and asked anxiously whether things had already gone so far in Germany—that some Germans could regard their fellow citizens as foreigners.

This was rather an unusual and singular incident, but still there were reasons for apprehension. Often, for instance, the question was raised whether the refugees were not given undue preferences; we had so many unemployed ourselves, so many hunting for a home, so many in charge of public welfare. Others declared that the majority of the refugees had not been exposed to serious dangers at all, and would have done better staying at home.

We have never rejoiced at the high numbers of refugees. Like many others, I also have worried about the depopulation of the zone. But I have always taken the point of view that we could only *ask* our countrymen not to flee unnecessarily; we were, however, not in the position to constitute ourselves as judges over those who could no longer live under the Soviet German domination—even if they had in some individual case not been exposed to bodily dangers but were only seeking a better life. It is not a crime to give way to pressure and have the wish to improve one's situation—especially in one's own country.

I have always sponsored the maintenance of as many personal contacts with the Soviet Zone as possible. This was not only a matter of letters, and parcels, and visits—as far as they were permitted. It was not only a question of our Eastern visitors being able to partake of West Berlin's cultural life. It was not the least of our duties to help the victims of the Communist terror, and their families

I have declared myself emphatically against "political adventures," against mixing up welfare activities with politics or even with intelligence work, not because I wanted to please the Communists, but in the interest of the people concerned. As for the rest, I stood and stand on the right to help and comfort the victims This is not only a right but also an obligation If someone calls this objectionable or subversive, let him. But the Communists are not at all fit to play the part of censors of political morals.

Of the fate of the political prisoners I was not only informed in reports and by moving appeals from the zone, I had personal friends among those who for their convictions —or merely as victims of a blind despotism—were tortured, sentenced to long years of hard labor, and sent to Siberia. At the beginning of 1949, I was suddenly informed one night that a member of the East Bureau of the Social Democrats whom I knew very well had been abducted from the French sector. He was beaten terribly and had to endure horrible tortures. It did not particularly surprise me that some weeks later the obligatory "confession" appeared in the Eastern press in which I was called an "agent of the Norwegian Intelligence Service." But I was overjoyed—and astonished—when after some seven years my friend was released. He himself could not quite believe it when an amnesty opened for him the way to a new life.

During the time of National Socialism as well as later on I had the experience that a totalitarian regime is by far not so hard to influence as people often think. The dictators are not completely indifferent to world public opinion. Many a life has been saved, many sufferings could be mitigated by breaking through the walls of silence, tearing apart the veil of anonymity. Therefore, I have repeatedly stood up for the deported, the political prisoners, and the prisoners of war, arbitrarily kept in captivity.

In the summer of 1952, I submitted to the *Bundestag* the case of Dr. Walter Linse, a lawyer who had been abducted from West Berlin, I stated that this was a provocation, a challenge to the whole nation. I denounced kidnaping as the worst abuse of human rights:

"There is the saying that he who courts danger must expect to perish therein. We say, he who assists the population of the zone, who tries to enforce the law, deserves well of the nation and of the state; as much as everyone deserved well of the nation and of the state who offered resistance to Nazi despotism and helped its victims. We appeal to the conscience of the world. Knock with us at the prison door until it opens. There must be an end to kidnaping!"

In April 1953, I spoke in the *Bundestag* about the fate of journalists imprisoned in the Soviet Zone. I particularly interested myself in the case of Herbert Kluge, a colleague of mine who on a trip from Berlin to West Germany had been dragged out of the autobus and was sentenced to fifteen years of hard labor for his work as a journalist. Our endeavors had at least the result that the greater part of his penalty was remitted I declared in Bonn:

"The name Kluge stands today for all those innocent victims of despotism. We are indebted to all of them: the civil- and the war-prisoners in the jails of the Soviet Zone and in the camps which lie farther east. My political friends and I have no greater wish than that there may be a *détente* in international affairs, and we hold that German politics must actively and boldly pursue this aim, but on the premise only that the solution is sought on the basis of freedom and humanity. He who wishes a peaceful co-existence of the nations ought at least—and first of all—open the prison gates to those who have been innocently condemned and imprisoned."

2

In our fast-moving times the memory of even important political occurrences does not last long, particularly since in the last decades we have been swamped with historical events, many of them have been called "turning points in history," although they were by no means so decisive as the exaggerating chroniclers of our era chose to depict them. To attract the attention of the public every election, every speech, every conference of the foreign ministers is called "historical"—an inflation of big words which made people indifferent even to the essentially important events.

And yet we are not guilty of rhetorical exaggeration if we say today that the seventeenth of June, 1953, is a historical date. This day, together with the twentieth of July, 1944—has given us the right to call Berlin the Capital of Resistance.

The uprising of the people in East Berlin and the Soviet Zone was more than an outbreak of despair—it was of international significance. This was recognized even quicker and more clearly beyond the borders of Germany than in certain circles of the Federal Republic.

On the other hand, what was often overlooked abroad was the twofold character of the rebellion. It did not only result from the yearning for *national* freedom, but also for *social* liberation. The workers—and they were the vanguard and the body of the insurgents—rebelled against a system that had disguised slavery under the shabby cloak of an abused, so-called "socialism."

The unmasking of communism as the enemy of the weak, of the helpless, of the workers, whose advocate and guardian it always had claimed to be, had consequences which no countermeasures of the Kremlin could undo. Those consequences strongly influenced the political development in the countries under the Soviet rule. Immediately after those events I wrote a pamphlet titled "Worker and Nation." The following extracts give, I think, a good picture of those days. I wrote:

"At first sight it may be surprising why the workers in Central Germany started the riots just at that time. Sure enough, the dictatorship in the Soviet Zone had become more and more unbearable. At the beginning of 1953 the supply of food and basic commodities had almost completely collapsed. But on the other hand, the rulers had at the beginning of June just announced measures which promised a certain relief and some economic improvement."

Since Stalin's death the men in the Kremlin were obviously inclined to review their policy toward Germany. The mass flight from the zone—more than 50,000 refugees in March alone!—alarmed the Soviet authorities. They ordered the "Unity party" to slow down the pace of Bolshevization. The farmers were promised that the enforced collectivization would be restricted, artisans and businessmen were assured of considerable relief. Some thousand persons who had been condemned for minor "economic crimes," were released. But all these measures were regarded with much distrust by the population of the East Zone. The workers quite correctly felt that within the leading circles of the party there was uncertainty; the power apparatus seemed to go through a crisis, and they wanted to take advantage of it. And when at the beginning of June the rulers of the zone raised the norms of production, the signal was given.

According to the Communist propaganda the plants in the Soviet Zone belonged to the workers, therefore, it was unreasonable for them to strike "against themselves." But the workers knew that the nationalization was not at all to their advantage. They were faced with the most powerful and reckless employer. They had not been given co-determination in the factories, much less a chance for a democratic influence on the government.

The economic policy in the Soviet Zone was aimed at increasing productivity by a steady increase of output and decrease in wages. All demands to adjust the lower wages to those of the better-paid workers were strictly rejected. Thus, the gap was continually widened between the income of the privileged groups and the average wages The regime deliberately tried to tie a group of managers, leading engineers, and "activists" closely to its cause, and to play them off against the mass of workers and employees.

By an official decree dated May 28, all the norms were ordered to be raised by at least ten per cent till the end of June. In the building trade the consequences were particularly hard. Masons lost thirty per cent of their wages, carpenters more than forty per cent.

In May and in the first days of June stormy protests were raised in many plants against the increase of norms and the lack of food. Especially great was the dissatisfaction among the workers in East Berlin's Stalinallee. On the fifteenth of June work was stopped temporarily on several sites.

The morning of June 16 a party secretary declared in the Stalinallee that the increase of norms would be carried out in any case. Thereupon eighty men of block forty put down their tools. They wanted to submit a resolution of protest to the government. Behind a red sign with the watchword "We Demand a Reduction of Norms," the workers marched to the central office of the so-called *Freier Gewerkschaftsbund* (Free Trade Union Federation).

On their march they got reinforcements. The original eighty became hundreds, soon there were more than two thousand men. Their rhythmic shouts rang through the streets: "Mates, join in, this is the beginning!"

The workers found the doors of the *Freier Gewerkschaftsbund* locked. Thereupon the steadily growing procession marched on to the government building in Leipziger Strasse, the former Air Ministry. The excitement grew from minute to minute. People no longer shouted for higher wages and lower norms, they shouted for free elections, they demanded the overthrow of the government.

When the demonstrators were just about to retreat in good order, riot cars with loud-speakers appeared; it was announced that the Cabinet had countermanded the norms. Some hours earlier this news would most probably have calmed down the excited workers. But now they regarded it as a proof of the weakness of the regime. The knowledge of their own power was intoxicating. Already the workers demanded the general strike.

In the afternoon of this sixteenth of June the East sector of Berlin offered quite an unusual sight. At all street corners gathered large groups of debating people. Functionaries of the Communist Unity party, who had been sent out to bring the workers round, got laughed at; some got a good beating. The general strike could no longer be stopped.

It began in the night of June 16.

In the morning of June 17 ten thousand marched to the government quarter. They broke through the barriers of the police. From the suburbs of the East sector new columns of workers arrived. They carried black-red-gold flags, some of them adorned with flowers, and signs with the words "Free Elections" on them. The workers had set out just as they were: some wearing clogs, others with naked chests, their goggles pushed up to their foreheads, many with pokers and other tools.

Some 100,000 people had by now gathered in the Leipziger Strasse. Beside strong police forces Soviet troops had marched up to protect the seat of the government. But the workers could not be bullied. Again and again the Berlin wit broke through: "Ulbricht, Pieck, and Grotewohl, soon we'll put you in the hole!" "We do not need a norm, today we are in form!"

The rage increased from minute to minute. A group of demonstrators tore down the red flag of the occupation power from the Brandenburg Gate and hoisted the black-red-gold flag in its place. About 50,000 workers assembled in the Lustgarten. Everywhere in East Berlin riots started at the same time. The central office of the Communist Unity party was besieged by a huge crowd, tanks relieved it eventually. A building of the security police was stormed by another crowd. In front of the police headquarters overturned police cars were burning. The propaganda kiosks and sales stalls of the state-owned Commercial Organization, called HO, were smashed to pieces.

In the morning hours Russian armored cars appeared in the streets In the course of the day two armored divisions were concentrated. At noon tanks intervened. The workers greeted them with the song "*Brüder zur Sonne, zur Freiheit,*" the tune of which was well known to the Russians.

Presently the first shots rang out. But while youths and women turned to flee, the workers locked arms and advanced against the firing troops Here and there the ranks of the workers wavered, some workers were hit by bullets and had to be carried away, but the others stood like a rock.

At 1:30 P.M. the Soviet Commandant proclaimed the state of siege.

Still, the crowds did not disperse; they held their ground, workers continued to stream into the city from the suburbs. Not until evening did peace slowly return. Behind units of the People's Police and Soviet infantry tanks had driven up along the borders of the Russian sector. They secured "peace and order."

The open intervention of the Soviet forces made it clear to

the East Berliners that further actions were hopeless. It was impossible to continue the general strike under the state of martial law. And yet two days passed until the workers returned to their factories.

The news of the riots in Berlin spread through the Soviet Zone in a flash. On the seventeenth of June, and on the following days, riots, strikes, and demonstrations occurred in 272 towns and communities. Grotewohl declared before the Central Committee of the Unity party that "only" 300,000 workers had taken part in the strike. Actually, it was a powerful revolt of the people, especially in the industrial centers of Saxony and Thuringia, the traditional strongholds of the German labor movement.

The seventeenth of June was marked by the fact that the strike of the workers widely assumed the character of a mass revolt. The people did not only rebel against insufficient wages—they wanted freedom. Following the pattern of the great revolutions the fury of the crowd was directed against prisons and jails. Many of them were stormed, some thousand prisoners were set free.

The failure of the People's Police was remarkable. It proved unreliable in many cases. Remarkable, too, was the conduct of many Russian officers and soldiers, who openly showed that their sympathies were on the side of the workers. These soldiers shot into the air or calmly watched the demonstrators turn against the police.

The number of the victims has never been exactly ascertained, but it became known that sixteen death sentences were pronounced by Soviet court-martials. According to reliable estimates no less than four thousand people were arrested in East Berlin, sixteen thousand in the entire zone. The greater part was soon released, but thousands remained imprisoned.

Yet it would be wrong to say that the seventeenth of June

was "unsuccessful." The immediate aim of the East Berlin masons was realized, the work norms were reduced. The economic and social demands of the workers found a certain consideration in the following months. Travel between the two parts of Germany was facilitated; some years later, however, an inhuman passport law canceled these improvements.

A basic change in the general conditions could not be accomplished under the given circumstances. The government was powerless, but the Soviet tanks filled the vacuum. This was the hard lesson of those exciting summer days

On July 1, 1953, the *Bundestag* in Bonn decided to proclaim the seventeenth of June as the "Day of German Unity" —unfortunately, to many people in the German west it has become nothing more than an additional holiday. At that occasion I made a speech in the *Bundestag*, which by many people was criticized as too harsh. Yet, I was motivated only by my passionate desire to demonstrate to the people in the zone that they were not alone and not forgotten.

First, I pointed out that the uprising of the people in East Berlin and in the Soviet Zone had been the deed of those workers who could by no means be regarded as an indistinguishable mass without a creative will of their own: "These workers have not only as fellow combatants but also as champions proved themselves in the forefront of the fight for unity in freedom. As in all the great revolutionary crises, they have combined the fight for their immediate economic and social demands with the interests of the whole nation and have raised the fight for unity, the central desire of our nation, to a higher level."

I spoke of the world-wide echo the events in the zone had evoked and said:

"The struggle for a reunification in freedom has the precedence of all plans and projects in foreign affairs. We will not make any progress with the hesitation and timidity of those who apparently fear nothing more than the possibility that their own cherished plans might be discarded by a successful policy of reunification.

"The workers in the zone have recognized the moment when spontaneous actions could be started. Now it is our task in the Western world to recognize the moment when the German question can—if at all—be solved on an international level. Of course, no one of us is foolish enough to declare that a positive result is certain We are armed with skepticism. But in spite of skepticism and distrust we believe that negotiations ought to be attempted, and the attempt has to be made quickly.

"We cannot with a clear conscience tell the eighteen million in the East Zone to wait till doomsday. Neither by what we do nor by what we not do must we expose these eighteen million people in the zone to the danger that the powers which have been shaken and may eventually be overthrown by an all-German settlement become consolidated again.

"In the years past, those were guilty of illusions and of a lack of realism who did not take into account eventual negotiations between East and West. By the way, we still regard it as a great danger that for the time being the great powers do not talk about a solution of the German question at all.

"There is no other solution than the peaceful solution of the German problem. There is no other possibility than to negotiate about the German question. We demand more activity, more clarity, more determination in the fight for German unity in peace and freedom."

3

Those who had hoped the democracies would seize the opportunity of the seventeenth of June to put political pressure on the Soviet Union, at least show a new initiative on the diplomatic level, were soon bitterly disappointed.

In the zone there were many who had misunderstood the attitude of the Western powers and Adenauer's slogan of the "Policy of Strength." They had hoped that they would be given military assistance. This was a tragic error.

The Soviet government was—after Stalin's death—in a crisis. An attempt should have been made to take advantage of it, to strengthen the position of the West in Berlin, to lighten the burden of the suppressed people in the East of Germany. The advanced European positions of the Soviet occupation power could have been made the subject of serious negotiations. But the Allies seemed primarily determined to prove that they were in no way responsible for the East German rebellion. They did not want to get involved in the eventual consequences of the events. By their political passivity they left the field to the Soviet government.

In the Eastern camp serious doubts were raised about the reliability and trustworthiness of the West. The discrepancy between strong words and the actual passivity was in many places considered as very distressing. The rulers in the Kremlin and their satraps in Eastern Europe were the beneficiaries. Their self-confidence grew. Even Walter Ulbricht survived his disgrace and exposure on the seventeenth of June. The Communist regime was strengthened by the fact that parts of the anti-Communist population decided there was nothing doing, they had to get along with the regime.

The events in the German East Zone in 1953 were to become the precedent of the Hungarian tragedy three years later: a courageous uprising of the population, merciless intervention of the Soviets, stupor of the West.

But above all it was disheartening to see what faint echo the events found in the Federal Republic. Of course, the people were interested or even shocked; of course, the flags were hoisted at half-mast; of course, many speeches were made. But most of the speeches dealt with the elections for the second *Bundestag,* three months after the seventeenth of June. They ended with a great victory of Konrad Adenauer's Christian Democratic Union.

Those were elections in the wake of the *Wirtschaftswunder,* of satiated content, of materialistic egoism. All this was not so hard to explain. People were glad about the successful reconstruction and had, I think, good reasons to be proud of what they had accomplished in the postwar years—and what the Federal government in Bonn now took all the credit for. Many people forgot the Marshall Plan aid, which had been the initial source of the new prosperity. Others overlooked the fact that circumstances which originally had been heavy burdens proved blessings in disguise and initiated the boom.

The damages inflicted by the war and aggravated by the dismantling of plants and machinery also necessitated the reconstruction of a supermodern industry. The millions of displaced people from the East and the refugees from the Soviet Zone—a quarter of the population of the Federal Republic—had difficulty in finding their places in West Germany's economic life, but they also formed the pool which was supplying manpower for years. The reconstruction was largely performed by means of high prices and low wages. In a few years huge fortunes were amassed. But the rank and file of the population profited too. And, therefore, it was not astonishing that most of the people had only a sole aim: to make money.

A man like Ernst Reuter was shocked at the German people's lack of readiness to make sacrifices, and at the attempts of many to push aside difficult decisions and their obligations toward the community in order to indulge undisturbed in the—mostly rather modest—pleasures offered by the economic prosperity. He had asked that we should be ready to give our last shirt to recover freedom for the people in the zone. But this appeal corresponded very little to the frame of mind of people who were all too glad to have a few shirts in their wardrobe again.

In the circle around Ernst Reuter we discussed openly and on the whole justly the mistakes and weaknesses which had led to the defeat of the Social Democratic party in the general elections. I, too, was numbered among the "reformers"

Ernst Reuter was bitter, he had hoped for a change of course in Bonn. We did not know then how much his health was affected, how much his heart had suffered. He never complained, never consulted a doctor. His best friends did not know how ill he was So, his death came quite unexpectedly.

On that twenty-ninth of September I was at home, at my desk. A telephone call came from Oslo. The newspaper of the Norwegian government—though a member of the *Bundestag* I had not given up my journalistic activity—asked me to dictate an obituary on Reuter at once.

In the first moment I did not understand what they meant. Reuter dead? I could not believe it.

Fifteen minutes later I was in Reuter's little house in the Bülowstrasse.

When I walked home benumbed and troubled, I saw an unforgettable sight. In all apartments, in each street I passed, candles were suddenly burning in the windows. Nobody had called on the people for such a demonstration. The general feeling of personal grief wanted an outlet. And so people remembered that Reuter himself had asked them the Christmas before to put candles in the windows as a greeting to the prisoners far away—as a pledge of faith and solidarity with all the persons who were the dearest to each of them and whom they did not want to forget.

Those innumerable, flickering little flames behind the windowpanes looked like innumerable glittering tears. The Berliner wept wherever he received the news—at the radio, at the street corners reading the special editions of the newspapers. A whole city was mourning for its dead leader; the people were moved as many Americans were when in April of 1945 President Roosevelt left them forever. I had received the news of his death when I was among my friends in Stockholm; it had moved me deeply, too. Five years earlier in my hiding place near the Oslo fjord I had followed the discussion about the third nomination of the great President, whom I have always kept in high esteem, notwithstanding the mistakes he made toward the end of the war.

When on the first of October at a huge rally in the later Ernst-Reuter-Platz we Social Democrats of Berlin bade farewell to Germany's great son, I said:

"Berlin is weeping for its protagonist in the fight for its own right and the freedom of all. The young generation is not only mourning for the father of the people. You have been at the same time our teacher, our adviser, and our friend.

"You were master of the rare art to render complicated problems simple without ever becoming banal. Your words were always unpretentious, impressive, humane. You could speak as well to university professors as to workers.

"You never doubted of the victory of Freedom. Therefore, you were able to inspire those who worked with you, the whole population, but first of all the young people, with hope and confidence. Sometimes you have been called 'too much of an optimist.' What would have become of this Berlin without the stubborn will and without the faith that moves mountains!

"Your own struggle has made you aware of the fundamental motives of the Socialist movement, which will outlast every temporary program. Intellectual narrowness, boisterous mediocrity, and paltry quarrels were repugnant to you. What you did, you did thoroughly."

This was one of the greatest funerals Berlin has ever seen. And the following days brought many more commemorative addresses and manifestations of thankful memory. But nothing was, I think, as moving and solemn in its immediate expression of grief and affection as the silent parade of candles on the evening of Reuter's death.

Together with my friend Richard Lowenthal, who had acquired English nationality and had become political editor of the London *Observer,* I undertook the task of describing Ernst Reuter's life in a political biography which appeared in 1957. Through this work I have learned much for my own political activity.

4

When the second *Bundestag* was constituted, in the autumn of 1953, I was made a member of the Executive Committee of the Social Democratic parliamentary group. But I still was not admitted to the leadership of the party. I was defeated at the party congress in Berlin, in 1954, and two weeks later in Munich; not before 1958, in Stuttgart, was I elected a member of the Executive Committee of the Social Democratic party of Germany.

In the Berlin organization of my party, however, and on the political scene of Berlin in general, I had in the meantime gained some appreciation in spite of a strong hostility on the part of some functionaries. In the spring of 1954, at the request of some friends of Reuter's, I again ran for the post of chairman of the Berlin organization and was defeated by just two votes; I became vice chairman.

After Ernst Reuter's death the coalition of the three democratic parties in the Senate of Berlin had broken apart. The Christian Democrats and the Free Democrats governed for more than a year without the party which was by far the strongest. At the elections in December 1954 the Social Democrats, although they did not gain a greater percentage of the votes, received a bare majority of seats. I became President of the House of Representatives, as successor to Professor Suhr, who now, as governing mayor, was at the head of a Senate constituted by the Social Democrats and the Christian Democrats.

President of the House of Representatives—because of Berlin's postwar tradition, this was an honorable post and offered the opportunity of political activity beyond the confines of one's own party. But it also was a post of honor, though it took up much of one's time. I retained my mandate in the *Bundestag*, to the regret of some of my friends. There were some political reasons that could be stated in favor of this coupling of posts, but actually I too was distressed by the feeling that I could no longer concern myself with my parliamentary work in Bonn to the same degree that I had tried to do in the years past.

In Berlin my word carried weight with great sections of my own party, and not only there. In many a discussion, on many an occasion I was—which did not escape me—measured against Ernst Reuter. This was encouragement and obligation at the same time.

At the beginning of November 1956, I was pushed into the foreground in quite another manner than I would have liked. It was the reaction to an event which had occurred far from Berlin—the Hungarian revolt.

To protest against the brutal suppression of the revolt in Budapest, the parties in Berlin had called the population to a demonstration in front of the Schöneberg City Hall. They underestimated the tension of feelings, the rage of the Berliners; the news from Hungary roused the memory of the riots in East Berlin; wounds, scarcely healed, burst open again.

There were surely a hundred thousand people who assembled on that evening, a great part of them desperate and embittered. The feeling of impotency, the knowledge that the people in Budapest were being abandoned by the West just as the East Berliners had been three years ago, heightened their furious indignation.

The speakers at that rally had a difficult task. The well-meant words found no response. The chairman of the Social Democratic organization was hissed and booed. The chairman of the Christian Democrats, Ernst Lemmer, fared not much better, he could make himself heard only with great difficulty. Appeals to prudence and reason merely fell flat, the crowd wanted to see "action." The catcalls came down thick from all sides. Someone in the crowd shouted: "To Brandenburg Gate!" Others took up the cry: "To the Soviet embassy!" or "Russians go home!"

As a speaker, who had not been on the program at first, I could hardly make myself understood. But the people agreed with me when I reminded them of the responsibility of the United Nations. Emphatically I warned of slogans which, if practiced, would not help our cause, nor the cause of the Hungarian freedom fighters either. To prevent a wild march on the East sector, I asked the crowd to march with me to the Steinplatz and stage a demonstration in front of the memorial for the Victims of Stalinism.

Many of them followed me, others went home A first success was achieved. On the Steinplatz I found words which expressed rather adequately our feelings in this hour, and when I intonated the song of the "Good Comrade" they all chimed in.

Then, suddenly, alarming news came. A few thousand demonstrators, mostly young people, had formed a column and, with torches in their hands, had marched to the Brandenburg Gate. Another, greater part was stopped in the Street of the 17th of June by the West Berlin police. There had been bloody clashes, and with every minute the situation became more and more critical. Ruth and I jumped into a car and hurried to the Tiergarten; we had to prevent the worst. The worst were violent clashes on the border of the Russian sector. There were not only People's Police at the Brandenburg Gate, ready to fire, but also Russian tanks had driven up in the bystreets of the "Linden." If Soviet troops were attacked and started shooting, it could mean war.

From a riot car of the police, the panes of which had been smashed, I seized a microphone and addressed the infuriated crowd, most of them students and other youths, whose honest intentions were beyond doubt, whose feelings I well understood. But they were not aware of the consequences of their actions. I told them very bluntly that we would play into the hands of the Russians if we fought against each other and let the others provoke us. The pressure on the police barrier slackened. Ruth, who had disappeared among the crowd, gathered some levelheaded students about her; they helped to calm the crowd, reason was getting a hold on the people. Then the moment came when here too we could sing the song of the "Good Comrade"—demonstrators and policemen together, who a few minutes before had been at each other's throats.

At this moment I received a message urging me to come at once to the Brandenburg Gate; there the situation had come to a dangerous point. When I arrived some minutes later, the president of the police had already, by personal entreaties, succeeded in dispersing a part of the demonstrators. I jumped on the top of a car and bluntly explained again that a bloody encounter would not help the Hungarians a bit, but would probably provoke a war. Then I placed myself at the head of another procession, a smaller one this time, and led it away from the Brandenburg Gate, past the Russian war memorial, situated on West Berlin territory. Here I asked the people to sing defiantly the German national anthem. In political situations it is useful to remember that my German countrymen are fond of singing.

On the way I encountered several English military police who had been beaten, because some West Berlin youngsters wanted to let them suffer for the faults they found with the British action in Suez—which, of all times, took place during the events in Hungary! Some days later I invited the poor MPs and their officers for a glass of beer, and they exhibited a grand and very intelligent attitude.

Credit was not due to me that the demonstration for Hungary did not end fatally for Berlin. In such a situation the individual—whatever he does and however he may act—does not count much. The actions of a huge mass of people are directed by its own laws. Luck more than anything else, help from external circumstances is needed to assert oneself successfully.

But that evening certainly helped Ruth and me to win the hearts of the Berliners. When we intervened we were only anxious to avert a catastrophe. We did not feel at all heroic when later in the night we sat with friends in my office. Ruth had a delicate sense of the imminent danger of war that then was hovering above the heads of all mankind. Hungary and Suez coincided in a fatal way. Berlin played only a very small part in the great drama.

5

Otto Suhr, the governing mayor, a conscientious, industrious, learned man, was already in the first year of his term of office afflicted with a serious, malicious disease. It was a tragic fate, and it was rather distressing to me that in 1956 I was here and there called his potential successor.

I had never really aspired to the office of mayor of Berlin. I rather regarded it as my task to work as a Berliner in the field of Federal policy.

At the beginning of 1957, a few months before I became governing mayor, I was subjected to particularly vicious attacks. My intervention at the Hungary protest meeting provoked from some people more envy than praise. Political opponents of another group tried to use my refugee past against me. A veritable campaign of slander was started. I defended myself in a civil suit, which offered me the welcome opportunity to have my whole political life openly and judicially ascertained.

Meanwhile my health had suffered somewhat. I had overstrained myself.

In the late summer of 1957, there was another election campaign, which again ended with a victory of Konrad Adenauer, although the Social Democratic party won more votes than in the previous elections. But before the campaign was over, in the end of August—I happened to be at an electoral rally in Kehl on the Rhine—I received the news that Otto Suhr would not survive the day. A few hours later I was in Berlin.

In the following days it was the Berliners who, in spite of some intrigues from my own party, carried their point with its leaders. They wanted to have me at the head of the city, and they got their wish.

After some tug of war I was almost unanimously nominated by my party friends, and elected by the House of Representatives with a great majority. It was a heavy burden that I took upon me. But I was not entitled to complain. Nobody forced me to shoulder this burden.

Theodor Heuss, President of the Federal Republic, whom I admired very much and who was our fatherly friend, wrote to me then, in the beginning of October 1957: "As you may imagine, your personal and political fate worried me very much during the past weeks—the musical accompaniment from Berlin sometimes alarmed me considerably. But I only wanted to write you after the decision had been made; that is to say, I have never doubted the outcome. Now these lines shall express my sincere congratulations and good wishes—your deliberate calmness and your courageous energy will master the task."

*

CHAPTER THIRTEEN

Berlin Reborn

1

In order to understand what we in Berlin have done and accomplished in the past few years it would be advisable to visit the city: he who sees with his own eyes and can make his own comparisons, will best evaluate the progress and realize what has become of the desert of rubble of 1945, and how childish the propaganda slogan is that describes West Berlin as a "cancer and a danger spot."

Many observers from all over the world had the chance to ascertain the truth. Last year we had more than 400,000 visitors, 20,000 alone from America. And no one felt entitled to a medal of valor for having made this trip.

In spite of the difficult isolation which, according to the Soviet propaganda, demands immediate redress, Berlin, its life, its economy has become rather extensively normalized

A few figures illustrate our work of reconstruction. The most heartening statistics show the steady decrease of unemployment.

In 1950, the year after the blockade, we had 300,000 unemployed and many ten thousands of short-time workers For every two employed workers we had one unemployed. When in 1953 we declared our intention to push the level of unemployment below the 100,000 limit, many doubted that we could ever reach that goal. But in the fall of 1959 we had only 38,000 unemployed left.

At the beginning of the Berlin crisis I did not worry about the fighting spirit of our population, about its will to resist the Russian threat. But my co-workers and I worried about the economic development. Would we have to face a flight of capital? Would big industries leave the city? Would orders from abroad be canceled? Would a new wave of mass unemployment engulf Berlin?

Even such a crisis would have not forced us to abandon the road which we had chosen But it was good that we were spared such a test. On the contrary, we experienced in the first year of the new Berlin crisis a remarkable boom. That the Communist attack against our economic stability failed was a result of the determination of the Berliners and of their confidence in the Allies. It was also the result of the additional help which we received from West Germany.

On December 19, 1958, a few weeks after the ultimatum, I met with a group of influential businessmen from West Germany in the little Westphalian town of Altena. Fritz Berg, the president of the Association of German Industrialists, had called the meeting. The gentlemen understood the need of the hour, and in the following months many new orders poured into our Berlin factories.

I regard it as a great victory, won with peaceful means, that in the last nine years we have created approximately 350,000 new steady jobs and have reached in West Berlin the impressive figure of 900,000 steadily employed people. Public and private initiative have complemented each other very well.

Many people deserve credit and praise for their contribution; among them I can name here only one: Paul Hertz, the Senator for Economy, whom Ernst Reuter at the end of 1949 called back from his American exile and to whom the administration of foreign aid was entrusted.

Nine years ago half of our needs had to be met with the help of our friends from abroad and from the German West. Today we live on more than eighty per cent from the fruits of our own work From year to year we stand more firmly on our own feet The nasty description of Berlin as a "bottomless barrel" has been proven a stupid lie.

Since 1950 our exports have risen tenfold. Two thousand West Berlin firms export to 137 nations.

In the foreground of our economic life stands the electronics and machine industry. The second place is held by the textile industry. Berlin fashions have gained recognition beyond Germany's borders. But many other industries flourish in Berlin also: chemical and pharmaceutical products, beer and chocolate, printing and cigarettes, hosiery and canned food. From the big dynamo to the finest wedding dress and the most exquisite china—Berlin produces it

The economic progress has created a problem for us which no one could foresee a few years ago: the need for skilled workers. This is a problem of great importance, especially if the division of Germany continues for an indefinite period. In normal times a city like Berlin attracts each year many people from all parts of the country. Since the last war this has changed. Many skilled—primarily young—people immigrated to the West because they found better chances there.

The need for bringing young skilled workers to Berlin becomes all the clearer if one thinks of the structure of our population. We have an unusually high percentage of women, the highest in Europe. We have also a relatively "old" population. Half of our citizens are over fifty years old, seventeen per cent over sixty-five—in West Germany only eleven per cent. This fact explains our high social budget, the urgent need for hospitals and old-age homes.

This is, however, only one of our worries. We have greater ones. Among them I do not count the fear of a new blockade. First, Moscow knows too well that we would win additional sympathy in the whole world if the weapon of starvation would be raised against us again. Second, Moscow knows that this weapon has lost its edge. It has become blunt because with the aid of the Federal government we have systematically accumulated great reserves of food and raw material. Even under a new blockade we could live on a limited but passable level for many months without supplies from abroad.

And yet the Communists could create great difficulties for us in the field of communication—by administrative harassment, in the form of a creeping blockade. This danger we must recognize. Therefore, all nice words about the freedom and integrity of West Berlin do not count much unless they are coupled with clear agreements about the free access to Berlin.

It is true, the roads to Berlin pass through the Soviet-occupied zone. But it is also true that the Western powers have an original right to a free access to Berlin. The Four Powers—the Soviets in unison with the three Western Allies—agreed at the Paris Foreign Minister conference of June 1949 to re-establish the status that existed before the Berlin blockade. They went even further and agreed to improve the communications of Berlin with the different zones.

This is, and remains, a good basis for a new settlement. I would have been pleased if the Foreign Minister conference at Geneva in the summer of 1959 had taken up the Parisian agreement more firmly The general formula of free access is not enough. It ought to be concretized. What improvements should be made in the interest of all concerned should be spelled out clearly.

2

Figures make boring reading for most of us. And it is difficult to see the living people behind dead statistics. Sometimes, however, dry economic facts assume a visible form and appear before our eyes in a dramatic manner.

What Berlin has accomplished in the last few years in the construction of houses, of streets, and last but not least, in the cultural field can be well understood without looking at statistics. A short drive by car, a few extensive walks through our city suffice.

At the end of the war more than a third of our dwellings were completely destroyed, another third badly damaged. Because of a lack of funds our reconstruction started later than in the German West. Nevertheless, since the blockade we have built 160,000 apartments—23,000 in 1959 alone. A respectable achievement, I think. The need has not been met by a long shot. It is true, every seventh Berliner now has a new apartment. But many families are still without a real home.

Although much remains to be done, we can, in my opinion, be proud of what we have accomplished. We have tried to explore new ways in the reconstruction of our city. We have tried to develop a new style in architecture, which mirrors the ideas and suggestions of noted city builders and architects of our time. Building is, in our opinion, not only an important part of our economic and social policy; it is first of all cultural policy in the broadest sense of the word.

In the last generation the main task of the city builders seemed to be to take the people out of the desert of stone into the light and sunshine of the suburbs. Today we must—and not only because we cannot grow beyond the city limits—

bring light and sunshine, trees and flowers into the city itself. Thus Berlin has become a city in the green. Where once ugly tenement houses with sunless back yards stood, today new settlements rise with airy balconies surrounded by lawns. The law says that only a third of any real estate can be used for buildings; the rest must remain free for lawns and parking space.

One of our architectural high points is the new Hansa district. There, at the border of the Tiergarten, a unique little town has come into existence. It was the main feature of the International Building Exhibition in 1957. Noted and renowned architects from all over the world were given a chance to demonstrate their ideas of a new architectural style not on mere models—they built complete apartment houses which remained and form today a whole settlement by itself. It has become a Mecca for all people interested in modern architecture.

Some of these buildings seem even to the Berliner, in general openminded, "too modern." And the popular sarcastic wit has invented for them descriptions which are not always very flattering: The Academy of Music is called "Music Garage." A church whose tower is a rather bold construction of steel is called "The Soul-Borer," another church—because of its unadorned façade of concrete—"Power Plant Jesu." Because of its unusual roof the Congress Hall, built by the United States, is referred to as the "Pregnant Oyster."

Yet, different and original as the architectural designs are, the Hansa district has, nevertheless, a uniform character. Besides, the practical result of this experiment must not be overlooked: 1200 families have found modern apartments here.

Approximately ninety-five per cent of all new apartments have been built with public funds. In West Germany the percentage is much lower However, in the West there is more capital available for construction, or more wealthy people who can finance their own housing. In Berlin about a third of the apartments built yearly is reserved for people with low incomes.

For those who knew Berlin from before the war and who see it now, it must be very surprising to find that this city which from old has been situated on a plain—in the proverbial sandbox of Brandenburg—is now surrounded by hills. They are planted with maples and acacias. Here we find parks, swimming pools, playgrounds for young and old. One can hardly believe that these hills were originally nothing but heaps of rubbish. After the war the mass of rubble and ruins piled high in Berlin yards was partly used as raw material for new buildings. But a large part could not be used at all, and it would have been too expensive, or even impossible, to clear it away. It was decided to pile up that rubble, and thus these hills emerged. Fertile soil was put on top, trees and flowers were planted. These "mountains" are the special joy of our children.

According to a joke Berlin is situated no longer at the River Spree but at the "detour." And in fact, one has the impression that nearly every street is blocked and has to be detoured. That is not surprising since at the end of the war most streets were completely destroyed. Many have been reconstructed, eighty-seven bridges have been rebuilt.

Aside from houses and apartments, streets and means of transportation, we have built schools, playgrounds, children's homes, hospitals, old-age homes. Today every eleventh child finds a place in a day nursery. We must do better, to give working mothers the chance to leave their children in good care.

It would be tempting to cite more details about our communal reconstruction. I have to resist this temptation. However, I want to say that my work at the head of a large community gives me much satisfaction. Here one is not faced with the problems of "high policy," here one deals with living people whom one can help and with whom one can rejoice in the common success Free communities are essential for a living democracy They are, especially in our time, a counterpoise against the danger of anonymous forces and against the feeling of impotency that overcomes the average citizen in the presence of the concentrated power of the state. In the city, in the community we can have a voice in our own destiny and carry a part of our common responsibility.

3

As the *Regierender Bürgermeister* of Berlin I am by law chairman of the board of trustees of the two West Berlin universities. But this is not the only reason why I am vitally concerned in the academic and intellectual life of my city.

It is no exaggeration when I say that the Free University, improvised in the winter of the blockade, is today an institution recognized beyond the borders of Germany. The two thousand students who enrolled in the first semester have by now grown to twelve thousand Due to a lack of space and facilities, more students cannot be admitted at present; besides, it is very doubtful whether it is not more practical to limit the attendance so as to secure a more personal contact between students and teachers.

Similarly rapid was the development of the Technical University. After the war fifteen hundred students gathered here in the midst of ruins. Now they are almost eight thousand. The reconstruction of both universities has proceeded very satisfactorily; how far our more ambitious plans can be realized will depend on our financial resources.

We also have in Berlin a number of smaller specialized colleges with three thousand students, among them special technical schools for engineers, whose importance in our time need not be stressed.

In the field of adult education we have not remained idle either. With the reconstruction of our libraries we had to start from scratch.

Some years ago we built a new theater, the Schiller Theater, and it will not be long until our new opera will open its doors. Our theaters, the municipal and the private, have not yet reached the artistic level to which we aspire. But even severe critics count them among the leading theaters of Europe.

Our efforts were greatly helped not only by the Federal government but also by our American friends. The Free University would have never been born without the sympathetic understanding and the support of the American authorities. It would not have become what it is without the wonderful help of the Ford Foundation. We also owe to the United States our Memorial Library, the already-mentioned Congress Hall, the new Student Village of the Free University. And last but not least, substantial American contributions made possible our most modern hospital, one of the biggest on the Continent; the cornerstone was laid in 1959. Eleanor Dulles, the sister of the late Secretary of State, has been our loyal and staunch supporter in all these efforts.

The Berliners know that they owe a debt of gratitude to the American government, to American institutions, and finally to the American taxpayer. They also know how important the cultural contact is which expresses itself in the exchange of professors and students, or in the participation of foreign artists in our International Film Festival and the Berliner Theater Festival, which take place every summer and fall.

More than a fourth of our students come from the Soviet Zone. We also have many visitors from Eastern European countries. Among our students we find hundreds of young people from the underdeveloped countries. Here in Berlin they can study better than anywhere else the theme "East versus West" and gain a personal impression of the peaceful competition which lately has become the main topic of Soviet propaganda.

I am of the opinion that we have nothing to fear from a peaceful competition, on the contrary, I am very much in favor of it. I think we must not avoid intellectual discussions and cultural exchanges, as long as we are sure that we represent the better cause.

A special lesson of the Polish and Hungarian events, also my experience with young Germans from the Soviet Zone, has made an inextinguishable impression on me. This lesson affirms what we have already seen in many other places—namely, that the young generation cannot be molded according to the whims of certain dictators. Even under a totalitarian regime the best part of the youth languishes for greater independence, for truth and beauty and humanity. Questions of security and military defensive fronts are at present very important. Yet there are other fronts on which we can fight a successful battle, and we must fight it.

On this front of cultural competition Berlin is an important sector. It will only fulfill its real duty if through extraordinary efforts, through inspiration and courage, it becomes the intellectual center of Germany. Again and again we have to face the question: shall Berlin be only a city among many cities? A voice among many in the federalistic concert of the German states? Or will we succeed in overcoming our special position at the border of the free world?

In Berlin itself, in the German West, and also abroad I have repeatedly appealed for help so that we can make our city the cultural center from which liberal energies and great accomplishments emanate, an example for the seriousness of its scientific work, a model of what the Germans can contribute in liberty and in the fight for liberty.

4

The governing mayor of Berlin is not only charged with the administration of a big city. Since Berlin has the status of a Federal state he acts also as a kind of prime minister. Furthermore—in view of the present world political situation—he must interest himself in foreign policy much more than it would be the case in normal times. I am not only chairman of the board of trustees of the two universities, but also on the board of the Bank of Berlin and the Electric Company. In 1957–58 it was my turn to act as the President of the Federal Senate, and during the two trips abroad of the Federal President Theodor Heuss I had to substitute for him.

These many and varied tasks and duties have a strong influence on my political and on my private life.

When I was elected mayor I promised myself that I would spend at least one hour every day with my family. I could not keep this promise very often. When I reach our little house in the suburbs where we continue to live after my election, it is usually late in the evening, my boys are already in bed. Lunch or dinner together we can have only on Sunday, but many a Sunday I am out of town on official business.

It is hard for me, not being able to devote myself to Peter and Lars as much as I would like. Boys of their age—Peter is eleven, Lars eight—need the guidance of their father. I can only hope that soon there will be more peaceful times which will grant me a more normal life. Fortunately, both my wife and the boys are intelligent enough to accept the inevitable, though the boys have asked quite often why their father could not find a decent job so that he could be at home at a definite hour like all other fathers.

Last year I had to travel extensively. I visited many capitals of Europe, toured the United States, went half around the world. My wife accompanied me on most of these trips. She was—and not only on these travels—an inestimable help to me. Her naturalness, simplicity, and charm made her an excellent ambassador of Berlin. To me she has always been a great support in the haste and turmoil of the political life.

Many of my friends have asked themselves and me quite often whether I do not spend too much time on "official functions," instead of concentrating my energy on the "great policy."

I had to answer that I was not master over these functions. My co-workers are trying hard to spare me all the superfluous paper work, and yet I have to attend personally, every day, to a mass of letters and documents—mostly in the evening. My co-workers also do their best to limit all my personal appointments to a minimum, and yet my day is crowded from morning to evening with all kinds of official and semi-official engagements. Prominent visitors expect to be received by the governing mayor. At many a congress or conference I have to appear as a representative of the city.

As far as the "great policy" is concerned, one must not forget that West Berlin—because we ourselves wanted it that way—is represented in its foreign policy by the Federal Republic. We have no ambition to conduct our own foreign policy, even though we are often accused of such aspirations.

However, what we have done here in Berlin in the interest of the security of our city, our effort to interest statesmen, politicians, and world publicists in our fate, and to secure for our problem the place it deserves in the international negotiations—all that has not merely local significance but is in itself world politics.

In the center of my endeavors is, of course, my concern for my city, whose spokesman I am. What we do locally has a decisive bearing upon the future of the whole of Germany. One can state it simply. what is good for Berlin is also good for Germany.

In the first year after my election as governing mayor I had to prepare and conduct an election campaign so that I could continue my work supported by the confidence of the voters. The elections of 1958 have manifested this confidence very impressively. In my own district, a former Communist bulwark, I won an especially gratifying victory.

In the face of the new Berlin crisis—if not for other reasons —it was important to present a united front. Therefore, we have decided to collaborate with the Christian Democratic party, although the Social Democrats would have been quite able to form the government alone. I am convinced that the coalition of the two parties is in the best interest of Berlin. That doesn't imply political conformity. It means that we do not want to add to the misery of the division of Germany internal political quarrels and dissension. Berlin has remained an island of common responsibility of all democratic parties. It would have suffered very dangerous consequences if we had in this respect followed the pattern which exists in West Germany.

In order to fulfill my task I followed the advice of my friends and in 1958 ran for the office of the chairman of the Social Democratic party. The identity of the leadership of party and government was a precondition of our victory in the elections. One can argue for a long time whether this dual leadership should not be separated The question has been answered differently in different countries at different times. This is not a question of principle but of expediency. In any event, a separation of the two offices makes sense only if there is a guarantee of a loyal co-operation between the leadership of the party and the government.

Since the spring of 1958, I have been a member of the Executive Committee of the German Social Democratic party. Thus, I have assumed that additional obligation of participating in its practical policy. I regard it as especially important to formulate a program and to develop a policy which could facilitate our efforts to assume the responsibility for governing the Federal Republic. The new program of my party, which was accepted in November 1959, was a decisive step in that direction.

5

In the first weeks and months after the Soviet ultimatum of November 1958 we not only had to hold the inner front, but also to make clear to the Soviets the grave risk that an attack on Berlin would entail.

A year later the problem has remained the same.

"Look at the people of Berlin and you will know what the Germans want!" I said at a mass demonstration in May 1959. It was the biggest meeting ever held in Berlin, attended by 600,000 people. The American trade-union leader Walter Reuther brought us the greetings from our friends abroad. I stated further:

"The day will come when the Brandenburg Gate will no longer be situated at our border. Until that day comes we beg, appeal, demand: 'Open the door! End the unnatural division!'

"We declare solemnly: the right of self-determination must also be granted to the Germans. The brutal intervention in the inner affairs of our people cannot be tolerated indefinitely. At a time when the colonial rule in other parts of the world is being abolished, we cannot tolerate a new colonialism in the heart of Europe."

At that time, in May 1959, the Soviet ultimatum had already been toned down. Meanwhile the British Prime Minister had been in Moscow and the conference of the foreign ministers in Geneva arrived at a temporary understanding. The Western powers manifested a marked desire to compromise the differences. In the Berlin question they went to the limit of what they possibly could concede. Nevertheless, no definite agreement was reached.

I thought it most unfortunate that the Western powers gave in so quickly to the Soviet demand to discuss Berlin independently from the general German problem and that they did not oppose strongly enough the Russian attempt to separate Berlin from the Federal Republic. The representatives of the Federal government, too, did not show the necessary clarity in this respect.

The fate of Berlin cannot be separated from the fate of all other Germans. Compromises would lead only to some kind of patchwork which, as we know from history, would plague generations to come.

The Soviet thesis that the unification of Germany is "up to the Germans themselves" is foolish. The German question is not a national problem but also a problem of the West-East relations—and not the least important of their problems.

The responsibility of the Four Powers for the solution of the German question must be kept; otherwise we will never arrive at the re-establishment of our national unity. I am, however, convinced that the unity of Germany will be realized not only because it is a vital right of our people but also because it is in the interest of world peace. No one can prove that a policy other than the one the Bonn Federal government has followed would have brought us closer to our goal. The fact is, that the official policy of Bonn has not helped us to advance on the road to national unity. It will depend on new efforts by new forces to find a new approach and to develop a new political strategy.

At Camp David the Soviet Berlin ultimatum was withdrawn; and we are most grateful to President Eisenhower that he spent so much time and energy to take this burden off our shoulders. But new dangers threaten.

Whatever further negotiations may bring, one thing is clear: Berlin must remain with Germany, and during the time of the division West Berlin must remain with the Federal Republic. This is the will of the people, and this is what our Constitution explicitly states. This has also been solemnly proclaimed by the parliaments in Bonn and Berlin.

Unfortunately, a perfect Berlin agreement is at present impossible. But it is not necessary that a change has to be made in a hurry—not until something better can replace the present status, unsatisfactory as it is.

*

CHAPTER FOURTEEN

My Credo

1 Where do I stand?

How does a man, who has lived intensely through the German and European turmoil of the last three decades and who has personally experienced the challenge of the totalitarian regimes, today determine his political position?

George Orwell coined the expression "double think"; he described the uncanny talent of the Communists to turn words and facts upside down.

Most of us never dream of substituting for dictatorship the word democracy, for slavery—freedom, for black—white. Yet, in the non-communist, non-totalitarian world, too, we suffer from a terminological confusion which makes any real understanding between people difficult, if not impossible. We use a vocabulary in its original concept without realizing that in the course of the last decade it has radically changed.

What is in today's politics "Left" and what is "Right"—what is "progressive" and what is "reactionary"? The specific meaning of many words is as hard to decipher as the inscription on worn-out coins. And yet we set them in circulation and demand that everybody should acknowledge the value which we ourselves place on them. Intellectual confusion, misunderstandings, even nasty conflicts are the result. UNESCO ought to commission a political dictionary, giving in detail the new definition of each word. Even if it would not help much it would make interesting reading.

But this lack of clarity, the confusion of ideas . . . is it not often intended? Is it not being cultivated in order to achieve definite effects?

This is first of all the case wherever, by means of modern propaganda, force, terror, and fear are falsified into an artificial enthusiasm. But the same happens also wherever demagogues gain influence and power; and against demagogues there will be no cure for a long time to come. Better schools and adult education alone do not prevent the mobilization of the least noble instincts against reason and intelligence.

In spite of the terrible heritage of Hitlerism, after the war we experienced dangerous relapses both in Europe and America. In the ten years of the Federal Republic we have witnessed examples of deceit, of misinformation, and obscurantism—for the end justifies the means, doesn't it? With nice irony and not so nice cynicism we were told that one "must distinguish between truth, real truth, and absolute truth."

The demagogues and power politicians have it easy because the course of social events becomes more and more difficult to follow. How shall the average citizen gain an intelligent opinion of the billion-dollar budgets of our days? How shall he comprehend the gigantic accumulation of power by trusts, and the complicated entanglement of economic and political interests? How can he find his way through the maze of foreign policy? Will he not be overcome by a feeling of impotency? Will he not, at best, be satisfied with placing his confidence in others, in men and women whom he votes for with the proviso that if necessity arises he will not vote for them again?

In one generation we have experienced greater changes than in centuries before. If someone had told us at the end of 1939 what radical changes the next two decades would bring, most of us would have taken him for mad: the progress of science and technology with their limitless possibilities for good and bad—the new weapons and strategic changes, including the exploration of the universe; the change in the political map due to the coming of age of the Afro-Asiatic world, Russia's rise to the status of a world power; the stirring of India; the challenge of China; the temporary decline of Europe, its division, its revival.

How often and how quickly the impressions of nations and of their representatives have changed! In the course of a few years the Germans, from an embodiment of everything that is hateful, have become the model pupils of democratic cooperation. Seen from Moscow, Tito was one day a fascistic reptile and the next day a dear comrade. In the eyes of Washington, Nehru—a statesman who impressed me most on my world tour—advanced from a half-communist to a respected partner of the democratic nations.

World history will not stop in 1960. In the next few years we will experience further radical changes. But although—or better *because*—the general confusion is so great and our time full of contradictions, the man who is active in politics must continually ask himself the question: Where do I stand? Where do I go?

2 Military action is not the answer....

As soon as I try to answer it, another basic question confronts me—the question of the "why" and "what for" of a modern, progressive party, dedicated to social reforms. What is the contribution a politician can make who has risen from the ranks of the German labor movement and is rooted in the European Social Democracy? Or has the ideological content of a social democracy outlived itself?

I want to speak first on two vital themes of our times: the preservation of peace and international solidarity in this divided world that yet strives more and more for unity.

The protection of peace is not a party issue. Only after I had written down these seemingly banal words did I discover by accident that F. D. Roosevelt, toward the end of the war, put the very same sentence on paper. Nobody will overlook the basic change brought about by the modern means of mass destruction: the decision for a new war will be identical with the decision for the continuation of the human race. I myself realized all the implications of that truth when in the spring of 1955 I heard Bertrand Russell speak.

A dreadful burden presses heavily upon all parts of the divided world—and primarily upon the two leading powers. They all are forced to establish an order which prevents the suicide of mankind. The road to a step-by-step controlled disarmament and to an international system of law and justice is stony, but there is no other.

Pure military thinking will get us nowhere. The decisions of our time fall on many, mostly non-military, fronts. On the other hand, the wishful thinking of those who neglect political reality and are ready to accept a one-sided weakening of the Western camp will not help us either. I am against that.

I remain a passionate opponent of those who misuse the human desire for peace for the sake of their own political advantages. At the beginning of 1959, I was sincerely happy when the venerable Dr. Albert Schweitzer sent me from Lambaréné an elephant tusk—indicating in an unmistakable manner his appreciation of the fact that the mayor of Berlin must show his teeth.

If we in Berlin had capitulated, the cause of world peace would have suffered. One must preserve the peace. But it is no less important to secure liberty and to fight for the triumph of justice.

The European labor movement, the camp of Social Democracy, and related movements in other parts of the world have never stopped advocating in their programs peace through the mutual understanding of peoples, and the reign of justice. They have always fought against any kind of imperialism, and proclaimed the solidarity between nations and continents.

This idea of solidarity and mutual aid across borders and oceans has been in the course of decades ridiculed, scoffed at, and falsified. One has misrepresented it as a denial of patriotism, whereas this idea simply puts the love of one's own country in the proper context—like an instrument in an orchestra or, to quote Jean Jaurès, like a flower in a garland.

Today nothing is more timely than this clear knowledge of the necessity of international co-operation and mutual help —and the determination to act upon this knowledge. Today we must also meet the challenge of a new imperialism which operates under an anti-imperialistic flag.

Much we can learn from reading. Much more we must see and experience for ourselves in order to really understand it.

This I realize when I receive visitors from the East Zone who are living examples of the sad truth that Ulbricht's "German Democratic Republic" is neither German nor democratic nor a republic. I had a similar lesson in contemporary history when I drove through the streets of Calcutta, saw the refugee camps near Karachi, witnessed a mass misery, the kind of which we in Western Europe and America can hardly imagine.

Provided the war danger between East and West can be banished, the next decision about the future of mankind will fall in those territories which we today call the underdeveloped countries. As far as the aid for these nations is concerned, something has been done, many chances have been missed, most remains to be done. This is a joint task of all those who think beyond the present day.

Two thirds of humanity are in rebellion. Advice and appeals to reason are as fruitless as the attempt to preserve—or re-establish—the status quo by force. We have only one choice: either we succeed in winning the confidence of the Asiatic, African, and Latin-American peoples through sincere co-operation and selfless aid, and thus help to guide their revolutions into somewhat reasonable channels, or Communist agents will, as they have already done in many countries with great success, steal the revolutions and misuse them for the aims of their masters.

3 Socialism and individual freedom

The question which, after my experiences of the last decade, occupies me most is: how can individual freedom be protected from the political, economic, and spiritual powers, how can it be defended against totalitarian threats and bureaucratic tutelage?

In the new program of my party it is stated: "The Socialists strive for a social order in which each individual can develop his personality in freedom and participate responsibly as a serving member of the community in the political, economic, and cultural life of mankind." Freedom, Justice, and Solidarity, so we read further, are the basic values of the Socialist program—solidarity understood as a mutual obligation resulting from our collective responsibility.

With this object in view it should be clear to us how wrong those well-meaning critics are who believe that the program of democratic socialism is honorable but long since outdated.

Certainly many of the demands which the rising labor

movement proclaimed and for which my grandfather fought under the flag of August Bebel have been fulfilled: from the prohibition of child labor to the seven-hour day and paid vacations, from the right to strike to collective bargaining, from relief for the unemployed to the insurance of the sick and old, from universal suffrage to the right of the workers to "economic co-determination."

New demands are on the agenda, new reforms will follow. They will usher in neither a paradise on earth, nor a boring conformity. But they will bring us a more harmonious social order, a constitutional state which will become more and more a social and cultural state. This is more than a program for a day, this is a goal toward which we must continually strive.

As I have said before, I cannot accept the often construed contrast between socialism and democracy. For me the question is not: freedom or socialism? It is: how can liberty, how can democracy be strengthened and expanded not only in the political, but also in the cultural, the social, and the economic field?

Since poverty, ignorance, and social discrimination are today no longer accepted as God-given, the majority of mankind in all countries insist that each and every one receives the same chances for his development and progress. But even in a country like Germany much remains to be done to overcome the privilege of wealth in education, and to tap the talents which lie dormant in all classes of the people.

It is simply illogical or pure demagogy to set nominal and real democracy against each other and, as the Communists in power do, to abolish the former for the sake of the latter. They liquidate as "insufficient" the political freedoms, painfully won in the course of decades, including freedom of the press, freedom of religion, and the right to form free trade unions—in order to open the road toward an allegedly more perfect freedom . . . "through the dictatorship to a real democracy." In fact, the dictatorship remains the permanent status, and real democracy is being postponed till doomsday.

I know too well how demagogic the contrary assertion is —namely that our Western democratic order guarantees each and every one the same rights and privileges. However, I want to state as emphatically as I possibly can that nominal and real democracy do not exclude, but complement, each other. Our task is to preserve all existing political and social freedoms, to cultivate them, to defend them with all our strength, and also to develop them in order to make them more perfect and more real. And in the countries without democratic tradition we must hail each little step forward, even if at first only partial successes can be achieved.

To me it seems decisive that we strive for a living democracy, and that means that each form of power must be placed under public control. Democracy must not be understood as something that once and for all is established in the Constitution, and that concerns us only insofar as it gives us a chance to put from time to time a little piece of paper in a ballot box. Democracy is not something final and definite but rather a constant striving for ever greater and further goals. In other words: an ever larger number of citizens should not only be formally *empowered,* but through the awakening of their interest and through greater knowledge should also be *enabled* to participate intelligently in the shaping of the common destiny.

For my German friends and for some of my European friends, this implies also the question of our own position in the state and of our attitude in regard to political power. When the German Social Democracy at its party congress at Godesberg presented its new program I stated:

"This is a program which, after the bitter and even now continuing experiences with totalitarianism, shows our party as an active democratic liberal movement in our times—a party which has the courage and the strength to appear as what it is. This program states more clearly than before our position in regard to the state and to its armed forces, in regard to the churches and in relation to the changed economic conditions.

"A constructive political force, or a pressure group plus a propaganda outfit—this is the question. Confidence will win only he who radiates confidence. Without the will to lead one will never gain power."

Democracy must be not only alive but also aggressive. No doubt it was legitimate that, according to the Constitution, the highest court banned the Communist party in the Federal Republic. But was it practical? I for one was glad that this decision of the Federal Constitutional Court did not apply to Berlin, so that we had the chance to liquidate with the ballot the reactionaries of the Communist Unity party.

Force alone is not enough. When the Soviets tried to conquer Austria from within, when they hoped to take Berlin, it was not "capitalism" that defeated their plans, but the broad masses of the population under the leadership of the Social Democrats. In the end, whether or not the Communists can win will always depend on the workers, the farmers, the white-collar employees and intellectuals. There is only one alternative for the Communist perversion of the struggle for social justice: an honest, positive, democratic and social policy. We will overcome communism best if we make it superfluous—by eliminating the sources that breed the bacilli of the communist disease.

In any event, Europe cannot renounce the solid democratic forces of the labor movement. That is not only the case in the Scandinavian countries, in England, in Germany. This applies also to France and Italy, where labor and great parts of the peasantry, at present lost to the Communists, must be won over to our side.

In America things are different. In America things are also often called differently. But what counts is not the label, but the contents of the bottle.

In the Afro-Asiatic world a new order will not be established without following the principles of Socialist solidarity. And for the countries in the Communist orbit there is no simple way back. The way forward leads through a gradual democratization, through the restoration of those humanistic elements of which even the cramped concept of a Lenin was not free and which later, under the regime of Stalin, were buried under an avalanche of terror.

4 Competition as far as possible, planning as far as necessary

Many a zealous opponent has pointed out that there are no "proletarians" in the modern industrial states and that the citizen of our times has not the faintest similarity with the "bourgeois" of the last century. Socialism, however, is being talked about and presented the way people understood it a hundred and fifty years ago.

It is noteworthy that the anti-Socialist crusaders never think in earnest to use the word capitalism in the meaning of that past. On the contrary. they point all the time to the gradual and basic changes capitalism has undergone. When the rhetorical question is asked, what is socialism without the proletariat, without the equalization of salaries and income? one is tempted to answer: what is capitalism without free competition, without unlimited profits, without personal risk? If the heroes of the early capitalistic era would come to life, those robber barons would today damn "the classic land of capitalism" as a socialistic community.

The truth of the matter is: today the Social Democrats list

the freedom of choice for the consumer, the right of the wage earner to choose freely the job he likes among the basic principles of their economic and political thinking; they regard free competition and the free initiative of the employer as essential elements of our modern economy.

The truth is: the profit motive without which the human society allegedly cannot exist is only one of the impulses of economic progress. The noted English liberal economist Barbara Ward stated: "The profit motive as such is not automatically either social nor useful. The profit motive has not automatically created wealth for the masses. Seventy, eighty years ago, large fortunes were accumulated but they remained in the hands of the few. Throughout the nineteenth century there were so-called 'crises of overproduction' because the masses still lacked purchasing power. In a democratic society an economy which provides for the luxuries of the few and does not serve the needs of the people will not, in the long run, be tolerated."

The most important problem of our time under the existing conditions in our modern industrial society is the control of economic power, not only when it is misused for political aims but also when it tends to eliminate the free market and free competition.

It is true, the general, all embracing planning, once a basic demand in all Socialist programs, has been rejected by the Social Democrats themselves. The so-called socialization of the means of production, which in former times was supposed to bring mankind "by necessity" greater freedom and true happiness, is today no longer regarded as a panacea or magic formula.

Especially here in Germany we have experienced and recognized the danger of a totalitarian-controlled economy. Therefore we have stated in the new program of the Social Democratic party:

"Competition as far as possible—planning as far as necessary.

"The private ownership of the means of production must be protected and cultivated, insofar as it does not hamper the development of a just social order

"State ownership is a legitimate form of public control which no modern state can renounce."

However: "Any accumulation of economic power, also in the hands of the state, is dangerous. The community is served best not through a central bureaucracy but through a responsible co-operation of all concerned."

One hundred and fifty years ago, the British, aghast at the police power in Napoleonic France, were so afraid that the establishment of a police organization would have "by necessity" to be paid for with the loss of individual freedom that they preferred to live under the rule of criminals and highwaymen. Nobody's freedom and life was secure any more, London was the city with the highest criminality in Europe —for the sake of the fiction of a non-existent freedom one sacrificed the real right to the protection of one's life. Until reason triumphed, and then it was proven that it was quite possible to have a police organization which served its purpose without endangering the rights and freedom of the citizen.

No intelligent person will advocate the removal of all traffic regulations—even when they sometimes get on his nerves —because everyone realizes that today we cannot exist without them.

In reality, today the question is no longer whether or not we should plan, but to what extent, by what means for what aim, for the benefit of whom. A tremendous and ever growing part of the social product is being regulated by state laws and used for public purposes. And those who in their pamphlets complain that the free economy is "in danger from socialistic planners" are mostly the first to demand interventions and controls by the state when they are confronted by economic setbacks or business reverses.

5 The example of the Scandinavian countries

There are still some who accuse the Socialists of being base materialists. Well, I found that in this respect hardly any "Marxist" can compete with the zealous advocates of "rugged individualism." The propagandists of "good old-fashioned capitalism" and the apostles of Moscow's "revolutionary" doctrine are brothers under the skin: they both do not recognize any other values but the ones that can be expressed in production figures. The democratic Socialist, on the other hand, in unison with other supporters of a modern economic policy, knows that there are higher values than the rate of production, that man does not live by bread alone, that his happiness is not determined by an icebox and a TV set.

There are also still those who predict that a modern economic policy "by necessity" will lead to a dictatorship. The Honorable Sir Winston Churchill argued before the British elections of 1945: in Germany the Nazis had a planned economy and a Gestapo; since in Great Britain Labor was in favor of a planned economy, they too would in the end establish a Gestapo.

In Germany the conservative forces have fought more than one election with the assertion that whoever wants to explore new economic methods does Moscow's bidding. Professor Ludwig Erhard, whose merits—especially as far as the dissemination of optimism is concerned—cannot be denied, has developed theories not at all consistent with reality. It is true: in the Federal Republic strong economic forces have been freed and great social tasks have been accomplished. But it is also true that in the Federal Republic income and wealth are especially unjustly distributed.

The clamor about the lack of freedom and the dictatorship which socialism "by necessity" entails, the assertion that democratic socialism is "an illusion," is as childish as the "historic truth" that capitalism turns the vast majority of the people into slaves and leads "by necessity" to wars.

The expression "by necessity" should be used more carefully.

In the Soviet sphere, the caricature which is hailed as liberal socialism bears as much—or as little—resemblance to liberal-socialist doctrines as does Franco's Spain to capitalist democracy.

Once more I want to mention the practical example of the Scandinavian countries of which I have spoken before. There for three decades, but for short intervals, Social Democratic parties have been in power. It is open to debate to what extent their policy has been bad or good in every respect—every few years the people in free and general elections decide on that. But incidentally, until now the decision has always been positive. In any case, nobody will assert with a clear conscience that in Sweden, Norway, Denmark "the middle road" has resulted in a limitation of democratic rights and freedoms. These countries in the course of decades have become richer, not poorer. There, democracy has not lost its vitality, but gained additional strength and power.

6 What shall youth believe?

Most people today are tired of politics, they mistrust ideologies. Practical questions are in the foreground of their interests How do I improve my position? How do I get a motorcycle? How can I trade in my motorcycle for a car? When can I buy this or that?

A great part of the young generation thinks and feels the

same way. Many of the young people show only a very limited understanding of our "constant fumbling" of the recent past. They approach the Hitler phenomenon as if it had happened in the days of Napoleon. Let us not forget: the thirty-year-old Germans of today were three years old when the National Socialist regime was established. Those who were born at the end of the war will, in a few years, have the right to vote.

It would be useful if we remained conscious of this fact. It would not be bad if—also for other reasons—in Germany and other European countries we tried to conduct our policy non-dogmatically, practically, pragmatically, instead of knocking out each other's brains over ideological differences and hairsplitting interpretations.

Yet, wrong as it is to overemphasize *ideologies,* it is as dangerous to underestimate the importance of *ideas* as a moving and decisive force in our lives. Berlin is an example, among others; but for me it is the nearest at hand and the most convincing: that spiritual forces and moral values can exert a definite influence also in the field of power politics. It is also an example of the role which clear-thinking minorities, elites in the good sense of the word, can play; a living democracy needs them like the earth needs its salt.

The same youth which scoffs at "ideological hairsplitting" is filled with a sincere desire to give its life a deeper meaning, an ideal content. Young people want to believe, to strive for great goals, to compete with great examples.

What shall they believe in? A car? Can they really give all their best for the acquisition of a TV set? The easier the material life becomes, the quicker and surer modern luxuries can be acquired, the more urgently will the best parts of the young generation raise the question of the "why" and "what for" of life They seek the exciting adventure—there is no greater one than the struggle for a new and better world.

Romanticism, and also the romanticism of the early socialism, may be a thing of the past. Hard manual labor does not ennoble—neither does it disgrace There remains the moral protest of the downtrodden and rejected. We cannot be satisfied to lose ourselves in the struggle for existence, to regard our work merely as a job which one does perforce, and the free time as so many hours which one does not know what to do with.

Liberal socialism is no ideal status which one achieves suddenly and once and for all. It is a constant task. It cannot aspire to a right of exclusivity. It respects conservative and liberal forces, since it has itself adopted liberal impulses and conservative elements.

The politician does not proclaim the last truth. The religious sentiments of men must not be determined by the party or by the state. Socialism is no substitute for religion. In the course of years I have learned to take questions of faith more seriously than in my early youth. I have also learned to understand what Christian ethos means in practical politics. On the other hand, I have also seen in what frivolous, even criminal manner religious values can be misused for political interests.

What is needed is a synthesis of practical thinking and idealistic striving. "Don't say: either-or, but: as well-as," August Strindberg recommended.

Berlin, in my opinion, exemplifies this struggle for a liberal order and a social democracy in an impressive and convincing manner.

I would like to have my own road to Berlin understood not only in a geographical sense. It has led me to clearer knowledge and deeper insights.

Even though Berlin cannot give the answer to the decisive questions which move the world today—sometimes it is important enough to raise uncomfortable questions and thus challenge the surrounding world to think over its problems carefully.

Berlin today is such a question and such a challenge: a question to the conscience of mankind, a challenge to its intelligence. No goal and no definite accomplishment, but sincere effort and courageous struggle.

I deem it my good fortune that fate has let me take the road to Berlin.

Lightning Source UK Ltd.
Milton Keynes UK
UKOW06f1940311017
311970UK00005B/629/P

9 781376 192223